A DELIVERANCE MANUAL FOR WOMEN

Woman! Thou Art Loosed

DR. D. K. OLUKOYA
ISBN 978-36917-1-6
Published Dec. 2003 AD
Reprinted 2004
Reprinted July, 2014
Reprinted August, 2018

Published by:
The Battle Cry Christian Ministries
322, Herbert Macaulay Street, Sabo, Yaba
P. O. Box 12272, Ikeja, Lagos.
www.battlecrystore.com
email: info@battlecrystore.com
customercare@battlecrystore.com
sales@battlecrystore.com
Phone: 0803-304-4239, 0816-122-9775

I salute my wonderful wife, Pastor Shade, for her invaluable support in the ministry.
I appreciate her unquantifiable support in the book ministry as the cover designer, art editor and art adviser.

All the Scriptures are from the King James Version

Foreword

The air waves and the print media, are inundated with bad news. Stories that bother on broken hearts, and homes, shattered dreams, demonic attacks and the like are being told, on daily basis.

The suffering of humanity is great. Much greater, are the harrowing suffering, traumatic experiences and satanic attacks which millions of women all over the world are going through. It is crystal clear, that the devil has targeted and shot his most wicked arrows at women. Therefore, untold number of women are grappling with problems at home and at work.

Several women, shed tears night and day. Those who are daring, comb the nooks and the crannies of the cities and villages in search of help, which is nowhere in sight. Several women are asking: Is there no help for women folk?" Others go about with gloomy faces whispering their own question: "Is there no hope for us?"

Against this back drop, came a voice charged with power, hope and deliverance.

Luke 13:12: And when Jesus saw her, he called her to him, and said unto her, **WOMAN, THOU ART LOOSED** from thine infirmity.

Wonderful words! It is music in the ears of the woman. This is a prophetic statement: "Woman, thou art loosed." These words offer hope to the hopeless, healing to the sick, deliverance to the captive, power to the faint, prosperity to the poor, unlimited possibilities for those whose lives have been placed under demonic embargoes and divine help for those who cannot find help anywhere.

"WOMAN, THOU ART LOOSED." Jesus spoke those words to a woman under demonic bondage.

Luke 13:11: And, behold, there was a woman which had a spirit of infirmity eighteen years, and was bowed together, and could in no wise lift up herself.

The woman in question was a victim of demonic attack. She had lived with her problem for close to twenty years. Deep within her, she knew that her problem was great and the level of her bondage high. This graphically describes the problem of many women today. The fact that the level of the bondage of women, is unusually high, is no longer news. The age long battles between the women folk and satan have continued unabated.

This book, offers an uncommon panacea for all the problems which women go through. One can safely say that the greatest thing that has ever happened to women is the release of this book **WOMAN, THOU ART LOOSED.** It offers digestible teaching, power packed deliverance prayers and comprehensive diagnosis of all hidden and known problems which women suffer. This is your victory tablet. No woman can make the maximum use of this book and remain the same.

This book, is vomited by the Holy Ghost to put an end to every problem sponsored by the kingdom of darkness in your life.

Be assured:

Romans 16:20: And the God of peace shall bruise Satan under your feet shortly. The grace of our Lord Jesus Christ be with you. Amen.

Pastor (Mrs.) Shade Olukoya.

Contents

And when Jesus saw her, he called her to him, and said unto her, Woman, thou art loosed from thine infirmity.
[Luke 13:12]

The Devil Versus The Woman

There is an age-long battle, between the woman and the devil. This battle,. has been fought by women of all races, colour and status. The devil has never concealed the fact that, he hates women with perfect hatred. He has continued to harass, molest, torment and destroy women.

A lot of women are suffering in silence; some have concluded that they are subjected to a life time of misery, woe and satanic attacks. Only very few have discovered the secrets of victory, in this peculiar area of their lives.

The Book of Genesis gives us the necessary insight into the topic. It traces what happened before the first battle, and the things that took place after the battle:

And God saw every thing that he had made, and, behold, it was very good. And the evening and the morning were the sixth day (Genesis 1:31).

God had just finished His creative work and decided to run the entire process through a test in His own laboratory. When His work of creation had passed through His Quality Control Department, He came up with the verdict that everything was in good shape. This shows us that God wants everything to be in a perfect state.

However, there was a particular situation which He declared to be less than desirable. This is highlighted below:

And the LORD God said, It is not good that the man should be alone; I will make him an help meet for him (Gen. 2:18).

God declared that leaving a man by himself without a woman was not good enough. The word 'help meet' in the original Hebrew language means several things. It refers to the following terms:

- ☞ Suitable company
- ☞ A shield
- ☞ Protection
- ☞ Defence

THE DRAMA

When God created a woman, He intended that she would fulfill a number of roles. These roles were crucial in His programme for mankind but the devil decided to thwart God's purpose for the woman by coming up with his own evil programme.

As soon as the devil came on the stage, we began to see the unfolding of one of the most challenging dramas in the history of mankind:

Now the serpent was more subtle than any beast of the field which the LORD God had made. And he said unto the woman, Yea, hath God said, Ye shall not eat of every tree of the garden? (Genesis 3:1).

We discover here that the devil did not direct his attack toward the man. He went straight after the woman because he realised that the woman had been earmarked to constitute a shield to the man. He knew that the moment the shield was removed, it would be easy to catch Adam.

Let us read what transpired between satan and the woman:

Now the serpent was more subtle than any beast of the field which the

LORD God had made. And he said unto the woman, Yea, hath God said, Ye shall not eat of every tree of the garden? And the woman said unto the serpent, We may eat of the fruit of the trees of the garden: But of the fruit of the tree which is in the midst of the garden, God hath said, Ye shall not eat of it, neither shall ye touch it, lest ye die. And the serpent said unto the woman, Ye shall not surely die (Genesis 3:1-4).

Eve fell for satan's bait. At the end, she accepted and ate the fruit. She did not stop there, but went ahead and prevailed on her husband to eat the fruit. That was the beginning of mankind's troubles. What happened at that instance, went beyond the fall of Adam and Eve. The incident marked the beginning of an intense warfare between mankind and the devil. God said:

> And I will put enmity between thee and the woman, and between thy seed and her seed; it shall bruise thy head, and thou shalt bruise his heel. Unto the woman he said, I will greatly multiply thy sorrow and thy conception; in sorrow thou shalt bring forth children; and thy desire shall be to thy husband, and he shall rule over thee. And unto Adam he said, Because thou hast hearkened unto the voice of thy wife, and hast eaten of the tree, of which I commanded thee, saying, Thou shalt not eat of it: cursed is the ground for thy sake; in sorrow shalt thou eat of it all the days of thy life; Thorns also and thistles shall it bring forth to thee; and thou shalt eat the herb of the field; In the sweat of thy face shalt thou eat bread, till thou return unto the ground; for out of it wast thou taken: for dust thou art, and unto dust shalt thou return (Genesis 3:15-19).

What you have just read in these verses, may appear very simple on the surface, but it is very deep.

One of the greatest tragedies in life, is for somebody to read the Bible with his eyes closed. A lot of deep things are revealed in this passage. Ignorance of what is revealed in the scriptures, will give the devil, the opportunity to continue to carry out his evil activities in one's life.

THE MOUNTAIN OF IGNORANCE

Ignorance is the greatest enemy of man. Eve's fall as well as her evil influence over her husband happened because of gross ignorance on her part. She was so naive, to have listened to her enemy. The devil has continued to utilise the same strategy. When one ignorantly or deliberately listens to one's enemies, one is heading toward the brink of a precipice. Listening to one's enemy brings confusion in the end.

Ignorance is terrible. It is the greatest form of bondage. Every man's mountain is the mountain of his ignorance. All tragedies of human experience, are due to ignorance. It has caused a lot of problems in the society. One's degree of ignorance determines the manner with which the enemy will defraud one.

Experience and thorough study of the Scriptures have brought the plight of women to the fore. The Lord has opened our understanding to a lot of things. For example, we have discovered that most women hardly enjoy their marriages. Immediately some make up their minds to enjoy their marriage, the lives of their husbands are cut short.

A lot of women have gone into evil covenants. There are territorial powers assigned to terrorise and attack women. They have suffered terrible agonies. If one travels to various parts of many nations of the world, one will be shocked to discover that in those places it is difficult to find good marriages. The Bible has given us the reason behind the mysterious problems amongst the womenfolk. The battle between the devil and women accounts for this problem.

IN THE BEGINNING

The battle against the woman did not just start in this century. It started way back in the beginning of creation. Knowledge of this truth will equip and challenge one to pray until one experiences victory.

As a matter of fact, satan and evil spirits have more than a common interest in women. They go to unimaginable extents just to carry out their evil intent. Satan targeted the woman right in the Garden of Eden.

The same strategy which the devil put to use at that time has remained unchanged. Satan is still targeting women and doing great havocs in their lives today.

On careful examination of the situation of things in our present generation, one will discover that satan is really at war with women.

For example, one may come across a well-trained lady from a very good home, who may decide to bring a boy who is a complete misfit to her parents, saying, "This is the man I would like to marry." Such a boy may be homeless, jobless and addicted to drugs; the lady will insist on getting married to him by all means.

There are other cases which border on aberrations among young women. They blindly go into error simply because they are targets of satanic attacks and manipulations.

STRATEGIC ROLE OF THE WOMAN

It is crystal clear, that the devil knows that if he can capture the womenfolk, he would control the world. Although women are often regarded as weak, the part played by them cannot be relegated to the background.

No matter how great a man becomes in life, there must have been a time when he was a helpless baby in the womb of a woman. The devil knows that the woman controls the womb, the cradle and the kitchen. If you meditate on the importance of these three areas, you will discover that the woman controls the world. The world is controlled by the womb, the cradle and the kitchen.

The devil is also conscious of the fact that women who want to be serious for God and occupy prominent places in history are potential threats to his kingdom. Such women have great battles to fight. The devil does not spare them, he fights them really hard.

If you take a second look at the plan of redemption, as revealed in the third chapter of the Book of Genesis, you will discover that the enmity between the devil and the woman is deeply rooted.

> And I will put enmity between thee and the woman, and between thy seed and her seed; it shall bruise thy head, and thou shalt bruise his heel (Genesis 3:15).

In God's plan of redemption, the seed of the woman was to bruise the serpent's head. What was referred to was not the seed of the man but that of the woman. It is clear therefore, that right from the beginning of the world, women have been giving satan nightmares.

Being aware of the fact that a particular seed of the woman would bruise the head of the serpent, the devil has resorted to attacking every woman since he does not know which woman would produce the dangerous seed. Thus he started an agenda against women by corrupting, polluting, demoting and downgrading the womenfolk. If women are under such terrible attacks, it is dangerous for any of them to remain ignorant. It is time for them to rise and fight against the stubborn enemy. Every woman should therefore rise in the power and strength of the Almighty and possess her possession.

Why don't you pray, at this moment? I rise by the power of God and possess my possession, in the name of Jesus.

These are some of the strategic roles of the woman:

- It was a woman who gave birth to Jesus
- Women supported the ministry of Jesus
- A woman anointed Jesus for death

- ☞ Women were at the cross
- ☞ Women were the first to see Jesus at resurrection
- ☞ It was women who first announced the resurrection of Jesus
- ☞ Women are more caring, loving and compassionate than men
- ☞ Women can pray better than men
- ☞ Women form higher percentage of the population after children
- ☞ A woman are she-man, a womb man
- ☞ Women are the mother of all living
- ☞ Women are the homemaker
- ☞ Women are life-multiplier and a world sustainer

DEMONIC EXPLOITATION

The devil knows that he can exploit certain characteristics found in women. For example, he knows that the woman is the weaker vessel, physically speaking and he does everything to exploit that weakness.

Again, the enemy knows that the woman talks more than the man. He also goes ahead to exploit that weakness.

The devil also knows that a woman can believe anything without any form of persuasion. He exploits that characteristic.

The enemy knows that women are simple and trusting. The enemy always exploits that area of weakness.

The enemy knows that women are easy to impress and he would do anything to exploit that weakness.

Right from Genesis 3, the devil started a two-pronged attack against women. These two forms of attack have affected many women. Consequently, many have become discouraged, low spirited and tired of their very existence.

Two strands of attack

The first bothers on the first born. All first born sons become his target. Since he was not sure who the Messiah would be, the devil targets his arrows against all first sons.

The second flows to the woman. If you are a very good reader of the Bible, you would have discovered that, it is difficult to find a first born son who lived a life that pleased God. This was a common problem in the Old Testament.

THE FIRST BORN'S DILEMMA

If you look at all the names of good Bible characters, you would discover that most of them were never the first born in the family. Characters like Abraham, Joseph, etc. were not first born.

The devil hates first born sons with perfect hatred. In his search for the seed of the woman, he has attacked every first born in the history of the world. He has embarked on a destructive mission with an eye on disqualifying first sons.

Cain was a first son. He was disqualified. Ishmael was another first son, he was disqualified. Esau was another first son, who had a promising future, he was disqualified. Reuben was also the first son and the devil trailed him until he became disqualified. Judah, who was also singled out as someone through whom our Saviour was to come, was not spared the devil's attack. His first son died mysteriously.

Incidentally, Jesus Christ is the first male son to defy the devil and his programmes. He is the true first-born son to dare the devil. The Bible refers to Him as the only begotten Son of the Father. He was the only first son who could look at the devil straight in the eye and declare: 'I must succeed'.

But before Jesus Christ came on the scene, the devil viewed every first born as a prospective messiah and attacked them.

One would have thought that the devil would limit his attack to first sons. Surprisingly, he has extended his attacks, and even anger, to first female children out of sheer wickedness. He has used first sons and daughters as torches or guinea pigs for his evil experiments.

Perhaps you are a first daughter or son and you have discovered that every child that came after you is doing well but you cannot make any headway, your problem can only be traced to the activities of the devil against first sons and daughters.

There is nothing anyone can do about it; there is an enmity between the devil and the woman. Nothing would ever change that enmity. As long as the devil remains the devil, that enmity will continue to persist.

Trouble starts, when any woman tries to mend fences with the devil and goes into a compromise. Any attempt at diluting the enmity between the devil and the womenfolk will lead the women to disaster.

If God has shown you your enemy, and you begin to befriend him, you are preparing the ground for an inevitable tragedy. Any compromise on the part of any woman, will only end in the issuing of a licence to the devil and inviting him to carry out his mission of destruction.

If you decide to make your enemy a friend, such an enemy will only become familiar with you and use that familiarity as a platform for evil attacks.

Familiar spirits are busy pursuing women. Witchcraft spirits are also pursuing women with common hatred. Many women do not really understand what is going on in their lives.

However, the truth is that if one befriends one's enemy, he (satan) would use the opportunity to launch severe attacks on one. Let me tell you this, "What God has separated, let no power or persons bring together."

The moment one knows that the devil is a wicked enemy, one should never make any effort to befriend him.

If a snake has ever bitten you, you will shudder when you see a harmless worm wriggling its tender body. If you have suffered pain as a result of a scorpion's poison, an ordinary spider will frighten you.

DEMONIC STRATEGIES

The devil is extremely clever. He thrives by concealing his wicked intents. All over the world, the devil has erected six structures through which he unleashes attacks against innocent women.

The following six strategies have been established and perfected as satan's instruments for attacking women.

Tradition

In most traditions in many parts of the world, the woman is regarded as a slave. She is seen as an object, to be used or toyed with. She is viewed as an object, to be ridiculed and relegated to the background.

In many cultures, women are supposed to be seen but not heard. Most traditions have been manipulated by the devil to put the woman down.

Many pastors have been embarrassed when they come in contact with cases that bother on the abuse of the womenfolk. A man suddenly dies, as a result of his waywardness and unGodly lifestyle and the family members pounce on an innocent Godly wife accusing her wrongly of being responsible for the death of her husband. Such family members often go as far as compelling the innocent woman to drink poison in order to prove her innocence. Such occurrences are a commentary on how women are abused by the society.

Under the cover of traditions, the enemy has dealt heavy blows on thousands of women across the world.

Religion

The enemy has also hidden under the cloak of religion, to perpetrate havoc in the lives of millions of women all over the world. False religious beliefs, have been propounded to completely cage women. Most religions put the women in a second class position. As far as they are concerned, there is no room for the woman in the front row. Only Christianity has offered hope to the womenfolk.

Societal values

The enemy has also hidden behind the canopy of societal values to attack women and push them backward. In many societies, women are shown as mere objects to be abused and used for advertisements. Thus anyone who has something important to sell finds an easy tool in the womenfolk. Thus, we have seen men parade near-naked women on a television screen just to advertise a product. Women have been used to portray all kinds of senseless emotions within the media.

Beautification activities

The enemy also hides under all forms of beautification activities. In trying to look more beautiful, many women have gone into serious bondage. Any attempt at brushing aside one's natural beauty for the artificial, will give the enemy an open doorway to enter into one's life.

Every woman has been endowed with a divine glory. Whoever trades this glory for any carnal form of beautification is responsible for any manner in which the enemy attacks her. Interestingly, the enemy also knows that many women are interested in beautification. Worldly fashions or make-up may appear dazzling, but be assured that they are doorways to demonic bondage.

The woman herself

One of the methods which the devil employs is the use of the woman against herself. He achieves this by making the woman keep unfriendly friends. The lives of many women have been ruined through the friends they keep.

An unfriendly friend, may appear nice outwardly, but would betray you at the earliest opportunity.

Food

Another avenue, through which the devil catches women is food. In African nations especially, the enemy has used food as a vehicle of attack. Many have innocently consumed food and drinks, which have led them into bondage and destruction. If the devil has been using food to attack you, you must dismantle such an evil structure today. Now is the time to dismantle every evil umbilical cord attaching you to the enemy. This is the moment to disconnect yourself from any power that wants to devalue your life. Today is the day when you must cry out unto the Lord for deliverance.

PERTINENT QUESTIONS

Perhaps your situation tally with what has been discussed so far, then you need deliverance.

Has the enemy afflicted you with sickness, which you want the Lord to heal today? Pray, and God will heal you.

What is the state of your marriage? Have you been struggling and sweating to make your marriage work, but all to no avail? You need divine intervention. Is your marriage upside down? You need deliverance.

Are you occupying the leadership role while your husband is doing nothing to fulfil his responsibilities as the head of the family? Have you become the breadwinner of your family while your husband has remained in a jobless state? Something is wrong somewhere.

Are you going backward in spite of every effort you have made to move forward?

Are you a young widow? Has the devil caged your husband? You need help. Has the devil killed your husband? You need help.

Have you been 'beaten' and 'battered' as a result of the rough weather which you have gone through? You need urgent help.

If you have discovered that your dream life has become an unending nightmare, it is an indication of the fact that the devil is really at work in your life. Do you dream of seeing horrible things when you sleep each night? You need to pray.

Have you discovered that you are trailed by marks of hatred wherever you go? You need help.

Do you go from hospital to hospital, looking for a cure without experiencing respite for one day? You need urgent help.

Are you reading this book and your home is at the verge of breaking up? You need deliverance.

Are you going through situations that make you feel the devil has vowed that you will never enjoy your life? It is time for you to rise and go into aggressive prayer warfare.

Now is the time to arise and do damage to whatever the enemy has planned against you. What you need at this very moment is deliverance.

WHAT IS DELIVERANCE?

You may ask: What is deliverance? In practical terms:

- ☞ Deliverance is the process, by which God sets free those who are attacked by the enemy.
- ☞ Deliverance means, closing every door that has been opened to the enemy.
- ☞ Deliverance is to deliver one from the evil pattern laid down for one by one's ancestors.

For example, if you have discovered that every marriage in your family line ends up with a tragedy, you need deliverance. If you have surveyed all the homes in your ancestral land and you discover that none is peaceful, you need to run yourself through serious deliverance. What you are suffering can only be referred to as an evil pattern or a demonic vicious circle. All evil patterns must be dismantled.

- ☞ It is the destruction of the works of satan in your life. Whatever has the semblance of satanic works, must be dismantled and destroyed.
- ☞ It also means to undo heavy burdens.

  There are people whose lives are filled with burdens that are too heavy to be borne by them. These burdens must be removed.
- ☞ Deliverance centres on, the breaking of evil yokes.

  Many women today are under serious satanic yokes. Such yokes can only be broken through deliverance.
- ☞ Deliverance, also entails the recovery of what has been stolen by the enemy.

  In the lives of many women, virtues have been stolen, blessings have been hijacked and valuable goods have been carted away.
- ☞ Deliverance means, the destruction of every form of infirmity.
- ☞ Deliverance centres on, the release of God's judgement upon every stubborn pursuer.
- ☞ Deliverance also grants you victory in your dream life.
- ☞ Deliverance bothers on the killing or the annihilation of any satanic embargo.

There are women who cannot move forward, no matter how hard they try. Such women need deliverance. There are certain forces behind the lack of progress in the lives of many women.

This reminds me of a serious case which we handled several years ago. A woman looked forward to being happily married and did not bargain for the type of violent attacks she experienced. The wedding was conducted successfully. But unknown to her, the greatest shock of her life was waiting for her at home on her wedding day.

As the new couple prepared to go to bed on that momentous day, the husband came up with a surprise; "Do you know who I am?" he asked the innocent wife.

"Of course, I do. You are my darling," she replied.

"Wait a minute," the husband said. Before the wife could figure out what was happening the husband slapped his head thrice and within a split second, he had transformed into a fearful serpent. The woman was frightened stiff. While she was about to scream, the husband cautioned her: "Don't ever tell anyone what you have just witnessed. It must remain a secret between you and I. Should you ever tell anyone, I'm going to transform myself into a serpent and swallow you alive."

That was what led the woman to run to the church for help. Of course, she knew that going back to her parents was out of the question, as they had sufficiently warned her against getting married to the man. It was during a deliverance session that she was set free.

- ☞ Deliverance, bothers on the breaking of every evil covenant and revocation of every curse.
- ☞ Deliverance, is to deliver your destiny from the power of your father's house.
- ☞ Deliverance means, getting to a point where you become too hot for the enemy to handle.
- ☞ It is the destruction of every evil marriage.
- ☞ Deliverance, is to identify and destroy every evil habit.

☞ Whatever reduces God's blessings in your life is a form of bondage.

For example, if you had been very rich in the past and are now very poor, you need deliverance.

Are you troubled by sexual immorality? You need deliverance.

Have you ever carried out an abortion? You need deliverance. You need to pray so that the blood of the aborted babies will stop crying against you.

Do you know you are supposed to be a winner and not a loser? If you discover that you are constantly losing out, you need deliverance.

One must face the devil squarely and fight until one experiences deliverance. The devil does not have any good agenda for any woman. He is always looking for how to hurt and destroy them. Until you rise to fight the battle, the devil will continue to have his way.

Several years ago, a woman was happily married to her husband. Her home was peaceful and her business was booming. She thought things would continue in that manner.

One day, the husband came home with a weird announcement:

"You must move your things from this apartment to the boys quarters."

"Is anybody coming to take my place?," she tried to query her husband.

"Who is this person, by the way?"

The husband looked up and said, "It is the housemaid, of course." The woman almost collapsed. The housemaid, who had been living in the boys quarters, was brought into the main flat. Things moved from bad to worse. The woman's business collapsed. All her companies began to fold up one after another. All the building projects she had embarked upon were abandoned. All her personal cars were grounded.

At that point, she knew that she was in the midst of a serious battle. She began to pray.

When her personal efforts were not enough, she ran to the church for help. We gave her some prayer points. The title of the prayer programme handed to her was: 'Sending Confusion to the Enemy's Camp.' She prayed after midnight for a number of days.

After one prayer session, she had a dream in which she saw a fearful looking serpent coming toward her direction, poised to attack. The serpent wrapped itself around her. She screamed: "Jesus, help me!" An angel from heaven gave her a big stick with which she battered the head of the serpent until it died.

By 6 o'clock the following morning, she was woken up with the news of her father's death. She decided to go home as a result of the news. By the time she got home and examined her father's corpse, she discovered that the corpse's head was battered. She tried to find out if anybody had attacked her father. All she was told was that the father screamed from his sleep and was found on the floor with injuries on the head.

Then it dawned on the woman, that her father was behind all that she had been going through. For the first time in her life she became conscious of the fact that her travail in life came from the camp of household wickedness.

The greatest tragedy, in a woman's life, occurs when her battles and problems are engineered by enemies from the home front.

Are you suffering because of the activities of household witchcraft? Are you under any form of attack? Do you eat in your dream? Do you have sex in the dream?

Do you swim in the dream? Do you come across dead people in the dream? Do you generally have unGodly dreams? You need deliverance now. It is time for you to arise and possess your possessions.

WAY OUT

How then can you overcome all forms of satanic attacks? What steps must you take in order to experience total deliverance as a woman?

The first step you must take is to surrender your life to Christ.

The second step is to know your enemy. You need a thorough knowledge of your adversary. The devil is your enemy. He is wicked to the core and bad beyond description. If you do not confront him eyeball-to-eyeball, he will continue to cheat you.

The third thing you must do today, is to wage war against the enemy. You shall soon do this as you utilize the prayer points below.

The last step you must take is to barricade your life against the enemy to prevent the hand of the oppressor from being laid upon you.

PRAYER POINTS

1. Every plantation of spirit husband, in my body, die, in Jesus' name.
2. Every power of the spirit husband, over my life and my marriage, die by fire, in the name of Jesus.
3. Every pillar of witchcraft and familiar spirit, die, in Jesus' name.
4. Household witchcraft, loose me and let me go, in Jesus' name..
5. Every power, pursuing my blood, what are you waiting for? Die, in the name of Jesus.
6. Thou power of strange women and your spiritual consultants die, in the name of Jesus.
7. Satanic embarrassment, backfire, in the name of Jesus.
8. Every mark of satan in my body, go, in the name of Jesus

9. Every virtue of my life, stolen by the enemy, arise, locate me in the name of Jesus
10. Evil marital pattern, I say bye-bye to you, in the name of Jesus
11. Any power, any spirit, standing between me and my divine children, somersault and die, in the name of Jesus.
12. Any power, that wants me to die a barren woman shall die, in the name of Jesus.
13. Oh God, turn my body into a baby factory, in Jesus' name..
14. From the north, from the south, from the east and from the west, you my marital breakthrough, locate me by fire, in Jesus' name.
15. Every seed of poverty, in my foundation, what are you waiting for? Die, in the name of Jesus.
16. Every devil inside me, by fire and by force, come out and die, in the name of Jesus.
17. Inherited bondage, die, in the name of Jesus
18. Every power of cancer, I command you to die, in Jesus' name.
19. Every wicked power of my father's house, die, in Jesus' name.
20. Oh God, arise and deliver me from the wickedness of unfriendly in-laws, in the name of Jesus.
21. Every stubborn spirit, using my children to punish me, what are you waiting for? Die, in the name of Jesus.
22. Satan, hear the word of the Lord. You will not break my marriage anymore, in the name of Jesus.
23. Anti-marriage arrows, go back to your senders, in Jesus' name.
24. I dissolve, by the Blood of Jesus and the Holy Ghost fire, every divorce in my family life, in the mighty name of Jesus.
25. You arrow of death and hell, fired to kill my husband, my life is not in your bondage, in the name of Jesus.

The Dragon's Anger With The Woman

The devil is given various attributes and names in the Scriptures. These titles and names, speak volume concerning his mission of destruction in the life of mankind in general, and women in particular. One of the titles is the word "Dragon."

And there appeared a great wonder in heaven; a woman clothed with the sun, and the moon under her feet, and upon her head a crown of twelve stars: And she being with child cried, travailing in birth, and pained to be delivered. And there appeared another wonder in heaven; and behold a great red dragon, having seven heads and ten horns, and seven crowns upon his heads. And his tail drew the third part of the stars of heaven, and did cast them to the earth: and the dragon stood before the woman which was ready to be delivered, for to devour her child as soon as it was born. And she brought forth a man child, who was to rule all nations with a rod of iron: and her child was caught up unto God, and to his throne. And the woman fled into the wilderness, where she hath a place prepared of God, that they should feed her there a thousand two hundred and threescore days. And there was war in heaven: Michael and his angels fought against the dragon; and the dragon fought and his angels, And prevailed not; neither was their place found any more in heaven. And the great dragon was cast out, that old serpent, called the Devil, and Satan, which deceiveth the whole world: he was cast out into the earth, and his angels were cast out with him. And I heard a loud voice saying in heaven, Now is come salvation, and strength, and the kingdom of our God, and the power of his Christ: for the accuser of our brethren is cast down, which accused them before our God day and night. And they overcame him by the blood of the Lamb, and by the word of their testimony; and they loved not their lives unto the death. Therefore rejoice, ye heavens, and ye that dwell in them. Woe to the inhabiters of the earth and of the sea! for the devil is come down unto you, having great wrath, because he knoweth that he hath but a short time. And when the dragon saw that he was cast unto the earth, he persecuted the woman which brought forth the man child. And to the woman were given two wings of a great eagle, that she might fly into the wilderness, into her place, where she is nourished for a time, and times, and half a time, from the face of the serpent. And the serpent cast out of his mouth water as a flood after the woman, that he might cause her to be carried away of the flood. And the earth helped the woman, and the earth opened her mouth, and swallowed up the flood which the dragon cast out of his mouth. And the dragon was wroth with the woman, and went to make war with the remnant of her seed, which keep the commandments of God, and have the testimony of Jesus Christ (Revelation 12:1-17).

Here, we are introduced to a woman. A very special woman. We are also introduced to a fearsome-looking dragon. The principal actors are mentioned in this passage: the dragon and the woman. On the other hand is the picture of a woman with a glorious destiny.

And it is clear in this passage that God has a hand in the life of the woman. She was ready to be delivered of a child. However, the enemy was against both the woman and the child. Raging against the woman and her child was a personality referred to as a red dragon.

To understand these two characters we need to take a second look at Revelation 12:17:

And the dragon was wroth with the woman, and went to make war with the remnant of her seed, which keep the commandments of God, and have the testimony of Jesus Christ.

Here, we see a picture of an angry dragon. The victim of the dragon's violent anger happened to be a woman. To understand what you have just read in the Book of Revelation, you must go back to the Book of Genesis.

And I will put enmity between thee and the woman, and between thy seed and her seed; it shall bruise thy head, and thou shalt bruise his heel.

This was the beginning of the rage of the dragon against the woman. Although the rage started thousands of years ago, it has not stopped. It has continued up till this moment.

One may wonder what the woman had done to attract such wicked anger. The woman happens to be a new creature designed and created by God. When God created the heavens and the earth, He spoke them into existence. When God created man, He formed him and breathed life into his nostril. But the woman was fashioned after God had already breathed the breath of life into the man. Hence, the woman is the last and best of all creations.

When the serpent was looking for a victim to attack, he did not go for the man; he went for the woman. The devil knew that if he could succeed in controlling the womenfolk, he would succeed in controlling the whole world.

The importance of the woman is brought out through Jesus' birth. When the Lord was to be born, he had to pass through a woman. Therefore, the devil has contrived a very terrible strategy against the woman. Technically speaking, the bulk of the world's wealth is in the hands of women.

Even, when we look at the entire population of the Christian communities, all over the world, we discover that more than half are women. The Bible tells us that women were the first to witness the resurrection.

Hence, the woman is very important when we consider the divine agenda. In fact, she is the most important ingredient in God's plan for human procreation. Therefore, the devil hates the woman with perfect hatred.

THE DEVIL'S AGENDA

Don't be deceived. The devil is never interested in helping any woman. His agenda for all women is destruction. The Bible states it very clearly: "And the dragon was angry with the woman:" Perhaps you have wondered why the dragon was angry with the woman.

The dragon knew the details of the role the woman would play in God's programme for mankind. He also understood the destiny of the woman. He also understood that the child to be born by the woman would constitute a terror to him. The devil decided to nip God's plan in the bud. He must have believed that the moment he breaks the egg, there would be no chicken. His plan has never changed.

Today, the devil is still against every gifted woman. He has perfect hatred for every woman of destiny. Therefore, if a woman goes to seek help from the devil, she is only seeking help from her enemy.

Right from the Garden of Eden, the devil has made the woman his target of attack. The attack has not ceased. It is the devil's plan to make the woman the gateway of every evil under the sun. Dark powers can go to any length to pursue that evil programme.

The satanic agenda for women centres on frustrating God's plan on the one hand, and using the womenfolk to carry out their evil intent on the other hand. In view of this fact, most women suffer in silence as a result of satanic oppression.

The problem of the womenfolk is compounded by the fact that many angry territorial powers are specifically assigned the duty of attacking women.

One of the major strategies of the devil centres on ensuring that women do not enjoy marriage. The enemy also ensures that majority of women are initiated unconsciously into evil societies.

The purpose of writing this book, is to address, squarely, how to get at the dragon. By the time you are through with this book and you get involved meaningfully with the prayer programmes, you will come up with wonderful testimonies.

TWENTY-ONE WICKED STRATEGIES

The devil has designed 21 strategies for carrying out his rage against women. These major forms of attack are being carried out by the dragon.

1. He attacks women through the power of familiar spirits.

When you survey the entire landscape of familiar spirits, you will discover that over two-thirds of all the cases come from women. Some victims voluntarily take up the spirit while others are forced into it.

2. The devil attacks women with the spirit of witchcraft.

There are three levels of witchcraft possession.

(a) Conscious witchcraft

(b) Unconscious witchcraft

(c) Forced witchcraft

We have discovered that witchcraft is more prevalent among women. Consequently many women's lives have been ruined by the forces of witchcraft.

3. Spiritual marriage

The devil also attacks the womenfolk through spiritual marriages. He ensures that, as many women as possible are forced or led into spiritual marriages. Most women suffer attacks from spirit husbands. Some women even have spirit children and parents. The dowries of some women have already been collected in the spirit world.

Such women have problems in their physical marriage.

4. Loneliness

This is another form of attack against women. It is possible for someone to live in a crowded house and still be lonely. A woman can be married and still experience loneliness. Some women have children, yet they are lonely. Loneliness is an arrow which the devil uses against the woman.

5. Anti-marriage spirit

The devil uses anti-marriage forces to attack women. There are all forms of anti-marriage spirits attacking many women. If women could open their mouths and talk, you would be shocked at what anti-marriage spirits are doing in their lives.

Recently, a married woman told me of something strange that was happening in her family. The husband refused to pay the school fees of his daughter simply because the wife caught him sleeping with the daughter and stated that it is an abomination for a father to sleep with his daughter. The power of anti-marriage spirits is responsible for such an aberration.

6. The spirit of Jezebel

The spirit of Jezebel is one wicked weapon which the enemies use against women. What is the spirit of Jezebel? It is the dominating spirit which the devil has used to ruin the lives of very many women.

7. The evil pattern

When this attack is in place, every woman in a particular family follow the same pattern.

8. Poverty

The devil has afflicted many women with poverty. Immediately poverty is injected into the lives of the women, other problems follow.

9. Womb problems

This is another way in which the devil attacks women. Women have suffered all kinds of complex gynaecological problems. Unfortunately, most of the problems have refused to respond to medical treatment.

10. The spirit of rejection

This is another form of attack against women. When women who are under this attack go anywhere, they encounter rejection. It is a spiritual attack.

11. Evil covenants

Some powers have led the womenfolk into evil covenants. Some women have entered into covenants consciously while others have done so without knowing the implication of what they were doing. If these covenants are not broken, the women continue to live a bad life.

12. Bad health

A lot of women are attacked in the area of health. They are sickly and run from one hospital to another. Many have spent their family fortunes on hospital bills and medication. The dragon fires the arrow of infirmity against women on a daily basis. You must pray for every arrow of infirmity to go back to the sender.

13. Curses

The moment a woman notices that she is battling with forces that have vowed to place her life upside down, she is under a curse. If you have discovered that something goes wrong each time you want to do something good, you are under an attack.

14. Sick tongue

Most women are victims of this kind of attack. They say what they are not supposed to say and thereby put themselves into trouble. So many women have leaked their secrets to their enemies. This can also be referred to as 'verbal diarrhea.'

15. Bad marital foundations

The devil gets husbands that are deficit for women with good potentials. He also leads boyfriends who are possessed to young ladies with good destinies.

16. Demonic in-laws

This is another weapon the enemy uses. Demonic in-laws have ruined many marriages.

17. Demonic marks

A woman wakes up in the morning, to find physical marks all over her body. These marks affect her physically. Wherever she goes, she experiences hatred.

18. Anger

Women who have angry spirits or manifest hot temper, will suffer greatly in the hand of the devil. The enemy will use the spirit of anger as a vehicle for introducing all kinds of problems into their lives.

19. Dream attacks

The enemy tries to pollute the dream lives of several women. He gives them all kinds of terrible dreams that lead them into confusion and sorrow.

20. Sexual perversion

These include all forms of looseness, fornication, adultery and every form of sexual perversion. Anything like oral and anal sex are demonic manipulations engineered by the devil to put women under bondage.

21. The power and activity of strange women

The devil has dispatched all kinds of strange women into the society and set them against homes. These powers have injured many women spiritually, socially, emotionally and materially.

Are you a victim of any of these demonic strategies? You need to pray. Do you find yourself eating in your dreams? You need to pray. Are you affected by evil spirits? The dragon is after you. Do you constantly experience hatred? Something is wrong somewhere. Have you ever attempted suicide? You are under attack. Have you lost property and money mysteriously? You need deliverance. Do you bed-wet as an adult? You are under attack. Do you often find yourself going backward when you ought to move forward? The dragon is after you.

Are you constantly going to the hospital? Have you suffered mysterious financial losses? Are you suffering from an incurable ailment? The dragon is after you. Have you experienced strange objects moving all over your body? You are a victim of the attack of the dragon.

Do you experience attacks after serious prayers? The enemy is at work. Have you discovered that each time someone wants to help you the fellow runs into problems? The dragon is after you. Do you dream of swimming, getting married, having sex with an unknown person, or seeing dead relations? The dragon is after you. Are you enduring your marriage rather than enjoying it? You need to pray. Do you suffer family distress? The dragon is after you.

WAY OUT

What then can be done to quench the rage of the dragon?

Repent from your sins. If you don't repent, the dragon will continue to carry out his evil activities on your life. The fact that you go to church regularly does not mean that you are born again. To be free from the power of the dragon, one must be free from all known sins and hand over one's entire life to Jesus.

Ensure that you do not have any strange object with you. Take an inventory of your entire possessions and whatever does not belong to you should be returned to its rightful owner. Whatever is an abomination in your house must be removed.

Wage war against the dragon. This is the third step, which you must take to quench the rage of the dragon. Someone has said that the best military strategy for defence is to attack. You must arise and detach every cobweb of the enemy attached to your life. You must close every door which you have opened to the enemy. You must arise and do permanent damage to the work of the dragon in every department of your life.

Now is the time to break every yoke and possess your possession. This is the moment of freedom. Your hour of deliverance is now. You must remove every satanic wind which the devil is blowing against your destiny.

Now is the time to kill every serpent and scorpion attacking your dream life. Now is the hour of releasing the judgement of God upon every stubborn pursuer. It is time for you to decide to declare that whether the devil likes it or not, you are moving forward.

The Marriage That Must Die

1 Cor. 2:11: For what man knoweth the things of a man, save the spirit of man which is in him? even so the things of God knoweth no man, but the Spirit of God.

There are some terrible powers known as spirit spouses. More than any other power, these spirits have destroyed marriages.

Many women suffer from astral sex regularly. Astral sex is the ability to project one's spirit man into the victim's body and have intercourse with it. This practice is very common amongst satanists. They leave their physical bodies in a dormant state while they project their spirits into the body of whomever they want to have sex with.

Many men and women wake up sexually aroused for no particular reason, and assume that they just had a sexual dream. But it was not. There have even been cases where the spirit lovers leave money under the pillow after each session. There have also been cases where physical wives and husbands have been terribly beaten up by the spirit lovers. There have also been instances where people find semen all over their bodies after the operation. These are terribly wicked operations.

It is a day of tragedy when you find yourself sleeping with dead persons. These spirits rape women to a point of haemorrhaging. These same spirits rape or control masturbation in men. These spirits feed on fornicators, marriage vow breakers and adulterers. They have unstable personalities.

They are very proud or arrogant. They are responsible for divorce, abandonment of children, moral decay, seductive attires, bad company, and abandonment of good things / projects. These spirits lodge themselves deeply into the reproductive organs. Extreme violence is needed, to dislodge them. They can assume either sex, in order to pollute human beings. Many prostitutes are women with spirit husbands. They are never satisfied with one man.

People with spirit husband or wife masturbate many times daily. Constant wet dreams are evidence that one has a spirit spouse. These spirits are so terrible that they can suck a man dry. They collect sperm and transfer them to witchcraft covens. Many people are ignorant captives of these powers.

114 SIGNS OF SPIRITUAL MARRIAGE

In addition to some of the symptoms of a spiritual marriage given in chapter one of this book, I would mention about 114 major signs of the terrible attacks of these spiritual marriages.

1. Marital distress
2. Sexual relationships in dreams
3. Hatred of marriage
4. Being jilted
5. Unpardonable sexual error
6. Wrong decisions
7. Neglect and abandonment by the opposite sex
8. Demonic dream assistance
9. Swimming in the dream
10. Missing one's menstrual period in the dream

11. Pregnancy in the dream
12. Breast-feeding a baby in the dream
13. Backing a baby in the dream
14. Having a family in the dream
15. Shopping with a man / woman in the dream
16. Seeing a man sleeping by one's side in the dream
17. Hatred by earthly spouse
18. Serious gynaecological problems
19. Having a miscarriage after sexual dreams
20. Dream marriages
21. Always regretting one's present marriage
22. Marital non-commitment
23. Wealthy in the dream but poor in real life
24. Playing with snakes in your dream, or having snake coil around you
25. Constant feeling that one's marriage will fail
26. No marital proposal
27. Terrible and irritating skin rashes
28. Being proposed to by unserious partners
29. Being proposed to by those only interested in sex
30. Acidic business poverty
31. Victim of persistent rape
32. Fiancé impregnating another lady after consolidating all marriage proposals
33. Violent parental opposition to your choice when you are over due (maritally); while mean parents fail to provide alternatives

34 Death of spouse when marriage date has been fixed
35. Death of husband while pregnant with first child
36. Loss of job immediately after marriage
37. Calamity after marriage - fire accident, motor accident, imprisonment, deportation, etc
38. Inability to make love with your partner
39. Fault-finding in family life
40. Complaint and nagging
41. Inability to control sexual thoughts
42. Seeing your wife as being older than her real age
43. Marital frustrations
44. Total rejection by in-laws
45. Contemplation of divorce based on flimsy reasons
46. Always changing husbands - four children for three different men
47. Strange, negative powers always retaliating on one's behalf against those who offend one.
48. Dual personalities
49. Always tired when you wake up
50. Not wanting to be intimate because of the erroneous belief that men or women are unreliable
51. Disapproval of all your ways by your partner
52. False and wrong accusations
53. Persistent suggestion in your mind that you made a mistake in marrying your partner
54. Voices asking you to pack out of your matrimonial home
55. Decision to stay single because of the fear of marital failure

56 Cutting off relationships for no reason at all
57. Disappearance of wedding ring some days after marriage
58. No compassion from spouse
59. Seeing a river in the dream
60. Husband keeping late nights to avoid the wife's company
61. Your spouse avoids going out with you
62. No marital intimacy
63. Spouse turns a drunk, chain smoker or drug addict after marriage
64. Persistent boasting by husband to force you out
65. Shabby dressing
66. Abandonment of self to obesity and shapelessness
67. Terrible menstrual pain
68. Migraines and aches during menstrual period
69. Serious waist pains during menstruation
70. Symptoms of pregnancy when not pregnant
71. Home separation jobs
72. Inability to receive the opposite sex's attention
73. Living separately with no intention of divorce
74. Monitoring spirits, animals or birds
75. Strange gynaecological illnesses
76. Terrible anger that breaks unity
77. Green blood during menstrual period
78. Fear of rivers
79. Falling into demonic comas
80. Strong soul-tie to mother or father

81 Driving expensive cars in the dreams, but bad cars or none physically
82. Being informed in the dream that you cannot marry in life
83. Occasional mental trouble
84. Fearful thoughts when alone
85. Inability to control your thought life
86. Seeing strange objects or beings when in the dark
87. Seeing bleeding cuts, nail cuts or teeth bites or scratches on your body when you wake up
88. Semen on your body when you wake up
89. Moving objects
90. Hearing strange voices
91. Missing personal properties, like one's underwear
92. Perceiving a terrible odour from partner
93. Academic failures
94. Single-parent spirit
95. Incorrigible and lack of submission
96. Looking older than actual age
97. Multiple operations
98. Multiple tragedies
99. Adult bed-wetting
100. Unsteady marital life
101. Not interested in marriage or anything relating thereof
102. Unexplainable termination of steady love relationship
103. Shopping with a strange man in the dream
104. Persistent periodic sexual harassment in the dream

105 Miscarriage or bleeding after sexual dreams
106. Always being told that your marriage is a regrettable mistake
107. Not caring whether marriage succeeds or fails
108. Wrong men interested in one
109. Unexplainable impotency
110. Fault-finding, accusation and complaint
111. Single-lady spirit syndrome
112. Strange powers retaliating on one's behalf
113. Burning of wedding albums or certificates
114. Physical appearance of spirit husband

HOW TO KILL EVIL MARRIAGE

☞ Surrender your life to Jesus.

☞ Carry out systematic deliverance of every organ in your body.

☞ Engage in regular personal deliverance.

☞ File divorcement and fasten it to the heavenlies.

☞ Define demonic doorways and temple-defiling sins.

☞ Break all sexual curses and covenants.

☞ Do regular night spiritual warfare.

Release from Evil Spiritual Marriage

The supernatural world is as real as the physical. What takes place in the spiritual realm affects us physically in our day to day lives. Ignorance is no excuse. The fact that you are not aware of a bad situation, does not mean that you will not suffer its consequences.

It is unfortunate that, some people go through terrible situations in life while remaining in darkness as regards the source of their problems. A lot of people beat about the bush, without knowing the cause of their sufferings and problems. They ignore the root of their problems and search for solutions where none exists. The greatest good you can do to yourself is to go back to the root. Your present problems might have been caused by supernatural forces.

You must ask the Holy Spirit to open your heart to the realities of the supernatural world. That may be the beginning of your miracles. By and large, one will discover that certain yokes, covenants and evil linkages must first be dealt with, if one must live a happy, holy, healthy and prosperous life.

The subject of the evil spiritual marriage has been grossly mis-understood by many people. While some hold erroneous views, others demonstrate partial knowledge of this all-important subject.

What we are considering in this chapter goes beyond the popular concept of spirit husbands and spirit wives. It goes beyond that point and teaches the evil of succubi and incubi actions. The problem of evil marriage goes beyond dilettantish purposes.

Evil marriage is a deep subject. It affects many people. From our spiritual research and statistical findings, we have gathered that seven out of ten ladies who profess to be born again are involved, consciously or unconsciously, with evil spiritual marriage. In the same vein, seven out of every ten Christian men are, consciously or unconsciously, affected by evil spiritual marriages.

If you gather ten ladies together and ask them questions about their dream experiences, their marital lives and certain mysterious happenings in their lives, you will discover that they are involved with spiritual partners or husbands.

The easiest index is this: If you have ever had an immoral affair with anyone who is not free in every sense of the word, then you can be sure that your relationship, as simple as it appeared, has led you into a spiritual relationship. It is difficult to know those who are free from those who are not. Even if you had never been involved in any immoral act, you are still targeted as a possible spouse to those who have little or pronounced association with demonic powers.

You may be surprised to know that a spirit spouse may fancy you and decide to use his or her spiritual power to lead you into a spiritual marriage, which you may never be conscious of. The world in which we live in is more complex than we can ever imagine. That is why it is never safe to take anything for granted.

As you read this book, it will benefit you if you make up your mind to be a believer rather than a doubter. If you have a genuine problem along this line, you will save yourself heartaches, unpleasant experiences and enigmatic situations if you decide to deal squarely with it.

You would not have lost anything at the end of the day. Even if you did not have this kind of problem at all, at least, you are now aware. Your prayer would still be used by God to bless you and set you free from all kinds of hidden covenants or curses.

If you have listened to the kind of stories which I am bombarded with on a daily basis, you would have no doubt in your mind about the existence of extra-human powers which try to get involved with innocent human beings. Now, if the issue of evil spiritual marriages can be that serious in the church, then it is far worse outside the church. In other words, if the righteous is scarcely free, what is the fate of the unGodly?

To understand the true situation in the secular world, question your unsaved neighbour and he or she would tell you that there are lots of deep experiences which cannot be understood by man. Some of them would tell you that evil personalities come to them, as ladies or men, to violate or abuse their bodies while they watch helplessly. That something is wrong somewhere is an undeniable fact. It is a universal human experience.

There are no questions as to the source of evil spiritual marriage. Undoubtedly, the devil is the head of all evil spiritual marriages - simple or complex. This explains why majority of those who are involved with evil marriage are kept in the dark concerning their dangerous physical and spiritual states. Satan is generally more effective when his victims are totally ignorant of what they are suffering. That is why there are people who have remained in an evil spiritual marriage for 20 or 30 years. Sad enough, some people bear the yokes till their last days on earth.

This is a subject which no one can afford to dismiss with a wave of the hand. It is worthy of consideration by every sincere and serious-minded person.

Evil spiritual marriage is more complex and real than many people would imagine. Unfortunately, it is a legal marriage, even though it is contracted in the spiritual realm. The results are visible in the physical realm. We are aware that legal contracts are binding for those who are involved in it. Those who are legally married in the spiritual realm but have no inkling of the reality of the marriage are to be pitied.

A man or a woman, who is bound under the law to fulfil certain conditions but fails to do so, will face the consequences whether he or she likes it or not.

In 1992, a Christian sister came for counselling and narrated a strange experience which she had. She told me of a strange marriage which she had contracted with a strange man. The marriage was real. However, she was not conscious of the fact that it was more than a physical marriage. She did not know that she was married to a man who was not an ordinary human being. That was the first time I ever heard such a strange story.

She showed me a family photograph and said that right from the first day of their marriage, the man kept telling her that if she ever gave her life to Christ or joined the 'Jesus people,' she would look for and would never find him again. The woman never took him serious. She always joked about it, asking, "What do you mean? How dare you make yourself an enemy of God? You must be kidding." She thought he was joking. Everything went on smoothly with the family until the day she gave her life to Christ. She never suspected anything until she got home only to find that her husband had disappeared mysteriously.

To make matters worse, everything concerning the man had vanished. That was not all. Their four kids also disappeared. They were nowhere to be found. She did not know what was going on until it dawned on her, later, that she had married a spirit being. Her story really surprised me but the evidences were right before me. I saw her wedding photographs and those of her four kids.

She had married a spirit husband and given birth to spirit children who vanished the moment she violated the law of the evil spiritual marriage.

This kind of story may sound strange to many people, especially the academic or intellectual minds, who believe in only what can be seen, tasted, felt, handled and proved empirically. Some theologians may also doubt the reality of evil supernatural marriages. They may opine that we must prove such ideas theologically. They refuse to accept whatever does not agree with their theological school of thought. They relegate the supernatural to the background and emphasise theological knowledge while battling secretly with the problem of evil spiritual world and marriage.

I have come across theologians who find it difficult to get married at the age of 40 and above, when their problems are simply rooted in their involvement with spiritual wives or husbands.

Therefore, many cases abound of innocent sisters who wake up every day to realise that they were sexually molested or abused by strange men in their dreams. They become confused and begin to get angry with themselves. Sometimes, their days are affected negatively by such sexual dreams. Others find it difficult to get husbands.

An elderly woman came to me sometime ago, complaining that she had been unemployed for a very long time. However, she got a job after she was prayed for. She felt highly elated. She was so excited that she looked forward to her first day in the office.

On the night preceding her first day, she had a strange dream. She found herself in the midst of a wedding ceremony. Strange enough, she was the bride. It was a church setting. She saw the congregation, the pastor and a bridegroom. She found herself standing side by side with an unknown man and was supposed to be joined together with him in marriage. The whole situation seemed bizarre to her.

In that dream, she called the strange pastor and said, "Who is this man? I'm sorry I don't know him. What kind of strange wedding ceremony is this? Why must I get married to a strange face? Count me out of this wedding." The Pastor ignored her statement and continued conducting the strange wedding ceremony. She decided to run for her life and ran out at the middle of the service. The pastor, the bridegroom and the rest of the congregation ran after her. She woke up tired and fearful.

She did not understand the implication of such a dream until she resumed work the following day. Expecting to be shown the way to her office, she was shocked when they told her to hold on for an hour or two. She was later called into the office of the director who told her, "Madam, we are sorry to have wasted your time. Although we gave you a letter of appointment, we have discovered that we made a mistake. That letter was not meant for you. Please, forget about the letter of appointment. You can try your luck elsewhere. Goodbye."

It was as if the ground should open up and swallow her. She felt humiliated, confused and tired. She ran back to me to narrate how she lost a job she had just secured. She narrated her strange dream. I told her what to do. I instructed her to summon the strange congregation, the evil marriage partner and the strange pastor who was trying to conduct the wedding, renounce every form of involvement with such an evil gathering and destroy all satanic agents associated with it with the fire of the Holy Ghost. She carried out the instructions.

She went back to the same company which had rejected her. The director apologized profusely and gave her the job immediately. That was how she had a positive change in her life after dealing with evil spiritual marriage.

SONS OF GOD AND DAUGHTERS OF MEN

How real is evil spiritual marriage? Is it scriptural? Let us take a journey into the scriptures.

And it came to pass, when men began to multiply on the face of the earth, and daughters were born unto them, That the sons of God saw the daughters of men that they were fair; and they took them wives of all which they chose (Gen. 6:1-2).

Let us reflect briefly on this passage. Here we are told that 'the sons of God' saw that the daughters of men were fair. What is the significance of that statement? Just as a man sees a lady and he is fascinated or attracted to her, so a spirit being can admire a normal human being and decide to strike a compulsory marriage deal with her.

Let us examine Gen. 6:4:

There were giants in the earth in those days; and also after that, when the sons of God came in unto the daughters of men, and they bare children to them, the same became mighty men which were of old, men of renown.

Who are the people referred to here as the sons of God who married the daughters of men? Some people opine that they refer to the fact that the children of Seth in the Bible went to marry the children of Cain. We must explain Scriptures with Scriptures and allow the usage of biblical words to be clarified by parallel Bible passages.

SONS OF GOD

The terminology, sons of God, appear only five times in the Old Testament, in Genesis 6:1-4:

And it came to pass, when men began to multiply on the face of the earth, and daughters were born unto them, That the sons of God saw the daughters of men that they were fair; and they took them wives of all which they chose. And the LORD said, My spirit shall not always strive with man, for that he also is flesh:

yet his days shall be an hundred and twenty years. There were giants in the earth in those days; and also after that, when the sons of God came in unto the daughters of men, and they bare children to them, the same became mighty men which were of old, men of renown.

The same Hebrew expression is used in Job 1:6 and 2:1, describing, "When the sons of God came to present themselves before the LORD, and Satan came also among them." Angels are clearly of interest here, as it is plain from the only other occurrence of the term 'sons of God' in the Old Testament:

Where wast thou when I laid the foundations of the earth? declare, if thou hast understanding. Who hath laid the measures thereof, if thou knowest? or who hath stretched the line upon it? Whereupon are the foundations thereof fastened? or who laid the corner stone thereof; when the morning stars sang together, and all the sons of God shouted for joy? (Job 38:4-7)

Without doubt, God is referring to angels rejoicing at creation. So, if the term refers to angels here, and the same Hebrew words are used in the other two passages found in Job and in Genesis 6, then the term "sons of God" is an Old Testament designation for angels.

So, we have good angels rejoicing at creation and presenting themselves before God in the days of Job; and we have fallen angels who sinned with the daughters of men in the days of Noah. Both groups are known as "sons of God."

Old Testament use of "sons of God"

As has been said, the expression -'sons of God' is found only five times in the Old Testament: twice in Genesis 6 and three times in the book of Job (1:6; 2:1; 38:7). The passages in Job clearly refer to angels. Furthermore, in the account of Shadrach, Meshach and Abednego in Daniel 3:24-25 an angel is called the son of God. In Jude 6-7 we also read:

The angels which kept not their first estate, but left their-own habitation, he hath reserved in everlasting chains under darkness unto the judgment of the great day. Even as Sodom and Gomorrha, and the cities about them in like manner, giving themselves over to fornication, and going after strange flesh, are set forth for an example, suffering the vengeance of eternal fire.

If Sodom and Gomorrha and other cities committed fornication 'in a like manner' as the angels, then it is clear that the sin of these angels was fornication. According to Genesis 6 this sexual sin was committed with the 'daughters of men.'

Let us, again, look briefly at Job 1:6:

Now there was a day when the sons of God came to present themselves before the LORD, and Satan came also among them.

This passage shows that the sons of God were angels. This meeting did not take place on earth. It has nothing to do with the children of Seth. It refers to angelic beings.

Job 38:4 says,

Where wast thou when I laid the foundations of the earth? declare, if thou hast understanding.

This passage makes it clear that the sons of God were angelic beings not normal human beings, the same referred to as sons of God came to daughters of men and committed immorality with them. These angelic beings, otherwise called sons of God, were fallen angels. This is made clear in Jude 1:6:

And the angels which kept not their first estate, but left their own habitation, he hath reserved in everlasting chains under darkness unto the judgment of the great day.

What did these angels do to warrant such judgement? Verse 7 gives us the clue:

Even as Sodom and Gomorrha, and the cities about them in like manner, giving themselves over to fornication, and going after strange flesh, are set forth for an example, suffering the vengeance of eternal fire.

It is clear that these angels were doing things that were similar to what was done in Sodom and Gomorrha: fornication and sexual immorality.

If we now combine all the scriptures in the books of Genesis, Job and Jude, we shall gain insight into the existence of certain demonic beings who go into relationship with human beings.

Everything was perfect at the beginning. There were no fallen angels or demons. But satan later fell and drew the support of one-third of the angels of God. Satan and his angels fell from their elevated position and were cast out of heaven. The devil became the enemy of God, while his angels became fallen angels. They were no longer the sons of God as before. Or, if you like, they were fallen sons of God.

The incident in Genesis chapter 6 took place after the fall of man. That is where we first come across the incident of evil marriage between human beings and demons or spirit beings. Just as children were produced from that evil union, those who are involved with evil spiritual marriages today equally have children in the spiritual world. Such demonic children inhabit the earth, the sea and the sky above.

The example we have just given illustrates one form of the operations of spirit beings, which lead innocent people into evil marriages. There are other operations and manifestations. The same spirits which operate in the book of Genesis sometimes take up the appearance of men. They come as men to attack women thereby becoming their spirit husbands. They also come as women to attack men thereby becoming their spirit wives. This shows us that, many people are married in the spiritual realm.

THIRTY FACTS ABOUT ANGELS

Angels are mentioned 306 times in the Scriptures. The word 'angel' is mentioned 202 times and the word 'angels' 104 times (KJV Bible).

1. They were all created by God. *Gen. 2: 1; Neh. 9:6; Eph. 3:9; Col 1:16.*
2. They were present at the creation of the world. *Job 38:1, 4, 7.*
3. They are not to be worshipped. *Col. 2:18; Rev. 19:10.*
4. They report directly to God. *Job 1:6; 2:1.*
5. They announced Jesus' birth to the shepherds. *Luke 2:10-14.*
6. They do not marry. *Matt. 22:30.*
7. They are spirits, like the soul of man, but not incorporeal. *Ps. 10; Heb. 17:14; Ps. 104:4-7.*
8. They were created to live forever. *Luke 20:36.*
9. Their purpose is to glorify God. *Rev. 4:8.*
10. Some angels help human beings. *Heb. 1: 14.*
11. Some angels harm human beings. *Mark 5:1-5.*
12. They are invisible beings. *Rom. 1: 18-32; Col. 2:18; Rev. 19: 1 0; 22:9.*
13. They are innumerable. *Deut. 33:2; Matt. 26; Heb. 12:22.*
14. They rebuke idolatry. *Judg. 2:1-4.*
15. They possess superhuman intelligence and power. *Mark 13:32; Ps. 103:20 Dan. 9:21-22; 10:14; Rev. 19:10; 22:8-9.*
16. They possess intelligence. *Dan. 9:21-22; 10:14; Rev. 22:8-9.*
17. They appear to man in human form. *Gen. 18:2; 19:1,10; Acts 1:10.*
18. They possess will power. *Isa. 14:12-15; Jude 6.*
19. Imperfection is ascribed to them as creatures. *Job 4:18; 1 Pet. 1:12.*
20. They have the ability to display joy. *Job 38:7; Luke 2:13.*
21. They have the ability to display desire. *1 Pet. 1:12.*
22. They are stronger than men. *Ps. 103:20; 2 Thess. 1:7; 2 Pet. 2:11.*

23. They are more intelligent than men. *Dan. 9:21-22; 10:14.*
24. They are of different orders. *Isa. 6:2; 1 Th. 4:16; 1 Pet. 3:22; Jude 9; Rev. 12:7; Ezek. 1: 1-28; 10:20; Isa. 6:1-8.*
25. They are elect. *1 Tim. 5:21.*
26. They are examples of meekness. *2 Pet. 2:11; Jude 9.*
27. They are swifter than men. *Dan. 9:21; Rom. 14:6.*
28. They are not omnipresent. *Dan. 10:12.*
29. They are not omnipotent. *Dan. 10:13.*
30. They are not omniscient. *Matt. 24:36.*

The majority remain true to God. They will join all believers in the heavenly Jerusalem. *Rev. 5:11-12; Heb. 12:22-25.*

VARIOUS FORMS OF EVIL SPIRITUAL MARRIAGE

Conscious evil spiritual marriages

Some people are aware of the fact that they are involved in evil spiritual marriages. They are consciously involved in what is happening in their lives.

A brother once gave a challenging testimony of how he experienced victory over an evil spiritual marriage. According to him, a particular strange being comes to him at about 4.00a.m everyday. The lady, who was light-complexioned and attractive, would come and lay down by his side. Whenever she came, he was helpless. It was clear to him that certain powers usually took control of his will. He compulsorily went into sexual immorality with the lady until he was tired and exhausted.

By the time it was day break, he became useless, confused and sick. That went on for years. However, the situation changed when he learnt how to pray fire prayers. He was able to solve the problem because he was conscious of what was happening.

Those who are unconscious of their involvement with evil spiritual marriages

For those who are unconscious of their involvement in spiritual marriages, the problem exists all the same. If these people can examine themselves, they will discover that, they have a problem. If you find yourself thinking about immoral things or if you find yourself in a strange sexual behaviour, that may be a sign of your unconscious involvement in an evil marriage.

Those who are forced into evil spiritual marriage

People in this category are forced into sexual intercourse or raped in their dreams.

Those who can see their spiritual spouses physically

Those in this group, are not ignorant of what is happening in their lives. Sometimes they can identify their spirit husbands / wives physically. Whenever they are in a particular place, they can see their spirit spouse while others who are there cannot see these strange beings.

A strange event took place years ago, during a wedding ceremony. The bride and the bridegroom, were standing by the altar waiting to be joined together. The officiating minister turned to the bride and said, "Will you take this man as your lawfully wedded husband, and keep to him? . . ." The priest waited for an answer. The woman said, "No!" The church was thrown into an uproar. The priest felt that he did not hear her properly so he repeated the question: "Will you take this man as your lawfully wedded husband, and keep to him? . . ." Before he finished, the woman said an emphatic "No." Everybody was surprised.

Initially, the pastor did not know what to do. The bridegroom was equally nonplussed. The priest could not continue. He turned to the congregation and said, "Ladies and gentlemen, since the bride has stated before us all that she is not ready to get married to this man, can we continue this wedding ceremony by asking for volunteers? I am sure that the bridegroom will not mind getting a new bride right here."

Before he finished, three ladies rushed forward, signifying their intention and readiness to marry the man. Quickly a choice was made among the three ladies. That was how the man got married to a different lady.

What was the problem of the original bride? She had a spirit husband, who would not allow her marry. Unknown to the officiating priest, the bridegroom and the entire congregation, immediately the lady was asked, 'Would you marry this man?' her spirit husband stepped forward and told her "If you ever open your mouth to say yes, you will die on the spot. You are married to me forever. You can never marry any human being." This strange voice was heard only by the woman. The woman recognised her spirit husband and his presence was more real to her than the presence of the physical bridegroom. Even when the bridegroom pleaded with her passionately to say yes, the presence of the spirit husband was so intimidating, that she could not.

Those who cannot see their spirit wives or spirit husbands physically

Although people in this category cannot see their spirit spouses physically, yet, somehow, they know that they are involved in an evil marriage.

Those who have international spirit wives or spirit husbands

There are also, international spirit wives or spirit husbands. Those who are involved with them are conscious of their experiences. One day, they dream about having sex with an Indian, the next day they dream about a Caucasian man or lady. Some other time, they come across a black spirit wife or spirit husband.

Those married to local spirit wives or spirit husbands

These satanic agents sometimes take up the appearance of someone who is very close to one, for example, one's husband, wife, or brother in the physical realm.

Those involved with evil spiritual marriages

These are marriages, in which bride prices are fully paid and there is a ceremony.

Those in courtship

This category of people are not yet married. They are still courting. The involvement is not total or complete.

Those who are not very serious with the evil spiritual relationship

In this case, the commitment is not very deep. The spirits involved are just floating around, messing people up sexually. They go about as playboys or spiritual flirts messing around with whoever they come across. They are not looking for stable wives or stable husbands. They appear to disappear and re-appear, as they wish.

Those involved with monogamous spiritual relationships

Some men or ladies are married to one spirit wife or spirit husband. Those spirits are so powerful that, they cannot allow any other spirit to have any affair with their earthly wives or husbands.

Polyandrous and polygamous evil marriages

One lady can be a wife to as many as five spirit husbands while one man can be a husband to several spirit wives. Some of these wives, could come from the sea, others from the rock and some from the air. The spirit wives take their turn. That is why some ladies dream about three men fighting over them. It also explains why some men dream about sleeping with two or three spirit wives at the same time. The men are never able to have any meaningful marriage on earth because the spirit wives are generally jealous and possessive.

Normal human beings who decide to use demonic or occult power to attack a lady or a man who refuses to marry them

When some wicked men or women meet someone they like but who incidentally refuses their advances, they go into astral projection in the night to sexually molest him/her.

From what you have read so far, you can see that the problem of evil spiritual marriage is not an ordinary one. Why don't you take a short break and say this prayer point?

Every unprofitable linkage, I break you by fire today, in Jesus' name.

Now that you are aware that evil spiritual marriages are real, you must also know how to detect the occurrence of such ugly situation in your own life or in the life of anyone around you.

INDICATIONS OF INVOLVEMENT WITH EVIL SPIRITUAL MARRIAGES

Unclean dreams

Whenever one has dreams of sexual intercourse, it is an indication that one has a spirit spouse. Sexual intercourse is only normal among married partners who have the experience in the physical realm. For anyone to have sexual intercourse in the dream means that such a person is married (consciously or unconsciously) to a spirit being.

Sometimes, the person dreams of contracting marriage with a known or unknown person. If you continue to have these kinds of dreams, marriage may become impossible in the physical realm. It is worse when a woman finds herself giving birth to a baby in the dream.

Difficulty in child-bearing

These spirits interfere with marriages, sometimes thereby making child-bearing impossible. When they allow their victims to give birth to children, they ensure that such children are abnormal or useless to their parents. Or the children may end up being agents of demonic attacks. Such children may make statements like, "We are responsible for the lack of progress in the family. The sickness which has drained the family purse was caused by us."

Confusion and uncertainty

These spirits are also responsible for creating confusion in the hearts of young men and young women. Sometimes you hear of ladies, who have accepted marriage proposals, only to turn back to say no, as a result of confusion and uncertainty.

I have received hundreds of letters from men who are complaining of inability to find a lady to marry. I have often wondered why such men are suffering in the midst of plenty. The reason is that, some of them have been involved in invisible marriages with spirit wives, who are extremely jealous and would not allow them to get married to an earthly woman. If such men insist on marrying any lady, the spirit wife would descend on the lady.

Disharmony

If someone with a spirit wife or husband succeeds in getting married, he or she hardly lives, to enjoy the marriage. They experience strange things in their marriages. The situation is worse, when both partners are involved with a spirit wife and a spirit husband. The spirit wife would fight against her rival while the spirit husband would fight against his rival.

In any marriage, where the partners are quarrelsome, argumentative or irritable, they are suffering from the activities of spirit husbands and spirit wives.

It is clear that spiritual wives or husbands are marriage destroyers. They hate the institution of marriage with perfect hatred. They want marriages to break.

If you visit any divorce court, you will see that marriages are dissolved easily. As high as 90 per cent of the problems are caused by spirit wives and spirit husbands.

Many years ago, I met a woman in a street near our church. She was indeed a strange sight to behold. She was carrying all kinds of funny household utensils: pots, spoons, plates, brooms, pillow, lantern, palm oil keg, clothes, etc. It was a massive load. To make matters worse, a baby was strapped to her back and she was walking in the heat of the sun. I was moved to call her even though I did not know her.

'Madam, what is happening? Why are you carrying such a heavy load this sunny afternoon? Where are you coming from and where are you going?' I invited her to the church.

I was then a young minister. Her reply was embarrassing: "Don't mind that stupid man who calls himself my husband. He is a mad man. I am tired of living with him. I have just decided to pack my belongings and go to live with my aged parents. I am sure I will have peace of mind if I live with my parents."

I told her that she was wrong. After talking with her I asked her to go and apologise to her husband. She did, and they were re-united. But why did the woman leave her husband's house in the first place? Spirit husbands and spirit wives were responsible. They did not want her to live in her husband's house.

Some of these evil spiritual wives and husbands can kill, if they become very angry. They are very cruel in their jealousy. Sometimes you come across some cases in which wives are wrongly accused by their real husbands. They tell such innocent women, "Madam, I want to announce to you that you are a witch and that you are the one who is responsible for all my problems."

What is responsible for such a statement? Maybe the man had a dream, in which he was attacked by someone who came in the appearance of his wife.

When he woke up, he would accuse his wife, without knowing that it was a jealous spirit wife who wanted to cause a conflict, or if possible, a total breakdown in their marriage. The wife is not a witch. It is simply the manipulation of wicked spirit wives. On the other hand, the woman might take offence and decide to move out of her husband's house, without knowing that was the intention of the jealous spirit wives. That is how many marriages have been destroyed.

Spirit wives and husbands block good things from coming to the family. Their goal is to make life as difficult as possible.

Attack through female menstruation

Any lady, who is careless with her period may be in serious trouble. Remember that life is in the blood, and access to your menstrual blood by the enemy, can cause up to 20 problems for you. Let me recount to you the testimony given by a sister about four years ago.

After a prayer session entitled "Know the Secret", a sister was shocked to receive a female visitor from her home town, who knelt down before her and started begging for forgiveness. 'I can not recall that you have wronged me," responded the sister. The visitor then said, "I have been restless for the past one week and this is why I've come all the way to Lagos to look for you. I took your menstrual pad, about 20 years ago, to a shrine to prevent you from getting married and bearing children. After the rituals, I hid the menstrual pad inside a cracked wall. This is why you have found the issue of marriage and child-bearing problematic. Please, forgive me."

The sister dismissed her. Later, when she travelled home she found a dusty old menstrual pad inside the cracked wall. She took it out and burnt it. This was how she received her breakthrough.

The strategy of some evil people is to steal a woman's menstrual pad or to find out the dates of her menstrual period. Then the spirit of the owner of the menstrual pad is invited at night and the menstrual pad is shown to her to confirm ownership.

Thereafter, the menstruation becomes irregular and the sister may start putting on some demonic weight.

For total manipulation of menstruation, it is required that someone brings the sand, on which the sister has urinated. The first recognisable sign is intense stomach-ache during menstruation or at irregular periods. May the good Lord deliver us from those watching us of which we are not aware of.

The problems from local evil attack through female menstruation manifest as:

☞ Irregularity
☞ Protractedness
☞ Barrenness and miscarriage
☞ Contaminated children
☞ Problem in obtaining a partner
☞ Husband's lack of interest in the family
☞ Prostitution
☞ Breast cancer
☞ Things moving around in the womb
☞ Dreams of blood leading to miscarriages
☞ Covenants with spirit husbands
☞ Wrong choice of husbands
☞ Unexplainable constant sicknesses
☞ Uncontrollable sexual urge
☞ Family unrest and divorce

Development of polygamous tendencies by the husband

☞ Unexplainable internal heat

☞ Severe headaches during menstruation

☞ Total cessation of menstruation

☞ Prolonged pregnancy

These are local evil arrows. Since many sisters are always careless about their menstrual period, they easily become victims of these local attacks.

SOLUTION

Pray for divine revelation to expose the problem.

Pray to withdraw your blood and urine from any evil altar. (Use our book 'Pray Your Way To Breakthroughs,' or use the prayer points at the end of this book.)

Cancel the effect of evil attacks during the menstrual period.

Pray to recover what the enemy has stolen from you.

Attack through the male seed or sperm

Any man who sleeps with a woman, married or single, outside marriage, is digging his own grave. This is why the Bible has these deep statements recorded in 1Cor. 6:15-19:

Know ye not that your bodies are the members of Christ? shall I then take the members of Christ, and make them the members of an harlot? God forbid. What? know ye not that he which is joined to an harlot is one body? for two, saith he, shall be one flesh. But he that is joined unto the Lord is one spirit. Flee fornication. Every sin that a man doeth is without the body; but he that committeth fornication sinneth against his own body. What? know ye not that your body is the temple of the Holy Ghost which is in you, which ye have of God, and ye are not your own?

You might have "joined yourself" to a harlot many years ago.

And as a result, your sperm may be under the sea now. Most women who offer cheap sex in the streets are agents from the water sent to destroy men. They have 12 basic areas where they entice men for sperm collection namely:

☞ Hotels

☞ Universities

☞ Secondary schools

☞ Hair-dressing salons

☞ Betting offices

☞ Markets

☞ Cinema halls

☞ Night clubs

☞ Dead churches (especially where the leaders have many wives)

☞ Night parties

☞ Car-lifts (rides)

☞ Beauty shows/contests

May the good Lord, have mercy on sisters whose husbands' seed has been captured and stored beneath the water.

This has caused a lot of problems for men. Even if the male seed was collected as far back as when you were in the secondary school, you may still have some battles to fight now.

Here are some of the problems that may accompany such attacks:

Constant sexual relationship with spirit wives

- ☞ Low sperm count or none at all
- ☞ Total financial collapse
- ☞ Hatred by the opposite sex
- ☞ Inability to find a good wife or none at all
- ☞ Sticking to a demonic girl, no matter how hard the man tries to get out of the relationship
- ☞ Everything such a person touches will only prosper if he does not see or use water
- ☞ Regular sexual dreams
- ☞ Ceaseless masturbation
- ☞ Intense sexual thoughts

Foolish sisters, who employ women of 25 and 26 years as house helps m ay be trapping their husbands.

Also, sisters should check their friends, who visit when they are not at home, and only their husbands are at home.

Solution

Complete repentance and prayers for forgiveness.

Submit yourself for deliverance ministration or consult our book on 'How to Obtain Personal Deliverance.'

Pray to withdraw your semen from evil altars.

Pray to cancel whatever evil your semen has been used to do.

HOW SPIRITUAL WIVES AND HUSBANDS ARE ACQUIRED

How are these spirits acquired? How do men and women get into evil spiritual marriages? What are the avenues for such unnatural incursion into the institution of marriage?

The greatest problem we face today is that people find themselves in very complex situations that are difficult, or impossible for them to disclose what they are going through. Some who disclose their problems are often embarrassed by the reaction of the people they confide in. Such counsellors, or pastors often make statements like: "You mean this is what has been happening to you? Your case is very difficult. I have never come across this type of problem. I cannot promise you any help. If I decide to help you, the spirits who are attacking you, will focus their attention on me. You must be a strange fellow. Please, don't ever let anyone hear what you told me. I do not think that there is any solution to your problem."

What an unGodly reaction to the disclosure of a genuine problem. That is why, only very few people talk about their problems today. The majority are afraid of telling anyone the details of the mysterious things they are going through.

A member of our church had an experience which baffled her. A neighbour came to her house because she had a strange problem. The sister heard a knock at her door and got up to welcome the visitor. Behold, it was a pregnant woman. She welcomed the woman and asked her to sit down. The woman narrated her problem: "Sister, I have a problem and would like to confide in you. I am sure you have never come across my kind of problem but, please, I need your help. I want you to take me to your church."

The Christian sister wondered what the problem was, looked at the woman and said: "Don't worry, I will take you to the church. But what exactly is the problem? Tell me so that I can know how urgent it is." Then the woman asked the sister to put her ears near her stomach. The sister almost ran away when she heard the baby in the woman's womb talking. The sister said: "Please, I am coming. In fact, I was almost going out to see someone just before you came in. I am sorry, I won't be able to take you to the church. The address is No. 13, Olasimbo Street, off Olumo Road, Onike, Yaba. I advise you to go immediately. Don't wait any longer. In fact, I would like to close the door of my house right now."

The woman was still trying to ask more questions concerning the location of the church but the sister only said, "Just go, you won't miss it. Goodbye." She was happy that she had been able to push away a strange woman.

What kind of baby was that? Why should a baby talk in the womb? It sounds strange, doesn't it? What do you think would have happened, if that woman's husband heard the words of the strange baby? Won't he ask the woman to take her belongings and go away?

Seeking satanic protection

If you have ever sought protection from agents of the devil, you may end up getting involved with evil spiritual marriage. Let me make this very clear. There is nothing like ignorance, in the spirit world. If you are ignorant, you will pay dearly for it. Those who go for protection in satanic places usually get more than they bargained for. You may end up with an evil spiritual marriage.

Many innocent young girls, have been given away in marriage to evil spiritual forces. How does it happen? Maybe when the girl was a baby, she was taken to a "prayer house" or to the shrine of a fetish priest, where a bangle was put on her legs as a means of securing her life. No doubt, such power may prevent her from dying, but it will go beyond that.

The bangles may serve as an instrument of giving her away to a spirit husband.

Other young girls or babies, have incisions in all parts of their bodies. Some are dedicated to powerful idols, to ensure that they are protected from untimely death. These powers may protect the babies from death, but they may have to pay a very high price for the protection.

These evil powers may make up their minds, that the young girls they have protected would become their wives for life. Such girls , may then find it difficult to get any man to propose marriage to them when they grow up. Their parents wanted protection, but they have ended up getting spirit husbands for their children. This explains why, a lot of marriageable men and women, are finding it difficult to meet anyone who is genuinely interested in them. Such people should check their foundation and cleanse every spiritual contamination if they want to experience breakthroughs in every area of their lives.

Immorality

The Bible says:

Know ye not that your bodies are the members of Christ? shall I then take the members of Christ, and make them the members of an harlot? God forbid. What? know ye not that he which is joined to an harlot is one body? for two, saith he, shall be one flesh (1 Cor. 6:15).

It is clear that the moment anyone goes outside the bounds of marriage, such a person is open to satanic contamination. A lot of men and women have got into problems this way.

Satan is very clever. He sets clever traps, for careless people. If you allow the devil, to blindly lead you into immorality with a possessed lady, you may end up contracting marriage with her in the spirit realm. You will not know that such a spiritual marriage is real until you pray fervently. Then, the spiritual power behind the evil marriage will react. If you argue too much, they may tender the spiritual marriage certificate as an evidence against you.

Unprofitable gifts

A person may be entangled with an evil spiritual marriage through the acceptance of gifts. Today, many people are unconsciously married to spirit husbands and spirit wives because they received certain gifts. If you receive cheap gifts from people, you may be collecting objects of initiation into unGodly spiritual marriages.

If a man gives a present to a lady, and the man happens to be an evil agent, the lady will surely marry the spirit behind the man. If you have ever received a gift from a demonic man when you were a sinner, and now that you have become born again, you think that everything is over, you are wrong. It is when you intend to get married, that such a power will fight you. He will succeed in his effort, because you actually collected a gift from him.

Recently, we had to pray for a lady who had serious problems. She was a very beautiful lady, but her life was a bundle of complicated problems. The first man who approached her for marriage landed in the hospital after a serious fight. His skull was fractured. He managed to survive, opted out of the relationship and ran for his dear life.

Soon afterwards, another man came her way. The man was so interested in her that he promised to marry her. Again there was a serious fight between them. The man survived the fight, but lost an eye. The lady had used a broken bottle to remove his eye. That was the end of the relationship.

A third man came, who proved to be difficult. A fight broke out. The man fought with her, being a demonic agent himself. She broke the man's head and the man broke her head. Then, she discovered that she had a great problem and she decided to go for deliverance. The deliverance minister took time asking what her problem was, but she did not disclose anything. However, things took a different turn, when the minister said, "You demons, if you have refused to let her go because of the gift which she had collected from you, I break the link between both of you and I command you to let her go, in the name of Jesus."

All of a sudden the demon in her screamed: "I am coming out but she has to fulfil a condition. She must return the wrapper which she collected from us. Then, I will have nothing to do with her again." The minister had to destroy the wrapper and whatever it represented before she was set free. Have you collected any gift from agents of satan? You may have to return such unprofitable gifts if you must experience freedom.

Cultural dances

And when Aaron saw it, he built an altar before it; and Aaron made proclamation, and said, To morrow is a feast to the LORD. And they rose up early on the morrow, and offered burnt offerings, and brought peace offerings; and the people sat down to eat and to drink, and rose up to play (Exo. 32:5-6).

If you were involved in cultural entertainment and dancing, in the village or in an urban area, you have probably got involved with a spiritual marriage. The local idols, have their altars. If you danced before such idols, you might have become a bride or a bridegroom to them.

Check the lives of those who are involved in traditional dances. You will realise that, they are not spiritually free.

Inheriting satanic priesthood

An average African family has a family idol. These idols are inherited from our ancestors. Some of the idols, have been worshipped by generations, for hundreds of years. Various objects are worshipped by different families. Some people worship snakes, some worship coconut trees; while some worship other trees. Although we live in a modern age and many of these idols have been destroyed or thrown away because of civilization, the links with them have not been broken.

Families have priests, who minister to the family idol. What does a 'priest' mean? It basically means marriage to a deity. That is why many African priests and priestesses refuse to marry. They are already married to the deity whom they worship. Anyone who worships an idol is married to that idol. That is why those who worship the Lord Jesus, are called the brides of Christ.

There are two kinds of priests. One are well-known as devotees of certain idols, while the other appear like ordinary human beings. There are also priests in the spiritual realm. That is why you should not take certain things for granted. If someone comes to your house and jokes with your child saying, "This is my wife." Or "This is my husband," and such a person is a priest, he can lead your child into evil spiritual marriage.

Recently, a man was sick to the point of death and was summoned to his village by his parents . He was taken to a bush at the back of the family house where there was a huge black stone and was told to perform some rituals. The priest simply asked him to repeat the following words, "Oh deities, I have come to you today because I need your help. I am going to get married to you if you can solve my problem." The man repeated what the high priest said and was instantly healed. But that was not the end of the story. He also became married to the deity. One problem was solved only for a greater one to be ushered in.

Soul-ties

Many people, get into spiritual marriages through ungodly soul-ties. If you have ever had a demonic boyfriend or a demonic girlfriend, whom you gave your photograph, this may lead to soul-tie and eventually to a spiritual marriage.

A sister once came to me, to make a funny request. She said, "Here are the names of seven men. I am planning to marry one of them. Please, make the right choice for me. But please, note that the first two are prosperous and wealthy. Both of them have cars. The other five are still struggling. When can I come for feedback?" I looked at her and gave her a piece of my mind. I told her that I would not be involved with such a foolish exercise. I would not choose marriage partners for people. I also challenged her by saying, "You are covetous. What are you doing with the names of seven men? You must sort yourself out. You need deliverance." The truth did not go down well with her, so she ran away from me.

Eventually, she decided to marry the richest among them. Her home was like hell on earth. The man almost killed her. But surprisingly, she could not get out of the relationship. Her parents advised her to get out of the man's house to avoid being killed. She agreed with her parents and attempted to return to her parents, only to run back to the wicked husband the next day. This situation persisted until it dawned on her that the husband was not an ordinary human being. She decided to confront him. It took her a lot of courage to do so. Finally, she faced him:

"I have decided to talk to you today, because I am tired of all your wicked actions towards me. I have evaluated our relationship and come to a conclusion. You are not a normal human being. Your behaviour towards me, suggests that you are not free spiritually. You cannot deny the fact that you are a demonic agent and I think you are planning to kill me."

The husband looked at her, smiled, and said, "Oh, I pity you. I thought you knew that you have been married all these years to a demonic husband. I am not free. I have never been free. To tell you the truth, you have been married to two of us. I am a dual personality. I am your physical husband but there is another being who is always with me.

You are also married to that spirit being. That is why I have sometimes beaten you to the point of death. You are suffering under the wickedness of two satanic agents."

The woman opened her mouth and could not close it. All she managed to say was: "I know that Jesus will deliver me from both of you." She was indeed funny. Why did she want Jesus to deliver her, when she did not, in the first place, allow the Lord to lead her to the right partner?

Unholy sexy dresses

Seductive dresses lead ladies into evil spiritual marriages. Any dress, that reveals delicate parts of your body may drag you into an evil marriage. If you advertise your body, through highly suggestive and tight-fitting dresses, you may attract the attention of spirit husbands. That is why women, who dress carelessly and seductively, hardly have stable homes. They find it difficult to stay with any husband because they are involved in a marital relationship with spirit beings.

If a lady dresses as if she was coming out of the water, putting on clothes with wet looks, she may attract the attention of husbands from the marine world. Evil spirits are easily attracted by seductive dresses.

Covenants with first sexual partners

Unknown to most people, they enter into evil covenants with the first lady or man with whom they had sexual intercourse. We all know that when a virgin has an affair with a man, blood is involved. This may lead to a spiritual marriage. You can then imagine the number of evil spiritual marriages and demonic problems certain men who have slept with many virgins would have had.

Masturbation

A lot of people take certain things for granted. For instance, some go into masturbation, not knowing that they are opening themselves up for satanic attack and bondage. Such people do not know that, what they are doing have both physical and spiritual implications.

Circumcision

Circumcision is an age-long practice in many parts of the world. In many communities, both the male and the female are circumcised. The problem, however, is that the type of person who performs the rites of circumcision determines whether the person circumcised will get into an evil spiritual marriage or not.

Sexual perversion

Abnormal sexual practices like homosexuality, lesbianism, bestiality, oral sex, anal sex, etc. are channels through which people are led into evil spiritual marriages.

SOLUTIONS

What then are the solutions to all these problems? How can you get out of an evil spiritual marriage, if you are already involved in it? What must you do to regain your freedom?

Repentance

The first step you must take is to repent of all the sins in your life. Repentance has always been the key to liberty and freedom from bondage. Repentance is not a modern concept. If you refuse to repent, you cannot experience deliverance. Repentance leads to freedom. Repentance must be thorough and must cover every area of your life.

Go before the Lord to settle your account with Him. You will call a spade a spade. You will list out, as many as you can remember, all the men or ladies with whom you have been involved. You may have to itemise all the instances and thoroughly repent of them.

Then you must go ahead to break every covenant, which you have with all those sexual partners. General confession of sin will not help in this area. Confess the sins one by one.

Identify and locate the entry points of these spirits.

Make atonement by the blood of Jesus.

You may have to pray in this manner: ***I plead the redemptive power in the blood of Jesus. I redeem myself with the blood of Jesus. I set myself free from every evil marriage by the blood of Jesus. I use the blood of Jesus to wipe away every evil marriage relationship.***

Reject and renounce every evil marriage

You must remember that every evil marriage, is legally binding on those who are involved in it. The Bible says,

And Jesus answering said unto them, Do ye not therefore err, because ye know not the scriptures, neither the power of God? For when they shall rise from the dead, they neither marry, nor are given in marriage; but are as the angels which are in heaven (Mark 12:24-25).

This passage shows us that God does not approve of any attempt by any spirit to go into marriage. Spiritually speaking, it is illegal. The Bible makes it clear that species should reproduce after their own kind and the Scriptures cannot be broken. Here is what another Scripture says in 2 Corinthians 11:2,

For I am jealous over you with godly jealousy: for I have espoused you to one husband, that I may present you as a chaste virgin to Christ.

With this Scripture, you can challenge all illegal marriages. You can tell every spirit wife or spirit husband: "Jesus is my divine spouse. He is jealous over me with Godly jealousy."

Issue a bill of divorce

As soon as you have rejected every evil marriage, you are free to issue a bill of divorce against them.

Bind and cast them out of your life.
Command every spiritual deposit to depart from your body.
Execute judgement upon them

Let me end this chapter with Psalm 149:

Praise ye the LORD. Sing unto the LORD a new song, and his praise in the congregation of saints. Let Israel rejoice in him that made him: let the children of Zion be joyful in their King. Let them praise his name in the dance: let them sing praises unto him with the timbrel and harp. For the LORD taketh pleasure in his people: he will beautify the meek with salvation. Let the saints be joyful in glory: let them sing aloud upon their beds. Let the high praises of God be in their mouth, and a twoedged sword in their hand; To execute vengeance upon the heathen, and punishments upon the people; To bind their kings with chains, and their nobles with fetters of iron; To execute upon them the judgment written: this honour have all his saints. Praise ye the LORD.

You must deal with every evil spiritual marriage today. Those who are married but are suffering from spirit spouses can join hands with their earthly spouses to bring their real marriages before God. Then they can go ahead to destroy every evil marriage. If you are ready to take all these steps, you will experience deliverance and freedom, from the power of wicked spirit husbands and wives. The Lord will set you free. You will be free to live a normal life.

Deliver Your Family From Evil Traders

These are perilous times, for the family. The enemy has changed to the fifth gear in order to deal with any family with a colourful destiny. More than at any other time in history, Christian families are under the attack of the enemy. As a result, marriages are being destroyed at a rate, faster than man could count; divorce is climbing at an alarming rate. With it, there is an epidemic of delinquent children all over the place. There is a violent attack from the bottom of hell fire against families.

A man of God entered an aircraft. As he sat down, he found that the fellow sitting close to him was praying hard. Although he couldn't hear what the man was saying, he could see it was a very serious prayer and he was impressed. The man went on with the prayer for about 30 minutes. The man of God waited for him to finish and then said, "Hello, how are you? You must be a Christian. What were you praying about." To the amazement of the man of God, the fellow shouted at him: "I'm not a Christian! I've only been praying against Christian families."

You and I should therefore, know that, there is a violent attack against families now.

Some time ago, I read an advert about slave trade on the page of a book: "This is John Henry, handsome, strong, able to iron clothes at a fast rate, very obedient. He's on sale - $1." Likewise, today, a lot of families are advertised for sale by evil traders: "Wonderful families, colourful destiny on sale."

Who are these traders?

In Nahum 3:4 we read:

Because of the multitude of the whoredoms of the wellfavoured harlot, the mistress of witchcrafts, that selleth nations through her whoredoms, and families through her witchcrafts.

The traders, therefore, are witchcraft powers. They sell families and nations. But I thank God for what is written in Psalm 68:18:

Thou hast ascended on high, thou hast led captivity captive: thou hast received gifts for men; yea, for the rebellious also, that the LORD God might dwell among them.

This means that God has imprisoned the prison warder. I pray that, every family captivity shall be broken, in the name of our Lord Jesus Christ.

The Bible tells us in Isaiah 52:3:

For thus saith the LORD, Ye have sold yourself for nought; and ye shall be redeemed without money.

The above verse contains the promise of the Lord. This is a very dangerous period for the family. Many families have become victims of witchcraft traders and witchcraft robbers. As a matter of fact, and to be quite honest with you, while many families are advertised for sale, many have already been sold. There are different kinds of satanic markets for family auction. This is very sad.

Recently, I met a man whose father committed suicide.

His grandfather, too, committed suicide; his mother committed suicide and his sister committed suicide. His only surviving sister killed her husband and was consequently jailed for 60 years. She was already over 40 years. Her brother, was consequently, charged with the responsibility of looking after her children. This burden, again, steadily led the young man to contemplate committing suicide. When his wife was called to say what she could do to prevent the man from committing suicide like the other members of his family, her statement did not help matters. Obviously, this was a family in bondage.

There are different kinds of markets for family trading. There are selective markets, there are individual markets, there are collective markets, there is poverty market, there is the breadwinners' market, in which the brightest star is picked out for elimination. Also, there is the market for the first-born. A lot of first-borns are struggling with what they don't understand. In addition, when you get married without Christ, you become a legal target for the evil spirits around the person you marry.

The time has come, to raise a cry against the Pharaohs of family destruction. Unfortunately, for Africa, the enemy has also vomited polygamy into our midst which has given us what is called polygamous witchcraft. More than any other spirit, this one has destroyed so many potentials in Africa. For instance, a man is known to have married seven wives, six of whom were witches. All the six witches descended on the only one who was not a witch and were bent on making a mince-meat of her children.

The time has come to harass all the family prison warders. Perhaps you come from a family where all the men commit suicide; or where all the men are poor; or where nobody has been able to complete any building, and those who tried to do so died, or you come from a family where all the men are fed by their wives.

You must know that these families are on sale already. And evil traders may be on the throne of your marriage now. You need to cry out to the Lord that your family must be released from their hands. In fact, the first person to issue that kind of cry in the Bible was God Himself when He told Pharaoh, "Let my people go!"

In my counselling sessions, I have seen several terrible things. Sometime ago, a father and his son came for counselling and the son started by saying that his father needed deliverance and repentance. I asked him what his father had done and he said, "He is sleeping with my sister." I felt like taking a big stick and hitting the man on his head. But another shocker was in store for me. When it was the turn of the father to talk, he too accused the son of sleeping with his sister. Which meant that both father and son were sleeping with the same person. That family had been sold, though they had not known it.

Another time, I prayed with a person, whose family lost 11 people within one month. Sometime ago, also, a 13-year-old girl who had been impregnated by her father was brought to me. By the time they brought the father, he was not in any way repentant. In fact, despite our disgust, he looked at us straight in the eye and said in pidgin English, *"Na me born am, na me gif am belle. So, pastor, wetin be ya problem?"*

The family is the foundation of civilisation. The family is a church within a church; it is a republic within a republic, a world within a world. It is the building block of society and civilisation. It is the root and foundation of the church and the state. If things go right in the family, they go right everywhere.

Conversely, if things go wrong there, they also go wrong everywhere. It is like a book, with the children as the pages and the parents, the cover.

The family is the school of human virtues. The concept of family didn't come from man; it came from God. Therefore, there are diverse wicked spirits, specifically targeted at pulling down successful families. Unfortunately, none of us has a choice as to the sort of family we would like to be born into. I am sure that if some of us had a choice, we would have preferred to pick our parents elsewhere.

I once met a man who expressed such a sentiment. He came for counselling wearing a three-piece suit. I noticed that there was something hidden under his suit. As he stepped into my presence, he said, "Dr. Olukoya, the only question I want you to answer is this, Is my mother a witch? All I need from you is 'yes' or 'no'."

I asked him if I said yes, what was likely to happen. He said, "Well, I know what to do." At the end I said to myself that if that man had a choice he would have preferred to be born somewhere else.

Certainly you and I have no choice in this matter. All we can do is to pull down the stronghold that is caging our families. Please, pause here and answer these questions:

Do you come from a family where, when people start getting ahead, things would fall apart? Do you come from a family where you observe that, you are falling into the sins of your parents - that is, where mistakes made by your parents are being replicated by you, which seem to confer on you the unwholesome tag of "like father like son", or "like mother like daughter"? Have you noticed a trend in your mother's life that seems to be repeating itself in your own life?

Or have you been noticing that those evil negative things your parents said about you are becoming true? Do you come from a family where they are all liars or always colouring the truth?

Do you come from a family, where they don't mind to kill, to steal or to destroy in order to get what they want? Do you come from a place where they are always playing on other people's sympathy? Or they are always irresponsible, or have stubborn, evil self-will? Do you come from a family, where they always have skin disorders and are always crying?

Do you come from a family, where there is always marital turbulence, or a family that is hardly stable? Do you come from a family, where the women usually have children at a very young age? Do you come from a family, from which no one is willing to take a wife? Do you come from a polygamous family?

Do you come from a family, where adultery is the talk of the day? Do you come from a family, where from the father to the son, everyone easily gets angry? Or is there a history of mental disorder in your family, or that of wasted childhood?

Any one of the above-mentioned families, is already on sale in the hands of witchcraft traders.

Do you come from a family, where everyone is confused, or one where there is always bitterness? Have you noticed a trend in your family, that people are always abandoned by their friends at their hour of need, or that anybody they do good to always repay them with evil? Or have you noticed a trend of financial failure in your family?

Have you noticed hardship and poverty? Or have you noticed that all the male children always wish to belong to an occult society? Or have you noticed a trend of laziness in your family? You need to cry out to the heavens now.

Do you come from a family, whose lot is always any of the following: depression, alcoholism, involvement in accidents, memory failure, inexplicable health problems and premature death. You need to cry out against family traders.

Do you come from a family, where people always descend from the height of their glory to the depth of doom? Do you come from a family where the children are always rebellious so that, at any point in time, somebody from that family would be in prison? Do you come from a family where they engage in sexual perversion and addiction?

Do you come from a family, where generations keep inheriting poverty and things always fall apart for you, just at the last minute? Do you start projects and never finish them? Is there a particular type of illness killing members of your family from generation to generation?

While I was in England, I read an article about some ladies who, when they noticed that their mothers died of breast cancer, went to cut off their own breasts even though they had not been diagnosed as having such ailments.

Do you notice any ailment that goes from generation to generation in your family? Do you notice religious blindness in your family? Do you have people in your family, though with very high educational qualifications, but who are still not doing well, or are wearing uniforms of menial jobs? Do you come from a family where all the members are vagabonds? If you come from any of those families, you need to cry out to the Lord.

STRATEGIES OF EVIL TRADERS

Witchcraft traders, have their strategies which, when you are able to understand, you will know how to pray to counter their activities.

Bad marriage foundation

Their first strategy, when they want to sell off a whole family, is to lay a bad foundation for the marriage. Once any marriage has a bad foundation, it needs deliverance. It is not only human beings or materials that need deliverance; intangible things like marriages do too.

For instance, if one engaged in sex before marriage, or got married because of an accidental pregnancy, or as a child (when one did not know one's right hand from the left), one did a blood covenant before one's marriage, or married as a result of a demonic prophecy, one has already laid a bad foundation which family traders are sure to use against one. So, the first strategy of witchcraft traders is to lay a bad foundation for the marriage.

Generational curse

Number two strategy, is to introduce a generational curse. In this case, the enemy provokes you to annoy a person who would issue a curse on you, that would not be easily removed, just as the enemy pushed Gehazi to annoy Elisha who, consequently, issued a curse that went down Gehazi's generations.

Evil dedication

The third strategy is evil dedication. Most children are caged the day they are born. This affects them all through life, and even passes on to their own children.

Evil covenant

The fourth strategy the enemy uses is evil covenant. When a person names a child "Orisabunmi", meaning "the idol has given me this" the child is already dedicated to witchcraft.

Bewitchment

Strategy number five is bewitchment.

Collective strongman

Another strategy is a "collective strongman" planted in the family to cage everybody. This strongman may be the kindest man around who cooks food for everyone. Many strange things are happening in our world. People who we least suspect, hide under the cover of darkness and are doing evil against us. Some of these people are very nice to us outwardly, but they may be the most wicked strongmen in charge of the greatest problems in our lives.

Collective evil mark

Collective evil marks: It is possible for one's family, to suffer from problems emanating from collective evil marks. The enemy can put an evil mark on every member of the family. As soon as this mark is present, evil will begin to trail all the members of the family. Any family that has received a collective evil mark, will continue to experience negative circumstances.

Family sin

Some families are suffering as a result of the sins of their forefathers. Ancestral sins, are used against many families today. Satan keeps a register of all ancestral sins. He uses this, to lead many families into bondage.

Involvement in the occult

Those who get involved in any type of occultic movement and practise demonic instructions, will experience marital turbulence.

Any foothold of the occult in a family will create a standing place for witchcraft traders. The presence of a single member of your family, in the occult is enough to create problems for the entire family. While some members of the family would be grossly ignorant of what is going on, the whole family would be suffering as a result of the activities of wicked demons.

Spiritual marriage

Just as there are physical marriages, there are spiritual marriages as well. Whenever a spouse is involved with a spirit husband/wife, his or her particular family will be experiencing demonic attacks. It is worse, when a marriage is under the attack of a family spirit husband or wife. Such a spirit, will enter into a forceful spiritual marriage with every member of the family and everybody will be under an evil spell.

Poverty

Poverty has thrown many families into disarray, whenever it gains entrance into a family. It subjects every member of the family to unhealthy harassment.

Placenta manipulation

The problems of most families can be traced to placenta manipulation. When evil powers, locate the placentas of members of a family, they use it to wage war against the entire family. This happens, when they discover that the placentas were not properly disposed of. The placenta is a very powerful weapon that provides a very strong link with those who dispose of it carelessly. Once this link is established there would be evil attacks against the family.

Destructive habits

Some families, have been sold into spiritual slavery simply because some ancestors were involved in the slave trade. The enemy uses this to lead the families into bondage and to level against them all kinds of spiritual attacks.

The spirit of death and hell

The devil uses this spirit, to cause untimely death of adults and infants. You have to declare against premature death like this: "I will not die before my glory appears, in Jesus' name." You must refuse any harassment by the spirit of death and hell.

HOW CAN WE DEAL WITH EVIL TRADERS?

Become a friend of the Almighty. If there is any rift between you and God, settle it instantly. The Bible says that, it is wonderful to enter into partnership with God.

Peter allowed the Lord Jesus to use his boat, and consequently, he experienced deliverance from poverty. Are you willing to hand over the boat of your life to the Lord Jesus? The Bible says that, those who know their God shall be strong and do exploit. Are you willing to surrender the totality of your life to the Lord Jesus? Dedicate your life to the service of God.

Once you successfully align yourself with God, it will be suicidal for any power to venture into attacking you.

Recognise that the power of witchcraft has been defeated by Jesus. Of all the offences in the Bible, the only one for which God has issued a death sentence is witchcraft. My prayer for you is that, every power of witchcraft, working against your family, shall die, in the name of Jesus.

Challenge all witchcraft traders.

The challenge must be well targeted. If you summon the wrong person to the court of the Almighty, he will not be convicted. It is unfortunate that most of the time we are unable to track down the culprit and force them to face judgement before the spiritual court. The power that sells families, is the power of witchcraft which you must challenge.

Bind the activities of witchcraft in your family. Specifically address them and pray against them.

Recover your family, through spiritual warfare. If your children are not born again, if they hate the gospel, evil traders have captured them. Therefore you must pray until they are recovered. Failure to do so, is dangerous, as the enemy may use them against you later. Anyone who is not born again in your family, is a potential time bomb. Such a fellow is a danger waiting to happen.

Protect your family against further attacks. You need to pray prayers of immunity, for the family. Let your prayer level, usher protection into every department of your family.

However, if you are not sure of your salvation, you cannot win the war against the enemy. You cannot defeat witchcraft traders if you are not thoroughly converted. You must give your life to Christ today. Quit the camp of the devil and come into the camp of the Almighty.

My prayer for you is that, every root of successful curses upon your family should be uprooted, in the name of Jesus. I also decree that every generational spirit, that troubles your family must depart today, in the name of Jesus. My final prayer for you is that, all evil spirits trading with your family will fail woefully, in the name of Jesus.

Foundation Of Marital Distress

The prevailing situation of the modern age, points to the fact that this is the age of marital distress. It goes without saying, that many marriages are sick to the point of death. In fact, many couples have already packed up their marriages. Several men and women are exploring new ways of achieving satisfaction in life as they know that they have failed woefully in their marital lives.

Some successful businessmen, highly-rated professionals, technocrats, renowned politicians and men who seem to have made their mark in the world, are not finding the same level of success in marriage. Nine out of ten people are actually suffering from marital distress. The situation leaves much to be desired. The situation has continued to bother me as I survey the marital situation in the nation and in the church. If God's people are experiencing marital distress, what is the fate of the unGodly?

If Christians are finding it hard to achieve peace, stability and success in their marriages, what is the hope of those who have no relationship with God? One cannot afford to gloss over an issue as weighty as the institution of marriage. We must get down to the foundation and address this knotty issue.

The moment we are able to discover the root of marital distress, we are sure of receiving divine help which will, consequently, turn our marital situation around.

We need the wisdom of the Ancient of Days. Our human wisdom will fail us. Our skills may not suffice. My scientific and academic training has made me know that, erudition and human logic cannot hold the home together. There are renowned professors of psychology who are divorcees. I wonder what has happened to their knowledge of psychology. Why could they not bring psychological theories to bear on their marriage? Why are they so sound in human and animal psychology, but do not know how to relate with women who have no academic degrees? If some of these academic professors are sincere, they should seek for genuine help. How true are the words of the Bible:

> **Great men are not always wise. Neither do the aged understand (Job 32:9).**

Therefore, the greatest problem anyone can ever have, is to refuse to seek help from the Almighty. Solution to marital distress begins with definite steps toward bringing God into your marital situation. No marital distress is so acute that it cannot be taken care of by God. Perhaps your marital situation, is a far cry from what you anticipated several years ago. Perhaps you have actually come to your wit's end. It is also possible that you have decided to throw in the towel. Who knows, you might have vowed that you would never have anything to do with marriage again.

May I offer you some prophetic words of encouragement? Your situation will not remain the same. God will turn it around. Man's extremity, they say, is God's opportunity. What has been stumbling blocks before you, will soon become stepping-stones to marital success. Although you might have found yourself in the throes of marital distress, that kind of situation will not last forever.

A lot of people whose marital lives have become models of excellence, started out with problems, that they never thought about. I have discovered that a lot of people who have distress in their marital lives have potentials for achieving great exploits in marriage. The only problem is that they are ignorant of these potentials.

Therefore, many of them have given up, when they are supposed to make a little more effort to draw upon the grace and the power of God. If you are ready to receive divine help, your travails in the area of marriage will become a thing of the past. God will turn your marital distress to miracles, and your testimony will be an encouragement to a multitude.

Beloved, I want you to manifest violent faith in the Lord. Violent faith, is the faith that has no patience with the enemy. It is sad that many people have lost every sense of direction in the area of marriage.

A lot of people are being pushed back and forth by powers beyond them. Some, who are expected to have broken new grounds, in every department of marital life, are still struggling to get started. Many people have lost money, position and wonderful opportunities when they are expected to come up with unprecedented records of achievements.

A lot of people are confused, having met their enemies in every corner; enemies attack them in their business, family and social lives. It is possible, that what I have said so far has aptly described your situation. It is possible, that you have the feeling of being surrounded by terrible enemies.

There is no gainsaying the fact that, you know that God has something wonderful in store for you, but the problem is that you have found it difficult to reconcile your daily experiences with the good things, which you have continued to anticipate. I know that you have good dreams about the present and the future. I know that you are ready to pay the price of outstanding success and achievement in life. It is even possible that you have tried your best without any tangible result. I know that you have waited for the manifestation or fulfilment of the promises of God for quite sometime now.

I also know that it is possible that you are tired of waiting for your miracles. I have no doubt in my heart concerning the fact that you have tried every method that you know. I know that you are willing to go beyond your present level in life. The fact that you are reading this book means you are ready to receive help. Do not be intimidated by the fact that your previous attempt to solve life's problems in general, and marital problems in particular, did not yield the kind of result you desired. Just take one more step and your miracle is sure.

My heart goes out to those who are being hurt. I am burdened for men and women who know that their present position in life, is far away from where God wants them to be. I am praying with all my heart, for those who have continuously found it difficult, to attain their dreams, hopes and aspirations in life.

A lot of people are simply confused; they do not understand themselves. When such people are alone, they ask themselves questions like "What is wrong with me? What is happening to me? I have prayed, gone through deliverance, made several positive confessions and attended many Christian programmes. Why am I still suffering? Why is nothing working for me?

Why?" The greatest problem, which any man can go through in life, is that of marital distress. It is easier to cope with business distress than to cope with marital distress.

However, I have discovered that most marital distresses which people suffer have their roots in a deeper evil. Those who suffer marital distress do not know that evil powers are actually aiming at their lives. They are attacking their victims' marital lives only as part of a grand plan to get rid of them. Wicked satanic agents, are actually bent, on eliminating people who are complaining that they are suffering from marital distress. Yes, I know that your marital life is under attack, but that is not the end of the story. The devil and his agents are actually gunning for your life. That is why I want you to be angry with the devil. You must get to a point, where you are willing to talk back to the devil and say 'Enough is enough.'

I am aware of the fact, that some people are fighting a battle when they go to bed. Many people are restless because they sense the enemy's attack from day to day. Why should your life be converted to a battleground, when Jesus says:

Come unto me, all ye that labour and are heavy laden, and I will give you rest. Take my yoke upon you, and learn of me; for I am meek and lowly in heart; and ye shall find rest unto your souls. For my yoke is easy, and my burden is light (Matthew 11:28-30).

Why should you claim to be a believer, when rest is foreign to you? Why must you allow the devil to render the word of God of no effect in your life? God will change your situation. He is going to deal with your enemies and make them bow before you. You are going to experience the power of God today. It is possible that you have become an object of ridicule, simply because your marital life has been turned upside down by the devil. Now is the time for you to ask the God of Elijah to stand up on your behalf.

Get ready for a divine visitation, as you take these prayer points. Please, lay your right hand on your head as you pray with holy madness:

Every witchcraft arrow, come out by fire, in Jesus' name.

Every satanic twin sister/brother that is collecting my blessings, fall down and die, in the name of Jesus.

The Bible says:

If the foundations be destroyed, what can the righteous do? (Psalm 11:3).

The foundation of a building plays a crucial role in its stability. If it is faulty, the structure on it will not stand. Most of us who live in this generation are fortunate when compared with our ancestors. Many of the things which we address today, were not addressed in those days.

If you talk with those who got married 50 or 60 years ago, they would tell you that most of their problems can be traced to lack of opportunities. It is quite possible that your parents did not have access to the facts which you are reading today. Your parents would have been happier, if they had a good opportunity to lay a solid spiritual foundation for their homes. Many of them suffered because they did not have pastors or believers around them. You have the opportunity of laying that good foundation today. You have the opportunity of dealing with any enemy, that wants to fight against your marriage.

If you are single, you can use the weapon of prayer as a tool, for getting the right partner for your life. You have the opportunity of breaking yourself loose from all chains, which have put you into collective captivity. If you are able to clear a lot of things from your background, you will succeed in getting rid of problems that will arise later in your life.

LESSONS FROM CREATION

The foundation of everything in life is very important. We have a lot of lessons to learn from the story of creation. The book of Genesis shows us the process of creation. God created the world and He also created man. However, a crucial step was taken in Genesis when God created a woman. The Bible throws light on how God instituted the first marriage (Genesis 2:18):

And the Lord God said, It is not good that the man should be alone; I will make him an help meet for him.

God places a great premium on marriage. Your marriage is more important to God than you can ever imagine. God does not expect you to joke with your marriage. He actually states that it is not good for a man to be alone, neither is it good for a woman to be alone. Marriage is not an accident, neither is it a pass-time. It is a matter of life and death. It cannot be compared with a commuter bus, that one can board and alight from at will.

Once you board the vehicle of marriage, you are expected to remain on board, no matter what happens. You can jump into marriage, but you cannot jump out of it. It is easy to rush into marriage, but it is very difficult to rush out of it. You can choose to go into marriage with your eyes closed, but I doubt if you can remain in it without opening your eyes. God had a purpose, a design and a plan when He said: "It is not good that the man should be alone; I will make him an help meet for him."

How did God create Eve, Adam's wife?

And the Lord God caused a deep sleep to fall upon Adam, and he slept: and he took one of his ribs, and closed up the flesh instead thereof; And the rib, which the Lord God had taken from man, made he a woman, and brought her unto the man.

And Adam said, This is now bone of my bones, and flesh of my flesh: she shall be called Woman, because she was taken out of Man (Genesis 2:21-23).

The passage above gives us a very important revelation. Marriage is not based on human imagination. God the architect, the builder and the sustainer of the home, had a divine blueprint for every marriage. He brings two people together in marriage for a purpose.

God is meticulous even when it comes to the issue of marriage. He brings two people together with mathematical precision. He knows the man or woman who will make you fulfil His divine purpose for your life. If you are a sister, somebody's rib was used to create you.

If you are a brother, your rib was used to create a sister, once God has ordained that you will get married. The crucial question then is: how do I get to know my God-appointed partner? This is a question that you must answer. Your success in life depends on it.

The truth is that, your destiny in life is attached to your partner. Your divine helper is your partner.

Marriage is stronger than family tie. The consequences of getting married to the wrong person can hardly be enumerated. It is tragic to pick the wrong rib. Once you get married to the wrong person your destiny is affected. The devil is very intelligent. He knows the potentials that are inherent in a successful marriage. This explains why he hates any marriage that is capable of causing havoc to his kingdom. That is why he is the number one enemy of your marriage. He fights tooth and nail to destroy it.

Why are many marriages breaking down? Why are many couples contemplating divorce?

Why are many believers finding it difficult to successfully pursue their programme in the area of marriage? The only answer to these questions is that the foundation has been destroyed. If you desire a good home, you must take care of the foundation. Now is the time to look into the foundation of your marriage. A good start, will result in a good finish. The moment the foundation is solid, the building will stand the test of time. A home that is built on the solid rock will stand.

I had an experience when I was studying for my doctorate degree in England that I would ever live to remember. A Nigerian acquaintance of mine requested that I should accompany him to Gatwick Airport. I was somewhat curious and I asked to know what we were going to do there. He brightened up and said, "You are accompanying me to the airport because I want you to join me in welcoming my wife to England." I accepted to go with him since I wanted to share in his joy. The airport was unusually busy that day.

The fact that people were running back and forth signalled the arrival of a Nigeria Airways plane. The airport personnel as well as the security agents were all on the alert. Those in the aircraft began to alight one after the other. I expected my friend to locate his wife with ease but I was surprised when he brought out a photograph from his pocket trying to compare the face on it with the faces of some ladies who were arriving from Nigeria.

A lot of questions ran through my mind. After waiting for about 30 minutes, I could no longer keep quiet. I said to my friend: "I am sorry if this question will bother you. Do you mean you have never met your wife? Have you lost the memory of how she looks? Why have you continued to look at this photograph?" My friend smiled and came up with a shocking reply.

"Let me confide in you, I have never met her before. This photograph was posted from Nigeria. I am supposed to get married to her because my parents arranged it."

We waited for a long time. It was like waiting for eternity. Just when I thought the posted wife would not arrive, a light complexioned lady sauntered towards our direction. My friend looked at his photograph again, stole a glance at the direction of the lady and called a name that elicited a response from the unknown lady: "Yes, I am the one. Are you the man I am supposed to get married to?" That was how my friend's wife was posted to England. Unfortunately, the marriage never worked. Two years later, my friend's wife absconded with a German. What went wrong with that type of marriage? It was built on a wrong foundation. I have learnt to examine the foundation whenever I come across cases that bother on marital distress.

What is your basis for choosing a partner? Are you basing your choice on beauty, financial ability and academic qualification? That kind of foundation will not support a building that you intend to live in for a lifetime. If you fail to make God the foundation of your marriage, you will regret your action.

Every instance of marital distress, can be traced to a bad foundation. When you are planning to get married, you have to take a spiritual searchlight and examine the foundation.

CAUSES OF MARITAL DISTRESS

The following are the causes of marital distress:

Marriage relationships that were contracted when you were strangers to God.

Those who started their marriage without consulting God will experience marital distress. The way you handle your marriage can be likened to the way a computer is utilised. If you put garbage into your computer system what you get out of it is a well-packaged garbage. A bad foundation will give you a bad building, no matter the amount of money expended on it.Any relationship that is contracted or initiated when you are an enemy of God will fail. If a lady decides to hold on to a man who she met when she was in the world, she will build her marriage on the foundation of failure. Those who are partially born-again will automatically go for a relationship that has no God in it.

A man who decides to marry a lady who has no relationship with God, is storing up disaster for the future. If you get married to a godless man because of peer or family pressure, you will reap a bounty harvest of marital failure. If you join your hands with a child of the devil, that kind of marriage will not last; it will get into distress almost immediately you start it.

I have stated time and again that besides hell fire, nothing is as bad as marital distress. The consequences of leaving God out of the choice of a partner, far outweigh what you think you stand to gain. You can hardly afford to pay the price of self-management in the area of marriage.

Holding on to one's own choice and disregarding God's, is likened to walking into the jaws of a hungry lion. The catastrophic consequences can never be imagined. You will live to regret it. It is an expressway into trouble, confusion and total failure. Distress is inevitable. The Bible states unequivocally that, there is no fellowship or communion between light and darkness; they are diametrically opposed to each other.

There is no communion between the temple of God and the temple of an idol. There is no meeting point between children of light and children of darkness. Even if you chose to dine with the devil by cleverly using a long spoon you will end up being the loser. By the time you empty the content of the long spoon, it poisons your entire system. I pity men and women who choose to operate a 'buy now, pay later' system. Such people regret every step taken outside God's will.

I pity the smart Alecs of this world who think they can 'eat their cake and have it.' They have always ended up biting their fingers. You can join the bandwagon, but you will never get away from suffering the consequences. You can operate your life the way you like, but you must also be ready to pay the price. What you sow is what you will reap. A farmer who planted nothing and went about telling his friends that he has an hectare of apples will become ashamed when he has nothing to show them during the time of harvest. His story can be believed only for a short time and whoever tells it eventually bears the shame of self-deceit.

God expects you to burn the bridge that links you with the world, immediately you decide to follow Him. Your value, plans and prospects will be swallowed by God's perfect will. You must burn the bridge that is capable of taking you back to the world. Your employer may threaten to give you a sack, but you must consider the fact that it is easier to face the wrath of man than to face God's own wrath. It is better to lose a job than to lose the opportunity of getting to heaven.

Why must you succumb to the pressures of a man who keeps his own family intact, and wants to ruin your future.

I know of rich men who send their children to school in chauffeur-driven cars and lavish care and comfort on them while they are ready to destroy the lives of other people's children. Beware! You must break every relationship that is capable of constructing and establishing a bad foundation for your marriage. Burn the bridges, disregard the promises and return the presents given to you by those who are likely to lead you to the dungeon of separation from the Almighty.

Marriages based on accidental pregnancy

Many people are married today, not because they planned it that way, but because they were forced into it through accidental pregnancy. Such marriages are not based on love; they are born out of circumstances. That kind of marriage can best be described as a fire brigade arrangement. I do not know if you have ever watched fire brigade personnel in action. They are always in a hurry, they have no room for decorum.

A lady suddenly gets pregnant and everybody begins to panic. The parents of the two partners agree that the marriage should be contracted to avoid the shame of accidental pregnancy. Whenever some parents discover that their daughter has been put in the family way, they forcefully instruct the man responsible for the pregnancy to marry the pregnant girl.

Marriages that emanate from accidental pregnancies are based on lust rather than love. True love will not put the other partner into trouble. Lust is careless, but love is considerate. The people of the world often say, 'love is blind.' They are wrong. Perhaps what they meant to say is 'lust is blind'. Yes, lust is blind; it is also deaf and dumb. Lust makes people insensitive to the well-being of others.

Sex before marriage

Any sex outside marriage leads to marital distress and amounts to the construction of a satanic coffin. If you decide to construct a coffin for your marriage, you may end up being buried in it. The problem of pre-marital sex has become the order of the day. People now say, "if you cannot beat them, join them."

The situation is so alarming that teenage girls find it difficult to maintain chastity. Nowadays, girls in the early teens are so morally loose that they constitute painful embarrassment to their parents. By the time such girls gain admission to the university, they graduate into glorified academic prostitutes. That is how most lives have been destroyed. A lot of atrocities take place on university campuses and have left many people bewildered and confused.

A particular incident took place in 1995. Members of our prayer warrior team, were observing a prayer vigil, while a strange appearance of five strange birds caught their attention. They sensed that the birds were not ordinary ones and decided to issue judgmental curses against them. One of the birds landed on the ground, within the church premises, and transformed into an old woman. The members of the prayer warrior were surprised, but they knew that it was their fiery prayer that brought down the flying image.

This is no fantasy. I actually spoke with the woman eyeball to eyeball. She told me she came from a town located in the western area of Nigeria. According to her, she took off in the company of other powerful witches, to carry out an assignment at the University of Lagos. She made me know that their responsibility was to strengthen cult activities in the university. She said, "Man of God, we have no business whatsoever with your church. In fact, it is a no-go-area for our class of witches.

The only problem is that your church is located very close to the university campus. To get to our place of assignment, we have to pass through the precinct of your church. We did not know that your men were holding a prayer meeting."

I challenged her to give her life to Christ but she remained adamant saying, "It is impossible. I cannot. I have already sold my soul to the devil." Then she looked straight at me and said, "We know you. Your father died last year." I told her she was correct, I asked her to tell me how she knew that I lost my father. She reeled into a terrible laughter and said, "You are asking me how I got to know that you lost your father? We operate a very powerful network and we have our agents everywhere."

Can you imagine that an illiterate witch, was given the assignment of supervising a university campus? The devil is really wicked. You can imagine what will happen to the university ladies who sleep with men at random as well as male students in the university, who are in the occult. Your guess is as good as mine.

Female university students operate under a terrible licentious spirit. How can you explain the case of an 18-year old male, who goes about with dangerous weapons with which he harms innocent students? How can a young boy, hack a fellow student to death with an axe? Such students are operating under terrible satanic influences. What that old hag disclosed to me made me pity young men and women in the universities.

It pays to obey God. When the Bible says thou shalt not do so and so, such a commandment is for your utmost good. To get involved with premarital sex is to put your marriage into trouble. If you violate the word of God, your life will be invaded by terrible demons from the bottomless pit.

You may choose to commit immorality and your pastor may never know it, but the devil will surely know you have violated a spiritual principle and he will afflict you. You are waging war against yourself and digging your own grave. If you are 25 or 30 years old and about five men are sleeping with you, you need serious deliverance.

Marriages contracted after demonic consultation

It is common knowledge that many African parents visit soothsayers or diviners to find out what the future holds for their children.

Whenever some believers inform their parents that they have been led of the Lord to choose their partners, some parents would quickly ask them to give them the names of such would-be husbands or wives. What do they generally do with such names? They go to the house of local witch doctors to ask them to check the names with their gods. That is how many people's names have gone to demonic archives through consultation with fetish priests.

If you are very vigilant, you would have realised that African parents are fond of collecting the names of people they see around their children. If your marriage takes place after such a demonic consultation, it will end up in failure. Satan, being very clever, would use the information against your life, which will be the beginning of your marital failure. Whenever the soothsayer tries to consult with a higher demon, the devil will manipulate and seal your doom.

Satanic agents will not rest, until they have succeeded in luring one into an unprofitable union. Even if the person's name you have given to your parents was capable of leading you into confusion and marital failure, such a fellow is likely to pretend and dance to your tune until he has succeeded in destroying you.

If you are a lady, such a man will decide to 'accept' to join you in your church, and he would be regular until he has succeeded in taking you to the altar. You may experience the greatest shock of your life, when he takes you home after the wedding and you come across occult materials in his bedroom. He is likely to say, 'You can go to blazes. You are already married to me and there is no going back.' That is how the problem begins right from the first day.

How can the devil succeed in capturing such a lady? The devil knows that he can destroy people's destiny through leading them into destructive marital relationships. His intention is to lead as many young men and women to get married to their enemies. This is a very serious matter. You cannot afford to gloss over an issue as weighty as this.

I want you to close your eyes as you take this prayer point:

I shall not marry my enemy, in the name of Jesus.

Failure to address this issue may sentence you to perpetual suffering and regret. Even if you had never experienced what it means to suffer the consequences of bad marriage, you may have witnessed the travail of relatives and parents who are bruised by the jagged saw of marital failure.

Perhaps you can recall how your own mother suffered at the hands of your father. Perhaps you can also recall how another relative of yours was battered for life after receiving deadly blows from the hands of the monster called marital distress. Would you like to step into the shoes of those people? Of course, not.

Many women who started their marital life on a wrong note have lived to tell stories of misery and woe. For example, although they suffered together with their husbands, yet they hardly live to enjoy the fruits of their labour.

If you do not want to have such bitter experiences, you must spend quality time to pay attention to your foundation. Prevention, the adage says, is better than cure. Even if you eventually procured the solution to your problems, the time spent as well as the scars from the wound will remain unforgettable.

Marriages enforced by ignorant parents

Some parents are fond of forcing their children into injurious marital relationships. Some parents are too anxious to see their children married, thus they coerce them into marriage.

If your parents force you into a relationship, whatever you suffer will be borne by you. You will not be able to blame them, but even if you do, it will not change your situation.

If a lady is seen with two or three men, who appear well off, the parents will likely have preference for that particular man. Your mother may say to you, "Who is this new man who has started visiting you? I do not want to see him. I want you to get married to that young medical doctor, who visited here a few months ago. That is my stand." The lady may reply: "Mummy, I cannot marry that medical doctor. He is not my kind of person. He is a womaniser. With that kind of man one cannot experience marital stability." The mother may persuade her: "That is not a problem. It is very easy to tame a womaniser. Just satisfy him and give him good food and he will never go out again."

With that kind of statement, the mother may persuade her. If the lady succumbs to the pressure, she would eventually experience marital distress. No matter what she does, the man would continue to womanise. Of course, her mother will not be there each time the man comes home after a late night escapade. She can blame her mother but it is she (and not her mother) who would bear the suffering.

Some parents ignorantly commit their children to get married to someone from the same town or village regardless of what happens in the future. Such parents, bring negative influence to bear on their children, because they feel that if their children marry from the same community such marriages are likely to stand.

What do you do if everyone from your village or community is a drunkard, occult practitioner, chieftaincy title holder, member of the white garment (fringe) church, member of the Jehovah's Witness sect or a nominal church goer? Must you get married to someone from your community? If you build your marital life on the foundation of ignorant parents, you will regret your action.

Sexual pollution during your youth

In this environment, many young people are sexually assaulted or lured into immorality when they are very young. Such an ugly experience leads young men and women into sexual promiscuity. Unless such victims go through deliverance, their traumatic experience will affect their marital lives.

If an armed robber rapes a lady, she is likely to suffer marital breakdown. After such a lady has seen a medical doctor, she must also consult Dr. Jesus for spiritual sanitation and deliverance. Such a lady's life must be rid of all the evil things which the armed robber has transferred into her through sex. It is possible that some wicked spirits are bent on destroying your marital life.

Marriages in which blood covenants were formed

Many young people go into blood covenants to prove their loyalty to their partners. Some young men and women foolishly cut themselves with razor blades and form terrible blood covenants without knowing the implication of what they are doing. Such covenants will work against your future marriage.

Why should two young people who are yet to get married enter into any kind of covenant? If you said, "I am going to get married to you, if I disappoint you, let my days be filled with darkness and sorrow", you have formed a covenant. If you break it, you will come under a curse. Such people must go through deliverance, if they want to experience freedom from evil covenants and curses.

Marriage established on the principles of "it is better than nothing"

A common saying goes thus, "Half of a loaf of bread is better than none at all." Really? That sounds like a demonic philosophy. If you go for a half loaf of bread in your marriage, you are going to live with it.

Will you opt for a marital relationship which you are going to be managing when it is possible to receive God's best? Such a marriage will collapse like a pack of cards.

Marriages based on trial and error

Some people are ready to say yes to any man or woman they come across, perhaps because they believe they have waited too long. Such people normally come up with statements like, "I am ready to say yes to any man who comes to ask my hand in marriage. Anything goes. If I keep on waiting for Mr. Right, I might end up waiting forever. Let me try the relationship, who knows, it might work."

Such a trial and error approach will surely end up in failure. God never intended for us to approach marriage in a hit or miss way. God is the only genuine match-maker. He is the only manufacturer who can never make a mistake.

Marriages based on physical attraction

Physical attraction cannot sustain marriage. Beauty fades and appearance cannot give you a lasting satisfaction. If your marriage is based on physical attraction, it will fail when your spouse begins to age. The beauty you saw yesterday may not be there tomorrow.

Some ladies go about saying, "I am still looking for my kind of man. I will get married to a tall, handsome man. If a man is not presentable, I cannot marry him." You can go ahead and marry Mr. Universe or Miss World, but you will discover sooner or later that, beauty fades. Physical attraction will not survive, when you face the nitty-gritty of marriage.

Marriages based on material interest

If your choice of a partner is based on material interest, your marriage will not last. It is good to live a comfortable life, but prosperity and material comfort cannot sustain a home. I know many millionaires who are divorcees.

I pity ladies who go about telling everybody: "The man of my dream must be wealthy. He must have at least two cars, six digit bank accounts, and must not be a tenant. My man must also be able to afford occasional overseas trips. I can never marry a poor man. I am not going to suffer in the house of any man." Such a desire will lead you into a terrible mistake. There are lots of young men who are quick to go for ladies who are comfortable and have cars. Immediately they sight a sister who owns a car, they begin to pray. Within a short time they come up with a vision. Some careless brothers go to car parks to choose their wives. They ask the ushers and security personnel to give them names of rich, single sisters.

Once they are through with their enquiry, they run to the marriage committee with such names. Unfortunately, such sisters are too busy to pray, and might say "yes" without finding out the will of God.

. . .

Such ladies, who have waited for several years, generally grab whoever comes to them. It is after the marriage has been contracted, that the man realises that he has walked into a cage. If anything happens to the lady's fortune or wealth, the boat of their marriage will capsize.

Marriages based on satanic prophecies

When we talk of satanic prophecy, people are likely to think about visiting a voodoo priest. Respected or popular prophets in white garment churches dish out satanic prophecies. It is unfortunate that some people who are married today, were led by the nose, through satanic prophecies.

Some people attend churches where some so-called prophets and prophetesses speak saying, "Thus said the Lord . . . You are going to come across your wife beside a tree around noon tomorrow. Just walk up to her; she is your God's appointed wife." Such a man will be confused as he would not know how to locate the appropriate tree; and that is exactly how many men have picked a deadly bomb for a wife.

Marriages established by donation of a spouse at a young age

It is the practice in some African countries, that parents give out their daughters at the ages of eight, nine or ten to some wealthy businessmen or traditional rulers. The young girls grow up in the houses of their husbands. That kind of foundation will lead to marital failure. How can a young girl of 13 or 15 cope with marriage? She will end up going through the travail of marriage when she is supposed to be under the care of her parents. Such a marriage never works.

Polygamous marriages

Most African marriages in the past were polygamous. We thank God for the wonderful changes which the Gospel has brought to our society. Polygamy is not the will of God and will never work.

A lady may go into a polygamous marriage just because she is pressured into it. After a year or two, she is likely to begin to seek for ways of coming out of it. There are some ladies who decide to get married to rich men who already have two or three wives. Such ladies will discover sooner or later, that money cannot provide satisfaction.

Perhaps you come from a polygamous family, and you can remember what you have gone through. The problems often extend to the third or fourth generation.

Having examined these faulty foundations, you can now understand why many families are distressed. A bad foundation will not sustain any marriage. Even if the marriage ceremony was conducted in Europe or America, it would not stand.

The success of your marriage, is directly proportional to the strength of the foundation of your marriage. Salvation is the beginning of a successful marriage. The day you become a child of God, your life is taken away from a bad foundation and placed on Jesus the solid Rock, and with Him your marriage will never fail.

The Bible says,

If the foundation be destroyed, what can the righteous do.

The righteous can only rely upon what is written in Jeremiah 32: 17:

Ah Lord GOD! Behold, thou hast made the heaven and the earth by thy great power and stretched out arm, and there is nothing too hard for thee.

It is possible that your foundation is really bad, but you do not have to worry. God can change it. He will bring such a fantastic transformation in your situation that you will be pleasantly surprised.

Some ladies came to narrate their peculiar experiences: "Man of God, I do not understand what has been happening to me. Men used to pester me before I became born again. But since I gave my life to Christ no single man has spoken to me. Tell me, what is wrong with me?"

Such people need not worry. That kind of situation is an indication of the fact that the devil had terrible plans for their lives before they knew the Lord. The devil is now terribly angry that they have escaped from his kingdom. He will continue his attempt to prevent your divinely-ordained partner from receiving divine revelation. But he will not succeed.

STEPS TO BE TAKEN BY THE RIGHTEOUS

Identify your 'foundation'

You must ask yourself the following questions.

What kind of foundation or background do I have?

Have I identified all the problems that are capable of affecting my marriage?

Have I recognised what my parents did deliberately or ignorantly to affect my marriage?

Am I under any yoke, curse or bondage?

Am I trying to build my marriage along the lines of marital distress?

Have I covered anything which is capable of affecting my marriage?

Am I deliberately building my marriage on a bad foundation?

Have I sowed any bad seed that is capable of destroying my marriage?

You must provide answers to these questions. You cannot make any progress until you have identified your foundation. You must spend quality time on this important step. You must be ready to deal with all avenues for a satanic incursion into your marriage.

Confession of sin and repentance

You must confess your sins and repent wholeheartedly. Repentance, will earn you a transfer from the platform of bad foundation, to the mountain-top of victory and success in marriage. Confess your sins and tell God you will never go back to them.

If you conceal or hide your sins, the devil will continue to use them as a legal weapon for leading you into marital destruction. Repent today and you will experience a turn-around in your marriage.

Aggressive and well-targeted prayer

You can only build your life on a solid foundation by employing aggressive and well-targeted prayer. The devil is so wicked, that he is not ready to allow you to experience a successful marital life. He will not yield unless he is subjected to repeated prayer bombardments.

Many ladies and men will never get married unless they are ready to pray fervently. The devil knows that, if he allows you to have things easy in the area of marriage, he will lose the battle. That is why many people have fought their toughest battles in the area of marriage.

A lot of people will have to employ the weapon of dry fast, aggressive warfare prayer, vigils and serious prayers of agreement before the devil will shift his ground.

Breaking of evil covenants

Your marriage can only be successful, fruitful, progressive and trouble-free if you are ready to break evil covenants. If you go into marriage while evil covenants are still in place, that marriage will not succeed. Such a marriage is a miniature hell on earth. You must break every yoke and release yourself from bondage.

Breaking of curses

No man or woman should ever go into marriage when personal or ancestral curses are still operating in his or her life. A curse will cancel all the goodness which God has programmed for one's marriage. You must go through deliverance to get all curses in your life broken before you go into marriage.

Restitution

I have stated time and again that the devil is a legal expert. He is also the accuser of the brethren. If you fail to do your restitution the devil will have a case against you in the demonic kingdom. The moment you do your restitution, you become completely free.

Intercession

You can clear a lot of debris from your foundation through intercessory prayer. Prayer is the greatest pill that can grant you immunity from marital sicknesses. Intercession will also affect your partner and prepare him or her for a future marriage.

Finally, you have to take steps to clear satanic pollution from your marriage. You need to allow the divine axe to go right down to the root of your marriage and uproot unprofitable plantations.

You need to pray for the deliverance of your marriage from the polluting influences of anti-marriage forces. You need to paralyse and dismantle every evil pipe releasing pollutants into the foundation of your marriage. You need to invite the God of new beginnings into your home.

To end this chapter, pray this prayer point with fire in your voice.

Spirit husband/wife, release me, in the name of Jesus.

Forces Against Spinsters & Bachelors

There are diverse wicked spirits specifically fighting against successful marriages.

There are some marriages that the enemy considers ***"very risky"*** , i.e. marriages that would harm his kingdom. He (satan) fights hard to see that such marriages do not hold.

There are powers known as ***"Evil manipulators"***.

Their functions are four-fold:

1. To hinder right matches
2. Hinder people from getting married
3. Cause late marriage
4. Cause problems among married couples

Dark forces know the importance of marriage. Once a marriage is under the wicked authority of evil manipulators, they cause serious problems.

The first target of the enemy is the foundation. The Bible says, "If the foundation be destroyed, what can the righteous do?" Psalm 11:3.

The initial steps in setting up a matrimonial home are very important to the enemy.

The wicked forces attack marriages from the foundation. They sponsor marriages based on lust, or wild and foolish love. This means that such marriages are manipulated by the forces of darkness. If a marriage is based on lust, when old age sets in and beauty wanes, it breaks down.

The forces of darkness employ lust, senseless infatuation, forced marriage, parental manipulation, hurried marriages, sex before marriage, teenage marriages etc. to create bad foundation for the love.

If you are not led by the Spirit of God, your marriage cannot be put on a solid foundation.

Listed below, are the principal satanic forces, battling against bachelors and spinsters, particularly in our environment.

FORCES BATTLING AGAINST BACHELORS / SPINSTERS

Inherited anti-marriage problems

When one's marital status follows the evil trend affecting one's parents. E.g., when father or mother never married properly or have failed marriages.

The travails of the first born

When the first born has been covenanted to spirits offering counterfeit protection. Many first born are used as "torch lights", i.e. they opened the gate for others, but fail to prosper.

Spirit-husbands/wives

It is the situation whereby one is consciously or unconsciously married in the spirit world. The spiritual marriage is as binding as the physical marriage. The spirit wife or husband will fight with the last drop of blood to keep his/her partner. This relationship which is generally characterized by sexual dreams, prevents marital bliss or makes finding a partner very difficult.

Financial curse

Insufficient funds to settle down in marriage conveniently.

Bad names

Bearing names glorifying idols or linking to idols or dead relatives.

Bad marks

Spiritual marks of rejection and avoidance by would-be partners.

Spirit of rejection

Feeling unwanted, isolated and unloved.

Parental curses

Anti-marriage curses issued by parents.

Bad health

Chronic health disorders occupying the best of one's attention.

Spiritual blindness

Not plainly seeing God's choice for you.

Spiritual bride price

A situation where a person's bride price has been paid in the spiritual world, thereby preventing physical manifestation of marriage.

Spiritual wedding clothes and rings

Spiritual wedding rings and clothes block physical marriage

Anti-maintenance spirit

Constant amputation of relationships

Spirit of polygamy

Inability to maintain a monogamous relationship.

Evil covenants

Evil anti-marriage covenants block many marriages.

Evil linkage

Linkage to bad spirits.

Homosexualism

Whether past or present, this has serious spiritual implications for enjoying your marital life.

Lesbianism

Whether past or present, this, also, has serious spiritual implications for enjoying your marital life.

Broken homes

Children from such homes generally experience marital failures.

Amputators/emptiers

These are forces that amputate or empty marriage plans.

Prayer Warfare

DEFEATING ANTI-CONCEPTION FORCES

Personalise these confessions: Psalm 127:1-5; Isa. 8:18; Deut. 7:12-15.

PRAYER POINTS

1. Thank the Lord for He is able to do all things.
2. Lord, forgive me of all my ancestral sexual sins, in Jesus' name.
3. Let the lost glory of my family line, be restored to me, in the name of Jesus.
4. I bind and paralyse, the activities of the family strongman in my life, in the name of Jesus.
5. I bind and paralyse, any strongman in charge of my womb, in the name of Jesus.
6. Let all the doorways of the enemy, into my life, be closed firmly, in the name of Jesus.
7. I decree, the exit of all spiritual poison, that entered into my womb during my wedding ceremony, in the name of Jesus.
8. Spiritual poison, introduced into my womb through (pick from the underlisted), I command you to depart completely, in the name of Jesus:

- eating in the dream
- sexual intercourse in the dream
- drinking of dirty water in the
- dream demonic contamination
- abortion
- masturbation
- spiritual incision
- remote control mechanisms
- intercourse with demonic sexual partner(s)

9. I break and cancel, every curse, jinx and spell placed on my womb, in the name of Jesus.
10. Let all the spiritual parasites, feeding on the seeds of my womb, roast, in the name of Jesus.
11. Lord, correct supernaturally, any malfunctioning of my ovary, fallopian tube and womb, in the name of Jesus.
12. Let the fire and thunder of God, destroy any demonic padlock used by the enemy to lock my womb, in the name of Jesus.
13. Let all the demonic eyes, monitoring my body functions and progress receive blindness, in the name of Jesus.
14. I command, all evil plantation in my womb, to come out with all their roots, in the name of Jesus. *(Lay your hand on your womb and pray aggressively).*
15. Terminal pains, around my waist and beneath my belly, cease completely, in the name of Jesus.
16. Lord, activate my womb for conception, in Jesus' name.
17. Every vicious cycle of problems in my life, break, in Jesus' name.
18. Evil inner voice, speaking discouragement, unbelief and impossibility to my heart, be silenced, in the name of Jesus.
19. No devourer will devour the fruit of my womb, in Jesus' name.
20. I soak my womb, fallopian tube and ovary in the blood of Jesus.
21. I claim the promise of God concerning child-bearing, in the

name of Jesus. *(Confess Psalm 127:1-5 loudly.)*

22. Praise God for answered prayers.

WAR AGAINST MARRIAGE BREAKERS

Matt 19:6: Wherefore they are no more twain, but one flesh. What therefore God hath joined together, let not man put asunder.

PRAYER POINTS

1. Praise worship and thanksgiving.
2. I paralyse every architect of conflict and hostility in my home, in the name of Jesus.
3. I withdraw my marriage, from the hands of evil designers, in the name of Jesus.
4. Let every power, trying to re-draw my marriage map be put to shame, in the name of Jesus.
5. Let all household wickedness release my home, in Jesus' name.
6. I receive deliverance, from every evil plantation designed to bring me and my children under the bondage of the devil, in the name of Jesus.
7. I paralyse, every spirit of hatred and hostility militating against my home, in the name of Jesus.
8. I spoil and destabilize, every satanic plan against my home, in the name of Jesus.
9. I deliver my marriage, from the hands of home-wreckers, in the name of Jesus.
10. I pursue, overtake and recover my marriage from the hands of marriage breakers, in the name of Jesus.
11. Every evil effect of external interferences, in my marriage, be completely neutralized, in the name of Jesus.
12. Lord, dissolve and render to nought, every evil counsel fashioned against my home.
13. Every power, preventing me as a wife from accepting the headship of my husband, be paralysed, in Jesus' name.

14. Let every imagination, thought, plan, decision, desire and expectation of divorce and separation against my home, be nullified, in the name of Jesus.
15. Satan, hear the word of the Lord: You will not break my home, in the name of Jesus.
16. I bind, all powers eating away the determination of my husband to stay married to me, in the name of Jesus.
17. Let the satanic birds, eating away my love from the heart of my husband, vomit it, in the name of Jesus.
18. Pray in the spirit for at least ten (10) minutes.
19. Let all extra-marital relationship with other "partners" collapse and die, in the name of Jesus.
20. I break every soul-tie, between my husband and *(mention the name of the strange woman if you know it)* in Jesus' name.
21. I deliver my husband from the hand of evil seducers, in the name of Jesus.
22. I break the hold of the spirit wife upon my husband, in the name of Jesus.
23. I command failure, frustration and disappointment upon the strange relationship, in the name of Jesus.
24. I break the hold of the spirit of polygamy, upon my husband, in the name of Jesus.
25. Let the angels of the living God, pursue the strange woman out of the life of my husband, in the name of Jesus.
26. I refuse to be a second-hand wife, or a married-single lady, in the name of Jesus.
27. I break the power, of every evil manipulation, fashioned against my home, in the name of Jesus.
28. I paralyse every vagabond spirit, working in the life of my husband, in the name of Jesus.
29. I pull down *(pick from the underlisted)* stronghold fashioned against my marriage, in the name of Jesus.

- evil association
- planlessness
- carelessness

- weak family altar - pride
- unsaved partner or children - foolishness
- unprofitable imitation - deterioration of relationship
- communication gap - suspicion - evil counsellors
- misplaced priority - evil attachment to parents
- selfishness - unprofitable comparison
- incomplete "leaving" and incomplete "cleaving" of couple
- lack of knowledge of the word of God

PRAYERS TO ARREST UNPROFITABLE LATENESS IN MARRIAGE

1. Thank the Lord because your miracle has come.
2. Confess these scriptures out loud: Philippians 2:9; Colossians 2:13; Rev. 12:12; Luke 1:37.
3. Lord, make known to me the secrets of my inner life.
4. Help me, Lord, to discover my real self.
5. Let every imagination of the enemy against my marital life be rendered impotent, in the name of Jesus.
6. I refuse to co-operate with any anti-marriage spells and curses, in the name of Jesus.
7. I cancel every bewitchment, fashioned against my settling down in marriage, in the name of Jesus.
8. Let every force, magnetizing the wrong people to me be paralysed, in the name of Jesus.
9. I break, every covenant of marital failure and late marriage, in the name of Jesus.
10. I cancel, every spiritual wedding conducted consciously or unconsciously on my behalf in Jesus' name.
11. I remove the hand of household wickedness, from my marital life, in the name of Jesus.
12. Let every incantation, incision, hex and other spiritually

harmful activity working against me, be completely neutralized, in the name of Jesus.

13. I command all the forces of evil manipulating, delaying or hindering my marriage to be completely paralysed, in the name of Jesus.
14. Let all anti-marriage marks be removed, in Jesus' name.
15. Lord, restore me to the perfect way You created me if I have been altered.
16. Father, let Your fire, destroy every satanic weapon fashioned against my marriage, in the name of Jesus.
17. Lord, expose all the schemes and plans of satan ever devised against me through any source and at any time.
18. I forsake, any personal sin that has given ground to the enemy, in the name of Jesus.
19. I reclaim, all the ground I have lost to the enemy, in Jesus' name.
20. I apply, the power in the name and blood of Jesus, to my marital situation.
21. I apply, the blood of Jesus, to remove all consequences of evil operations and oppression in Jesus' name.
22. I break, the binding effect of anything of evil ever put upon me from any source, in the name of Jesus.
23. Let all the enemies of Jesus Christ, operating against my life be exposed, in the name of Jesus.
24. I sever myself, from any satanic linkage and any strange power, in the name of Jesus.
25. I remove the right of the enemy, to afflict my plan to get married, in the name of Jesus.
26. I break, every bondage of inherited marital confusion, in the name of Jesus.
27. I bind and plunder the goods of every strongman attached to my marriage, in the name of Jesus.
28. Let the angels of the living God, roll away the stone blocking

my marital breakthroughs in Jesus' name.
29. I remove my name, from the book of seers of goodness without appropriation, in the name of Jesus.
30. O God, arise and let all the enemies of my marital breakthrough scatter, in the name of Jesus.
31. Let the fire of God, melt away the stones hindering my marital blessings in the mighty name of Jesus.
32. Let the cloud, blocking the sunlight of my glory and breakthrough be dispersed in Jesus' name.
33. Let all evil spirits, masquerading to trouble my marital life be bound, in the name of Jesus.
34. The pregnancy of good things within me, will not be aborted by any contrary power in Jesus' name.
35. Lord, let wonderful changes, begin to be my lot from this week.
36. I reject, every spirit of the tail, in all areas of my life, in the name of Jesus.
37. I receive, my right match, in the name of Jesus.
38. I stand against, every spirit of discouragement, fear, worry and frustration, in the name of Jesus.
39. Lord, turn away all those that would jilt, disappoint or fail me, in the name of Jesus.
40. Thank God for the victory.

I RECEIVE IT

1. Thank the Lord because this year is your year of dumbfounding miracles.
2. Confess these Scriptures out loud: Philippians 2:9; Colossians 2:13; Rev. 12:12; Luke 1:37.
3. Lord, make known to me the secrets needed for my marital breakthrough.
4. Help me, Lord, to discover my real self.
5. Let every imagination of the enemy, against my marital life,

be rendered impotent, in the name of Jesus.

6. I refuse to co-operate, with any anti-marriage spells and curses, in the name of Jesus.
7. I cancel, every bewitchment fashioned against my settling down in marriage, in the name of Jesus.
8. Let every force, magnetizing the wrong people to me be paralysed, in the name of Jesus.
9. I break every covenant of marital failure and late marriage, in the name of Jesus.
10. I cancel, every spiritual wedding conducted consciously or unconsciously on my behalf in Jesus' name.
11. I remove, the hand of household wickedness from my marital life, in the name of Jesus.
12. Let every incantation, incision, hex and other spiritually harmful activity working against my marriage, be completely neutralized, in the name of Jesus.
13. I command all forces of evil, manipulating, delaying or hindering my marriage to be completely paralysed, in the name of Jesus.
14. Let all evil anti-marriage covenants, be broken, in Jesus' name.
15. Lord, restore me to the perfect way in which You created me if I have been altered.
16. Father, let Your fire destroy every satanic weapon fashioned against my marriage, in the name of Jesus.
17. I forsake, any personal sin that has given ground to the enemy, in the name of Jesus.
18. I reclaim, all the ground I have lost to the enemy, in Jesus' name.
19. Let the blood of Jesus, speak against every power working against my marriage.
20. I apply the blood of Jesus to remove all consequences of evil operations and oppression in Jesus' name.

21. I break, the binding effect, of anything of evil ever put upon me from any source, in the name of Jesus.
22. I remove, the right of the enemy to afflict my plan to get married, in the name of Jesus.
23. I break, every bondage of inherited marital confusion, in the name of Jesus.
24. I bind and plunder the goods of every strongman attached to my marriage, in the name of Jesus.
25. Let the angels of the living God, roll away the stone blocking my marital breakthroughs in Jesus' name.
26. O God, arise and let all the enemies of my marital breakthrough scatter, in the name of Jesus.
27. Let the fire of God, melt away the stones hindering my marital blessings in the mighty name of Jesus.
28. Let the cloud blocking the sunlight of my marital breakthrough be dispersed in Jesus' name.
29. Let all evil spirits, masquerading to trouble my marital life be bound, in the name of Jesus.
30. Lord, let wonderful changes be my lot this year.
31. Lord, turn away all those that would jilt, disappoint or fail me, in the name of Jesus.
32. Thank God for the victory.

POWER AGAINST SEXUAL PERVERSION

1. Thank God for His power to deliver from every bondage.
2. I break myself from every spirit of sexual perversion, in the name of Jesus.
3. I release myself from every spiritual pollution emanating from my past sins of fornication and sexual immorality, in the name of Jesus.
4. I release myself from every ancestral pollution, in Jesus' name.
5. I release myself from every dream pollution, in Jesus' name.

to come out with all its roots, in the name of Jesus.

7. Every spirit of sexual perversion working against my life, be paralysed and get out of my life, in the name of Jesus.
8. Every demon of sexual perversion assigned to my life, be bound, in the name of Jesus.
9. Father Lord, let the power of sexual perversion oppressing my life receive the fire of God and be roasted, in Jesus' name.
10. Every inherited demon of sexual perversion in my life, receive the arrows of fire and remain permanently bound, in the name of Jesus.
11. I command every force or power of sexual perversion to come against themselves, in the name of Jesus.
12. Father Lord, let every demonic stronghold built in my life by the spirit of sexual perversion be pulled down, in the name of Jesus.
13. Let every power of sexual perversion that has summoned my life be shattered to pieces, in the name of Jesus.
14. Let my soul, be delivered from the forces of sexual perversion, in the name of Jesus.
15. Let the Lord God of Elijah arise with a strong hand against every spirit husband/wife and power of sexual perversion, in the name of Jesus.
16. I break the hold, of any evil power over my life, in Jesus' name.
17. I nullify, every effect of the bite of sexual perversion upon my life, in the name of Jesus.
18. Every evil stranger and satanic deposit in my life, I command you to be paralysed and get out of my life, in Jesus' name.
19. Holy Ghost Fire, purge my life completely, in Jesus' name.
20. I claim my complete deliverance in the name of Jesus, from the spirit of fornication and sexual immorality, in the name of Jesus.
21. Let my eyes be delivered from lustfulness, in Jesus' name.
22. As from today, let my eyes be controlled by the Holy Spirit, in

the name of Jesus.

23. Holy Ghost fire, fall upon my eyes and burn to ashes every evil force and satanic power controlling my eyes, in Jesus' name.

24. I move from bondage to liberty, in every area of my life, in the name of Jesus.

25. Thank God for answers to your prayers.

SPEAK DESTRUCTION UNTO EVIL GROWTH

Confessions: Ps 31:2; Isa 58:8; Luke 18:8; Ps 102:2; Jer 1:12; 29:11; Ps 56:9; Mal 4:2; Gal 3:13-14; Col 2:14-15; Matt 8:17; Rom. 16:20; Matt 3:10; I Jn 3:8b; 2Tim 4:18.

1. *Spend quality time to stand against the effects of the evil fruits listed hereunder. Take each fruit one at a time and be violent. If you notice any reaction, stop and deal thoroughly with it before you proceed to the next point. Pray aggressively as follows: I speak destruction unto the fruits of . . . ., in the name of Jesus.*

- blood pollution
- parental curses
- open curses and threats
- spiritual confiscation
- periodic problems
- enchantment
- polygamous contamination
- peppery arrows
- marital downgrading
- dream harassment
- infirmity
- rejection

4. I recover every organ in my body from the hands of household wickedness, in the name of Jesus.

5. Every evil grip upon . . ., loose your hold, in Jesus' name.

6. I overthrow every demonic judgement directed against any organ in my body, in the name of Jesus.

7. Holy Ghost fire, destroy every garment of reproach in my life, in the name of Jesus.

8. I refuse every evil design and label placed upon my life, in the name of Jesus.

9. Any conscious or unconscious material eaten from the table of the enemy, depart from my life now in Jesus' name.
10. I dismantle, every demonic opposition to my marriage, in the name of Jesus.
11. I cast the spirits behind my problems, into the fire of judgement, in the name of Jesus.
12. Let the blood, the fire and the living water of the Most High God wash my system clean from . . .
    - unprofitable growth in my womb - evil plantation
    - evil deposits from spirit husband
    - impurities acquired from parental contamination
    - satanic poisons - evil stamps, labels and links.
13. Let every organ of my body become too hot for any evil to inhabit, in the name of Jesus.
14. Evil growth in my life, be uprooted by fire, in Jesus' name.
15. Let my body reject every evil habitation in the mighty name of our Lord Jesus Christ.
16. I pass out, any satanic deposit in my intestine, in Jesus' name.
17. I pass out, any satanic deposit in my reproductive organs, in the name of Jesus.
18. I pass out, any satanic deposit in my womb, in Jesus' name.
19. You foreign hand, laid on my womb, release me, in Jesus' name.
20. Let a creative miracle, take place in my womb and reproductive system, in the name of Jesus.
21. Father, I ask You in the name of Jesus Christ to send out Your angels and have them unearth and break all evil storage vessels fashioned against me.
22. I bind, plunder and render to nought, every strongman assigned to my womb, reproductive system and marital life, in the name of Jesus.
23. God, who quickens the dead, quicken my womb and

reproductive system, in the name of Jesus.

24. I release myself, from the hold of the spirits of sterility, infertility and fear, in the name of Jesus.
25. All spirits concerned with fornication, come out of my womb with all your roots, in the mighty name of our Lord Jesus.
26. All spirits concerned with sexual perversion, come out of my womb with all your roots, in the mighty name of Jesus.
27. I reverse, every evil manipulation done against my womb using my menstrual pads or dates, in the name of Jesus.
28. I release myself, from every inherited womb malformation, in the name of Jesus.
29. Let the blood of Jesus sanitise my womb and anoint it, in the name of Jesus.
30. I break every anti-marriage and anti-pregnancy curse, in the name of Jesus.

PRAYERS TO KNOW GOD'S WILL IN MARRIAGE

Bachelors and spinsters can use these prayer points to determine the following:

- whether a particular person is God's choice for them in marriage or not
- to discover secret things beneficial or detrimental to such relationship
- to implant God's wisdom into the foundation of the relationship.

Confess: Dan. 2:22; Eph. 1:17; Psalm 25:14; Deut. 29:29

1. Thank God for the revelational power of the Holy Spirit.
2. O God, to whom no secret is hidden, make known unto me whether . . . *(mention the name of the person)* is Your choice for me in marriage.
3. O Lord, remove from me any persistent buried grudges and half-acknowledged enmity against anyone and every other

thing that can block my spiritual vision.

4. Let every marriage-related idol present consciously or unconsciously in my heart be melted away by the fire of the Holy Spirit.
5. O Lord, give unto me, the spirit of revelation and wisdom in the knowledge of You.
6. O Lord, remove spiritual cataracts from my eyes.
7. O Lord, forgive me for every false motive or thought that has ever been formed in my heart since the day I was born.
8. O Lord, forgive me for any lie that I have ever told against any person, system or organisation.
9. O Lord, open my spiritual understanding.
10. O Lord, teach me deep and secret things.
11. O Lord, reveal to me every secret behind the marriage proposal, whether beneficial or not.
12. I refuse to fall under the manipulation of the spirits of confusion, in the name of Jesus.
13. O Lord, teach me to know that which is worth knowing, love that which is worth loving and dislike whatsoever is not pleasing to Your eyes.
14. I refuse to make foundational mistakes in marriage, in the name of Jesus.
15. Father Lord, guide and direct me in finding the partner You have ordained for me.
16. I stand against, all satanic attachments that may seek to confuse my choice, in the name of Jesus.
17. If . . . *(mention the name of the person)* is not for me, God re-direct his/her steps.
18. I bind the activities of . . . *(pick from the list below)* in my life, in the name of Jesus.

- lust - ungodly infatuation - ungodly family pressure
- demonic manipulation in dreams and visions
- attachment to the wrong choice - confusing revelations

- spiritual blindness and deafness

19. Lord, make Your way plain before my face.
20. O God, You who reveal secret things, make known unto me Your choice for me in marriage.
21. Holy Spirit, open my eyes and help me to make the right choice, in the name of Jesus.

CONFESSION AND PRAYER FOR SUPERNATURAL CONCEPTION

CONFESSIONS: Deuteronomy 7:13-15; Exod 23:25-26; Ps 91:10; Ps 113:9; Ps 127:3-5; Ps 128:3; Mal 3:10-11

Father, we thank You that children are the heritage of the Lord, and the fruit of the womb is His reward. Children are Your idea Father; You thought of children, family and home. You instituted the family in the Garden of Eden. You ordained children when You said to Adam and Eve, "Be fruitful and multiply." You say that the barren womb is never satisfied. Lord, Your word declares that 'I am fearfully and wonderful made by You.' Therefore, I'm perfect and able to conceive and have children. You said that I/my husband/my wife would be a fruitful vine by the side of our house and our children like olive plants around our table. We are not ashamed but happy because our quiver is full of children (or arrows, as You call them).

Thank You, Father, that You designed and fashioned my husband/wife and I to have children. You said in the Bible that barrenness is the exception and not the rule. That is not Your will, not normal, it is against Your plan and purpose. In Your goodness and faithfulness, every barren woman in the Bible who was godly and believed Your Word became pregnant; You opened her womb and blessed her, and she gave birth to a precious baby just as I/my husband/my wife will. You make the barren woman to keep the house and to be a joyful mother of children.

You said, Father, that because You are our God and we are Your people and have a covenant with You, that You will love us and bless us and multiply us and bless the fruit of my/ my wife's womb, and that neither male nor female among Your people would be barren. Father, we are redeemed from the curse of the law by Jesus, and being barren is under the curse of the law. Therefore, we will receive Your grace and have children.

Father, no plague and no evil shall come near our dwelling. We are healed by the stripes of Jesus. Sickness of any kind is taken out of our midst. You say we shall ask anything from You in Jesus' name and it would be done; and that if two of us on earth agree as touching anything, it would be done. So we pray and agree with You and Your Word, Father, that we will conceive and bring forth a healthy, precious baby to Your glory and honour. We pray all this according to Your Word and will. You say that this is the confidence we have in You, that if we ask anything according to Your will, You will hear us; and if You hear us, we know we have the petition we desire of You. We have it now. Thank You, Father, in Jesus' name."

1. I claim redemption, from the curse in childbirth, including the pain, in the name of Jesus.
2. I break myself loose, from the bondage of fear in childbirth, in the name of Jesus.
3. I speak, to each part of my body and command them to live in God's perfect working order, in the name of Jesus.
4. I command my body to come in line and agreement with the Word of God.
5. I cast out, fear of barrenness, in the name of Jesus.
6. I declare the curse of barrenness broken, in the name of Jesus.
7. I override all that doctors have said concerning my conception, in the name of Jesus.

8. I command every part of my reproductive system to conform to the Word and plan of God in Jesus' name.
9. Lord, I cry unto You, in the name of Jesus. Let my body conceive.
10. Lord, I cry unto You, in the name Jesus. Let my womb be pregnant.
11. I claim perfect ovulation, release of perfect eggs from the ovaries through fallopian tubes, fertilized by sperms and penetrated into healthy pregnancy, in the name of Jesus.
12. I pray for good solid attachment to my uterine walls, nourished and protected for nine months.
13. I claim unharmed and unhindered pregnancy, in Jesus' name.
14. I pray that the pregnancy grows to a perfect baby, in the name of Jesus.
15. Let the pregnancy be fulfilled, in the name of Jesus.
16. I decree it, in Jesus' name, and receive God's best.
17. I will not settle for anything less, in the name of Jesus.

FREEDOM FROM INORDINATE AFFECTIONS AND SOUL-TIES

1. Thank the Lord for His redemptive power.
2. Prayers of confession of sins and forgiveness.
3. I release myself, from all unprofitable friendship, in Jesus' name.
4. I come against, the dark powers which manipulated my friendship with . . . *(mention the name of the person)* and break their power over my life, in the name of Jesus.
5. I bind all demonic authorities, which motivated and controlled my relationship with . . . *(mention the name of the person)* and break their authority and power over my affections, in Jesus' name.
6. I command all evil remote controllers to loose their hold upon

my affections, in the name of Jesus.

7. I release myself, from the hold of every bewitched relationship, in the name of Jesus.
8. By the blood of Jesus, I remove myself from any strange authority, ever exercised over me.
9. I remove all evil soul ties and affections, in Jesus' name.
10. I come against every desire and expectation of the enemy to engage me in any unprofitable relationship, in Jesus' name..
11. I break, every ungodly relationship, in the name of Jesus.
12. I break and renounce evil soul-ties I have had or may have had with
    - secret societies - cults - adulterers - family members
    - close friends - organisations - husbands
    - past or present friends - wives
    - acquaintances - engagements - doctors
    - clubs - religious leaders - social organisations
    - preachers, etc. ,in the name of Jesus.
13. I renounce, all hidden evil soul-ties, in the name of Jesus.
14. I renounce, break and loose myself from all demonic subjection to any relationship, in the name of Jesus.
15. I break all evil soul-ties and wash them away with the blood of the Lord Jesus.
16. I remove myself, from any strange authority exercised over me, in the name of Jesus.
17. I remove, all mind control manipulations between me and any friend or family member, in the name of Jesus.
18. I claim deliverance, from any negative affection towards anyone, in the name of Jesus.
19. Let evil affections towards me, be wiped off the mind of . . . *(mention the name of the person),* in the name of Jesus.

request that they be in submission to the Holy Spirit.

21. Praise the Lord for answered prayers.

DISSOLVING UNPROFITABLE GROWTH

Make these confessions boldly and loudly:

Ps 56:9: *When I cry unto thee, then shall mine enemies turn back: this I know; for God is for me.*

Mal 4:2: *But unto you that fear my name shall the Sun of righteousness arise with healing in his wings; and ye shall go forth, and grow up as calves of the stall.*

Gal 3:13-14: *Christ hath redeemed us from the curse of the law, being made a curse for us: for it is written, Cursed is every one that hangeth on a tree: That the blessing of Abraham might come on the Gentiles through Jesus Christ; that we might receive the promise of the Spirit through faith.*

Col 2:14-15: *Blotting out the handwriting of ordinances that was against us, which was contrary to us, and took it out of the way, nailing it to his cross; And having spoiled principalities and powers, he made a shew of them openly, triumphing over them in it.*

Matt 8:17: *That it might be fulfilled which was spoken by Esaias the prophet, saying, Himself took our infirmities, and bare our sicknesses.*

Rom 16:20: *And the God of peace shall bruise Satan under your feet shortly. The grace of our Lord Jesus Christ be with you. Amen.*

Matt 3:10: *And now also the axe is laid unto the root of the trees: therefore every tree which bringeth not forth good fruit is hewn down, and cast into the fire.*

I Jn 3:8b: *For this purpose the Son of God was manifested, that he might destroy the works of the devil.*

2 Tim 4:18: *And the Lord shall deliver me from every evil work, and will preserve me unto his heavenly kingdom: to whom be glory for ever and ever. Amen.*

Jesus is Lord over my spirit, soul and body for the word of God tells me that at the name of Jesus, every knee shall bow. I can do all things through Christ who strengthens me. The Lord is my shepherd, I shall not want. Jesus has delivered me from the powers of darkness and has translated me into the kingdom of His dear Son. In Jesus I have redemption through His shed blood and forgiveness of sins. Jesus has blotted out the handwriting of ordinances that was against me which was contrary to me, and took it out of the way nailing it to His cross. I am the body of Christ. I am redeemed from the curse because Jesus bore my physical and spiritual diseases in His body. I have the mind of Christ and hold the thoughts, feelings and purposes of His heart.

Praise Worship.

1. Thank the Lord for His power to deliver from any form of bondage.
2. I apply the blood of Jesus on my spirit, soul, body and womb.
3. Let the fire of God saturate my womb, in the name of Jesus.
4. Let every design, against my life, be completely nullified, in the name of Jesus.
5. Let all evil labels, fashioned by the camp of the enemy against my life, be rubbed off by the blood of Jesus.

   Sing the song' HOLY GHOST FIRE, FIRE FALL ON ME with full concentration and by faith.
6. I vomit, every satanic deposit in my life, in the mighty name of Jesus. ***(Prime the expulsion of these things by coughing slightly. Refuse to swallow any saliva coming out from your mouth)***
7. I break myself loose, from the bondage of stagnancy in the mighty name of Jesus.

8. Lord, destroy with Your fire anything that will make Your promise to fail upon my life no matter the origin.

As you pray No 9, take 3 to 4 deep breaths determinedly expelling and flushing out spiritual contamination. Do so aggressively in the mighty name of Jesus.

9. Let the blood, the fire and the living water of the Most High God wash my system clean from:-
   - unprofitable growth in my womb
   - evil plantation
   - evil deposits from spirit husband
   - impurities acquired from parents
   - evil spiritual consumption
   - hidden sicknesses
   - remote control mechanisms
   - physical and spiritual incisions
   - satanic poisons
   - evil stamps, labels and links.
10. Let every area of my life, become too hot for any evil to inhabit, in the name of Jesus.
11. Evil growth in my life, be uprooted, in the name of Jesus.
12. Let my body, reject every evil habitation in the mighty name of our Lord Jesus Christ.
13. O Lord, reverse all evil arrangements attracted consciously or unconsciously to my life.
14. I reject, all evil manipulations and manipulators in the mighty name of Jesus.
15. I break the power of the occult, witchcraft and familiar spirits over my life, in the name of Jesus.

As you pray No. 16, prime the expulsion of the following things by heaving deeply and applying little force upon the lower part of your abdomen.

16. I pass out, any satanic deposit in my intestine, in Jesus' name.
17. I pass out, any satanic deposit in my reproductive organs, in the name of Jesus.

18. I pass out, any satanic deposit in my womb, in Jesus' name.
19. *In the name of Jesus, I declare before all the forces of darkness, that Jesus Christ Is Lord over every department of my life.*
20. You foreign hand, laid on my womb, release me, in Jesus' name.
21. In the name of Jesus, I renounce, break and loose myself from all: - demonic holds - psychic powers - bonds of physical illness - bondage
22. In the name of Jesus, I break and loose myself from all evil curses, chains, spells, jinxes, bewitchments, witchcraft or sorcery which may have been put upon me.
23. Let a creative miracle, take place in my womb and reproductive system, in the name of Jesus.
24. Father, I ask You in the name of Jesus Christ, to send out Your angels and have them unearth and break all evil storage vessels fashioned against me.
25. I loose myself, from every evil influence, dark spirit and satanic bondage in Jesus' name.
26. I confess and declare that my body is the temple of the Holy Spirit, redeemed, cleansed, and sanctified by the blood of Jesus Christ.
27. I bind, plunder and render to nought every strongman assigned to my womb, reproductive system and marital life, in the name of Jesus.
28. God who quickens the dead, quicken my womb and reproductive system, in the name of Jesus.
29. I release myself, from the hold of spirits of sterility, infertility and fear, in the name of Jesus.
30. All the spirits concerned with fornication, come out of my womb with all your roots, in the mighty name of our Lord Jesus.
31. All the spirits concerned with sexual perversion, come out of my womb with all your roots, in the name of our Lord Jesus.
32. All the spirits concerned with spirit husband, come out of my

womb with all your roots, in the name of our Lord Jesus.

33. All the spirits concerned with masturbation, come out of my womb with all your roots, in the name of our Lord Jesus.

34. All the spirits concerned with guilt, come out of my womb with all your roots, in the mighty name of our Lord Jesus.

35. All the spirits concerned with pornography, come out of my womb with all your roots, in the name of our Lord Jesus.

36. Sing this song: ***There is power mighty in the blood....***

37. Thank the Lord for your healing and deliverance.

POWER AGAINST DESERT SPIRITS

Make these powerful confessions and personalise them.

Ps 31:2: Bow down thine ear to me; deliver me speedily: be thou my strong rock, for an house of defence to save me.

Ps 143:7: Hear me speedily, O LORD: my spirit faileth: hide not thy face from me, lest I be like unto them that go down into the pit.

Isa 58:8: Then shall thy light break forth as the morning, and thine health shall spring forth speedily: and thy righteousness shall go before thee; the glory of the LORD shall be thy rereward.

Luke 18:8: I tell you that he will avenge them speedily.

Ps 102:2: Hide not thy face from me in the day when I am in trouble; incline thine ear unto me: in the day when I call answer me speedily.

Jer 1:12: Then said the LORD unto me, Thou hast well seen: for I will hasten my word to perform it.

Jer 29:11: For I know the thoughts that I think toward you, saith the LORD, thoughts of peace, and not of evil, to give you an expected end.

Ps 56:9: When I cry unto thee, then shall mine enemies turn back: this I know; for God is for me

Mal 4:2: But unto you that fear my name shall the Sun of righteousness arise with healing in his wings; and ye shall go forth, and grow up as calves of the stall.

Gal 3:13-14: Christ hath redeemed us from the curse of the law, being made a curse for us: for it is written, Cursed is every one that hangeth on a tree: That the blessing of Abraham might come on the Gentiles through Jesus Christ; that we might receive the promise of the Spirit through faith.

Col 2:14-15: Blotting out the handwriting of ordinances that was against us, which was contrary to us, and took it out of the way, nailing it to his cross; And having spoiled principalities and powers, he made a shew of them openly, triumphing over them in it.

Matt 8:17: That it might be fulfilled which was spoken by Esaias the prophet, saying, Himself took our infirmities, and bare our sicknesses.

Rom 16:20: And the God of peace shall bruise Satan under your feet shortly. The grace of our Lord Jesus Christ be with you. Amen.

Matt 3:10: And now also the axe is laid unto the root of the trees: therefore every tree which bringeth not forth good fruit is hewn down, and cast into the fire.

I Jn 3:8b: For this purpose the Son of God was manifested, that he might destroy the works of the devil.

2 Tim 4:18: And the Lord shall deliver me from every evil work, and will preserve me unto his heavenly kingdom: to whom be glory for ever and ever. Amen.

Jesus is Lord over my spirit, soul and body for the word of God tells me that at the name of Jesus every knee shall bow. I can do all things through Christ who strengthens me. The Lord is my shepherd, I shall not want.

Jesus has delivered me from the powers of darkness and has translated me into the kingdom of His dear Son. In Jesus I have redemption through His shed blood and also forgiveness of sins. Jesus has blotted out the handwriting of ordinances that was against me which was contrary to me, and took it out of the way nailing it to His cross. I am the body of Christ. I am redeemed from the curse because Jesus bore my physical and spiritual diseases in His body. I have the mind of Christ and hold the thoughts, feelings and purposes of His heart.

PRAYER POINTS

1. Thank the Lord for His power to deliver from any form of bondage.
2. I confess the sins of my ancestors (list them).
3. Ask the Lord for forgiveness.
4. Ask the Lord to forgive those sins you do not know about.
5. Let the power in the blood of Jesus, separate me from the sins of my ancestors.
6. I renounce any evil dedication, placed upon my life, in the name of Jesus.
7. I break every evil edict and ordination, in the name of Jesus.
8. I renounce and loose myself, from every negative dedication placed upon my life, in the name of Jesus.
9. I command all demons associated with the dedication to leave now in the name of Jesus Christ.
10. I take authority over all the associated curses, in Jesus' name.
11. Lord, cancel the evil consequences of any broken demonic promise or dedication.
12. I take authority, over all the curses emanating from broken dedication, in the name of Jesus.
13. I command all demons associated with any broken evil parental vow and dedication to depart from me now, in Jesus' name.

14. Ask the Lord to separate you completely from all the sins of your forefathers by the precious blood of Jesus.
15. Ask the Lord to remove the curse if it is from Him.
16. Command the curse of . . . to be broken, in Jesus' name.
17. Apply the oil and command all demons associated with the curse to leave at once, in the name of Jesus.
18. Command any demon afflicting the . . . or causing . . . to leave at once, in the name of Jesus.
19. Ask the Lord to heal all the damages done.
20. I dismiss and disband from my heart, every thought, image or picture of failure in these matters, in Jesus' name.
21. I reject, every spirit of doubt, fear and discouragement, in the name of Jesus.
22. I cancel, all ungodly delays to the manifestations of my miracles, in the name of Jesus.
23. Let the angels of the living God roll away every stone of hindrance to the manifestation of my breakthroughs, in the name of Jesus.
24. O Lord, hasten Your Word to perform it in every department of my life.
25. O Lord, avenge me of my adversaries speedily, in Jesus' name.
26. I refuse to agree with the enemies of my progress in the mighty name of Jesus.

(Pray the next four (4) prayer points according to the level of your faith)

27. O Lord, I desire breakthroughs concerning . . . today, in the name of Jesus.
28. O Lord, I desire breakthroughs concerning . . . this week, in the name of Jesus.
29. O Lord, I desire breakthroughs concerning . . . this month, in the name of Jesus.
30. O Lord, I desire breakthroughs concerning . . . this year,

in the name of Jesus.

31. Let there be turbulence, re-arrangement, revision, re-organisation and re-routing of circumstances in order to give path to my desired miracles, in the name of Jesus.
32. Let every hole, present in the container of my life be mended, in the name of Jesus.
33. I bind, plunder and render to nothing every anti-testimony, anti-miracle and anti-prosperity force, in the name of Jesus.
34. The God who answers by fire and the God of Elijah, answer me by fire, in the name of Jesus.
35. The God who answered Moses speedily at the Red Sea, answer me by fire, in the name of Jesus.
36. The God who changed the lot of Jabez, answer me by fire, in the name of Jesus.
37. The God who quickeneth and calleth those things that be not as if they are, answer me by fire in Jesus' name.
38. I apply the blood of Jesus on my spirit, soul, body and womb.
39. Let the fire of God saturate my womb, in the name of Jesus.
40. Let every design against my life be completely nullified, in the name of Jesus.
41. Let all evil labels fashioned by the camp of the enemy against my life be rubbed off by the blood of Jesus.

Sing the song, "HOLY GHOST FIRE, FIRE FALL ON ME . . ." with full concentration and by faith.

42. I vomit every satanic deposit in my life, in the mighty name of Jesus. ***(Prime the expulsion of these things by coughing slightly. Refuse to swallow any saliva coming out from the mouth).***
43. I break myself loose from the bondage of stagnancy in the mighty name of Jesus.
44. Lord, destroy with Your fire anything that will make Your promise to fail upon my life no matter the origin.

As you pray No 45, take 3 to 4 deep breaths, determinedly

expelling and flushing out spiritual contamination. Do so aggressively in the mighty name of Jesus.

45. Let the blood, the fire and the living water of the Most High God wash my
system clean from:
- unprofitable growth in my womb
- evil plantation
- evil deposits from spirit husband
- impurities acquired from parental contamination
- evil spiritual consumption - hidden sicknesses
- remote control mechanisms
- physical and spiritual incisions - satanic poisons
- evil stamps, labels and links
46. Let every area of my life become too hot for any evil to inhabit, in the name of Jesus.
47. Evil growth in my life, be uprooted, in the name of Jesus.
48. Let my body, reject every evil habitation in the mighty name of our Lord Jesus Christ.
49. O Lord, reverse all evil arrangements attracted consciously or unconsciously to my life.
50. I reject all evil manipulations and manipulators in the mighty name of Jesus.
51. I break the power of the occult, witchcraft and familiar spirits over my life, in the name of Jesus.

Prime the expulsion of the following things by heaving deeply and applying little force upon the lower part of the abdomen.

52. I pass out, any satanic deposit in my intestine, in Jesus' name
53. I pass out, any satanic deposit in my reproductive organs, in th name of Jesus.
54. I pass out, any satanic deposit in my womb, in Jesus' name.
55. In the name of Jesus, I declare before all the forces of darkness that Jesus Christ Is Lord over every department of my life.
56. You foreign hand, laid on my womb, release me, in Jesus' name.

57. In the name of Jesus, I renounce, break and loose myself from all:
- demonic holds
- psychic powers
- bonds of physical illness
- bondage

58. In the name of Jesus, I break and loose myself from all evil curses, chains, spells, jinxes, bewitchments, witchcraft or sorcery which may have been put upon me.
59. Let a creative miracle take place in my womb and reproductive system, in the name of Jesus.
60. Father, I ask You in the name of Jesus Christ to send out Your angels and have them unearth and break all evil storage vessels fashioned against me.
61. I loose myself from every evil influence, dark spirit and satanic bondage in Jesus' name.
62. I confess and declare that my body is the temple of the Holy Spirit, redeemed, cleansed, and sanctified by the blood of Jesus Christ.
63. I bind, plunder and render to nought every strongman assigned to my womb, reproductive system and marital life, in the name of Jesus.
64. God who quickens the dead, quicken my womb and reproductive system, in the name of Jesus.
65. I release myself, from the hold of spirits of sterility, infertility and fear, in the name of Jesus.
66. All the spirits, concerned with fornication, come out of my womb with all your roots, in the mighty name of our Lord Jesus.
67. All the spirits, rooted and concerned with sexual perversion, come out of my womb with all your roots, in the name of Jesus.
68. All the spirits concerned with spirit husband, come out of my womb with all your roots, in the name of our Lord Jesus.
69. All the spirits concerned with masturbation, come out of my womb with all your roots, in the name of our Lord Jesus.

70. All the spirits concerned with guilt, come out of my womb with all your roots, in the mighty name of our Lord Jesus.
71. All the spirits concerned with pornography, come out of my womb with all your roots, in the name of our Lord Jesus.
72. Sing this song: ***There is power mighty in the blood….***
73. I reverse, every evil manipulation done against my womb using my menstrual pads or dates, in the name of Jesus.
74. I divorce, every satanic marriage to my father, in Jesus' name.
75. I release myself from every inherited womb malformation, in the name of Jesus.
76. Lord, grant my womb the power to retain, maintain and safely deliver my babies, in the name of Jesus.
77. Let the blood of Jesus sanitise my womb and anoint it, in the name of Jesus.
78. I command all satanic networks, against my having issues to be completely broken, in the name of Jesus.
79. I break every anti-marriage and anti-pregnancy curse, in the name of Jesus.
80. I bind every spirit of abortion and miscarriage, in Jesus' name

DAILY EXERCISE:

A. Speak to your womb to retain and maintain the pregnancy till birth.
B. Barricade your spirit with the hedge of fire and blood of Jesus
C. Bind household strongman from both sides of the family.
D. Command the spirit of abortion and miscarriage to depart from the womb.
E. Command the spirit of death to depart from the womb.
F. Thanksgiving.

POWER TO RETAIN

Confess these scriptures and personalise them.

Ps 31:2: Bow down thine ear to me; deliver me speedily: be thou my strong rock, for an house of defence to save me.

Ps 143:7: Hear me speedily, O LORD: my spirit faileth: hide not thy face from me, lest I be like unto them that go down into the pit.

Isa 58:8: Then shall thy light break forth as the morning, and thine health shall spring forth speedily: and thy righteousness shall go before thee; the glory of the LORD shall be thy rereward.

Luke 18:8: I tell you that he will avenge them speedily.

Ps 102:2: Hide not thy face from me in the day when I am in trouble; incline thine ear unto me: in the day when I call answer me speedily.

Jer 1:12: Then said the LORD unto me, Thou hast well seen: for I will hasten my word to perform it.

Jer 29:11: For I know the thoughts that I think toward you, saith the LORD, thoughts of peace, and not of evil, to give you an expected end.

Ps 56:9: When I cry unto thee, then shall mine enemies turn back: this I know; for God is for me.

Mal 4:2: But unto you that fear my name shall the Sun of righteousness arise with healing in his wings; and ye shall go forth, and grow up as calves of the stall.

Gal 3:13-14: Christ hath redeemed us from the curse of the law, being made a curse for us: for it is written, Cursed is every one that hangeth on a tree: That the blessing of Abraham might come on the Gentiles through Jesus Christ; that we might receive the promise of the Spirit through faith.

Col 2:14-15: Blotting out the handwriting of ordinances that was against us, which was contrary to us, and took it out of the way, nailing it to his cross; And having spoiled principalities and powers, he made a shew of them openly, triumphing over them in it.

Matt 8:17: That it might be fulfilled which was spoken by Esaias the prophet, saying, Himself took our infirmities, and bare our sicknesses.

Rom 16:20: And the God of peace shall bruise Satan under your feet shortly. The grace of our Lord Jesus Christ be with you. Amen.

Matt 3:10: And now also the axe is laid unto the root of the trees: therefore every tree which bringeth not forth good fruit is hewn down, and cast into the fire.

I Jn 3:8b: For this purpose the Son of God was manifested, that he might destroy the works of the devil.

2 Tim 4:18: And the Lord shall deliver me from every evil work, and will preserve me unto his heavenly kingdom: to whom be glory for ever and ever. Amen.

Jesus is Lord over my spirit, soul and body for the word of God tells me that at the name of Jesus, every knee shall bow. I can do all things through Christ who strengthens me. The Lord is my shepherd, I shall not want. Jesus has delivered me from the powers of darkness and has translated me into the kingdom of His Dear Son. In Jesus I have redemption through His shed blood and also forgiveness of sins. Jesus has blotted out the handwriting of ordinances that was against me which was contrary to me, and took it out of the way nailing it to His cross. I am the body of Christ. I am redeemed from the curse because Jesus bore my physical and spiritual diseases in His body. I have the mind of Christ and hold the thoughts, feelings and purposes of His heart.

PRAYER POINTS

1. Thank the Lord for His power to deliver us from any form of bondage.
2. I confess the sins of my ancestors (list them).
3. Ask the Lord for forgiveness.
4. Ask the Lord to forgive those you do not know about.
5. Let the power in the blood of Jesus separate me from the sins of my ancestors.
6. I renounce, any evil dedication placed upon my life, in the name of Jesus.
7. I break, every evil edict and ordination, in the name of Jesus.
8. I renounce, and loose myself, from every negative dedication placed upon my life, in the name of Jesus.
9. I command all demons associated with dedication to leave now in the name of Jesus Christ.
10. I take authority over all the associated curses, in Jesus' name.
11. Lord, cancel the evil consequences of any broken demonic promise or dedication.
12. I take authority, over all the curses emanating from broken dedication, in the name of Jesus.
13. I command all demons, associated with any broken evil parental vow and dedication to depart from me now, in Jesus' name.
14. Ask the Lord, to separate you completely from all the sins of your forefathers by the precious blood of Jesus.
15. Ask the Lord, to remove the curse, if it is from Him.
16. Command the curse of . . . to be broken, in Jesus' name..
17. Apply the oil and command all demons associated with the curse to leave at once, in the name of Jesus.
18. Command any demon afflicting the . . . or causing . . . to leave at once, in the name of Jesus.
19. Ask the Lord to heal all the damages done.
20. I dismiss from my heart, every thought, image or picture of failure in these matters in Jesus' name.
21. I reject, every spirit of doubt, fear and discouragement, in the

name of Jesus.

22. I cancel, all ungodly delays to the manifestations of my miracles, in the name of Jesus.
23. Let the angels of the living God, roll away every stone of hindrance to the manifestation of my breakthroughs, in the name of Jesus.
24. O Lord, hasten Your Word to perform it in every department of my life.
25. O Lord, avenge me of my adversaries speedily, in Jesus' name
26. I refuse, to agree with the enemies of my progress, in the mighty name of Jesus.

(Pray the next four prayer points according to the level of your faith.)

27. O Lord, I desire breakthroughs concerning . . . . today, in the name of Jesus.
28. O Lord, I desire breakthroughs concerning . . . . this week, in the name of Jesus.
29. O Lord, I desire breakthroughs concerning . . . . this month, in the name of Jesus.
30. O Lord, I desire breakthroughs concerning . . . . this year, in the name of Jesus.
31. Let there be turbulence, re-arrangement, revision, re-organisation and re-routing of circumstances in order to give path to my desired miracles, in the name of Jesus.
32. Let every hole, present in the container of my life be mended, in the name of Jesus.
33. I bind, plunder and render to nothing, every anti-testimony, anti-miracle and anti-prosperity forces, in Jesus' name.
34. The God who answers by fire and the God of Elijah, answer me by fire, in the name of Jesus.
35. The God who answered Moses speedily, at the Red Sea, answer me by fire, in the name of Jesus.
36. The God who changed the lot of Jabez, answer me by fire, in the name of Jesus.

37. The God who quickeneth and calleth those things that be not as if they are, answer me by fire in Jesus' name.
38. I apply the blood of Jesus, on my spirit, soul, body and womb.
39. Let the fire of God, saturate my womb, in the name of Jesus.
40. Let every design, against my life be completely nullified, in the name of Jesus.
41. Let all evil labels, fashioned by the camp of the enemy against my life be rubbed off by the blood of Jesus.

Sing the song, "HOLY GHOST FIRE, FIRE FALL ON ME . . ." with full concentration and by faith.

42. I release myself, from every curse issued against my child-bearing, in the name of Jesus.
43. I renounce and release myself, from every covenant of unprofitable lateness in child-bearing, in the name of Jesus.
44. I break myself loose, from every soul-tie contrary to child-bearing, in the name of Jesus.
45. I cast out, every spirit of death from my womb, in Jesus' name.
46. Let every power, attracting attackers to me during pregnancy be exposed and be destroyed, in the name of Jesus.
47. I break myself loose, from every spirit of lateness in child-bearing, in Jesus' name.
48. O Lord, perfect Your good works in my life.
49. I reject, every curse of miscarriage and pre-mature birth in my family, in the name of Jesus.
50. I declare that there shall be no barrenness in my life, in the name of Jesus.
51. Lord, remove the evil effect of anything that is unclean or destructive that has entered into my reproductive organs, in the name of Jesus.
52. I break, any curse contrary to child-bearing transferred to me by any boyfriend, in the name of Jesus.
53. I arrest, every hormonal problem, in the name of Jesus.

54. Let the walls of my womb be purged by divine fire, in the name of Jesus.
55. Let all the evil forces speaking defeat against my marriage be silenced, in the name of Jesus.

POWER AGAINST EVIL MARITAL MAGNETS

Scripture Reading - Job 11:4-20

Confessions:

Jer 1:10: See, I have this day set thee over the nations and over the kingdoms, to root out, and to pull down, and to destroy, and to throw down, to build, and to plant.

Gen 1:26: And God said, Let us make man in our image, after our likeness: and let them have dominion over the fish of the sea, and over the fowl of the air, and over the cattle, and over all the earth, and over every creeping thing that creepeth upon the earth.

Gen 3:15 : And I will put enmity between thee and the woman, and between thy seed and her seed; it shall bruise thy head, and thou shalt bruise his heel.

Luke 10:19: Behold, I give unto you power to tread on serpents and scorpions, and over all the power of the enemy: and nothing shall by any means hurt you.

Rev 12:9-10: And the great dragon was cast out, that old serpent, called the Devil, and Satan, which deceiveth the whole world: he was cast out into the earth, and his angels were cast out with him. And I heard a loud voice saying in heaven, Now is come salvation, and strength, and the kingdom of our God, and the power of his Christ: for the accuser of our brethren is cast down, which accused them before our God day and night.

Praises and worship to God

Prayer points

1. Thank God because He is going to intervene in your marriage through this prayer programme.
2. I destroy, anything that is going to stand between me and my prayers now, in the name of Jesus.
3. Anointing, to pray to the point of breakthrough in my marriage, fall upon me now, in the name of Jesus.
4. Lord Jesus, I invite You to come to my aid in every difficult situation in my marriage.
5. All my matrimonial properties, which the strange woman sits upon, I withdraw them, in the name of Jesus.
6. I withdraw peace, harmony, unity, love and continuity between my husband and the strange woman, in Jesus' name
7. Lord Jesus, let the strange and unholy love relationship between my husband and the strange woman die.
8. I withdraw, the favour of my husband from the strange woman, in the name of Jesus.
9. I stand against, every power of polygamy, in Jesus' name.
10. All spiritual evil arrows, fired from the strange woman at present into my marriage, loose your grip and go back to your sender, in the name of Jesus.
11. Let confusion, be the lot of every strange woman militating against my marriage.
12. Let irreparable division between . . . (mention the name of your husband) and . . . (mention the name of the strange woman if you know it), in the name of Jesus.
13. Angel of God, go straight and disconnect the relationship between my husband and the strange woman, in Jesus' name
14. Every strange woman, militating against my marriage, receive the judgement of God, in the name of Jesus.
15. I nullify, every evil judgement against my marriage, in the name of Jesus.
16. Let the hindrances, to the manifestation of my restoration to my rightful home depart from me and my marriage, in Jesus' name.

17. Lion of Judah, consume every fake lion of the strange woman roaring against my marriage, in the name of Jesus.
18. Thunder of God and fire of God, begin to scatter into pieces, the stronghold of the strange woman in the heart of my husband, in the name of Jesus.
19. You demons, energising the relationship between my husband and any strange woman, be rendered impotent and be roasted by the fire of God, in the name of Jesus.
20. Angels of the living God, brush off completely, the love of the strange woman from the heart of my husband, in Jesus' name.
21. Lord Jesus, create a new heart in my husband's life.
22. Every open door, that the strange woman is using to gain ground in my husband's life and in my home, receive the blood of Jesus and be closed, in the name of Jesus.
23. God of new beginnings, begin a new thing in my marital life, in the name of Jesus.
24. Blood of the Lamb, flow into the foundation of my marital life and give it a new life, in the name of Jesus.
25. Father Lord, let Your kingdom be established in my marriage, in the name of Jesus.
26. O Lord, put the wall of fire between my husband and the strange woman that they be separated forever.
27. Every evil veil, covering the face of my husband, receive the fire of God and be consumed to ashes, in the name of Jesus.
28. I recover, my legal rights, as the woman of the house from the hands of the strange woman, in the name of Jesus.
29. Every trap of destruction, fashioned against my husband by the strange woman, fail woefully, in the name of Jesus.
30. Let the stones of fire of God, locate the heads of my household serpents, in the name of Jesus.
31. I crush the head, of the ancient serpent, afflicting me and my household with the shoes of iron, in the name of Jesus.
32. Let the stronghold of the serpent and the scorpion, in my household receive the thunder of God and be dismantled, in the name of Jesus.

33. Let the habitation of the serpent and the scorpion, in my household become utterly desolate, in the name of Jesus.
34. Let the thunder and fire of God, expose all the secret places of my household enemies and consume them, in Jesus' name.
35. Let every legal ground of household wickedness, in my household be nullified by the blood of Jesus.
36. Every evil association of the serpent, with any member of my household, be terminated now, in the name of Jesus.
37. Let the custodian of my household serpent and scorpion, fall down and die, in the name of Jesus.
38. I dismantle, the head of all my Goliaths, in the name of Jesus.
39. Every power and spirit, attacking me in the form of snakes in my dreams, be buried, in the name of Jesus.
40. Every property of the enemy, in any area of my life, receive the fire of God and be melted out, in the name of Jesus.
41. I challenge, the root of any serpentine deposit in my body with the fire of God, in the name of Jesus.
42. I vomit, every poison and venom of the serpent and scorpion circulating in my body, in the name of Jesus.
43. Every serpentine pollution, affecting my health, be flushed out of my system by the blood of Jesus.
44. Every injury, inflicted on my marriage by household serpents, be healed by the blood of Jesus.
45. Every household serpent, affecting my breakthroughs, be neutralised by the blood of Jesus.
46. Every good thing in my life, swallowed by the household serpent, be converted to fire and be vomited into my hands, in the name of Jesus.
47. Every good thing in my life, paralysed by the poison of the household serpent, receive the blood of the Lamb and be made whole, in the name of Jesus.
48. Let all the activities of the serpent, in every area of my life, be totally paralysed, in the name of Jesus.

49. Henceforth, let no enemy trouble me for I bear in my body the mark of the blood of the Lamb of God.

POWER AGAINST MISCARRIAGE

CONFESSION: Exodus 23:26; Eccl. 3:14

Praise Worship

1. O Lord, make ways for me where there is no way, in Jesus' name.
2. Any of my clothes, that the enemy has set aside to afflict my conception, be roasted, in Jesus' name.
3. Any decoration in my apartment, that is bewitched, O Lord, reveal it to me.
4. Any cloth, that the enemy is using to destroy my pregnancy, be roasted.
5. Every demonic instrument of operation, set aside to abort my pregnancy, be broken into pieces, in the name of Jesus.
6. Every demonic doctor/nurse, delegated by satan to destroy my pregnancy, inject yourself to death, in the name of Jesus.
7. Every evil remote controlling gadget, being used to manipulate my pregnancy, be roasted by fire, in Jesus' name.
8. I render every weapon, fashioned against my pregnancy impotent, in the name of Jesus.
9. I close down, every satanic broadcasting station fashioned against my pregnancy, in the name of Jesus.
10. I refuse to harbour any pregnancy killer in any department of my life, in the name of Jesus.
11. I bind, every spirit of error, assigned against my pregnancy, in the name of Jesus.
12. I bind, the spirit of almost there. You will not operate in my life, in the name of Jesus.
13. I break, every hold of witchcraft, over my pregnancy, in the name of Jesus.

14. I paralyse, every opposition to my pregnancy, in Jesus' name.
15. Any member of my family, reporting my pregnancy to the evil ones, receive the slap of the angel of God, in Jesus' name.
16. Every territorial demon, working against my marriage, receive the thunder fire of God, in the name of Jesus.
17. I nullify, every satanic threat against my pregnancy, in the name of Jesus.
18. Every power/spirit, visiting me at night or in the dream, to terminate my pregnancy, fall down and die, in Jesus' name.
19. I nullify, every evil influence of satanic visitation upon my pregnancy, in the name of Jesus.
20. Let the plug of my womb, receive the power of the Holy Spirit, to carry my pregnancy to the point of delivery, in Jesus' name.
21. I reject, every manifestation of fever during my pregnancy, in the name of Jesus.
22. I reject, every satanic stress during my pregnancy, in Jesus' name.
23. Thank God for answers to your prayers.

PRAYER TO DISMANTLE MARITAL JERICHO

Note: Prayers to dismantle marital Jericho are to be done with holy anger, holy stubbornness, holy madness, violent faith and violent praises.

Confession: Psalm 65:2: O thou that hearest prayer, unto thee shall all flesh come.

Aggressive Praise Worship

1. O thou that troubleth my Israel, my God shall trouble you today, in the name of Jesus.
2. Thou rain of blessing, fall upon my marital life, in Jesus' name.

3. Magnet of favour in my life, arise and shine, in Jesus' name.
4. Powers of spiritual dowry, die, in the name of Jesus.
5. Let divine beauty, settle upon my life, in the name of Jesus.
6. Evil twin substitutes in the spirit, die, in the name of Jesus.
7. Evil spiritual parents, die, in the name of Jesus.
8. O God, make my life amazing to my enemies, in Jesus' name.
9. Before the cock crows, let my sun rise, in the name of Jesus.
10. O God, give me the very best You can, in Jesus' name.
11. Every cage of family witchcraft, release my divine partner, in Jesus' name.
12. Satanic substitutes, go away from my life, in Jesus' name.
13. My God-given partner, appear and locate me by fire, in the name of Jesus.
14. Arrows of permanent loneliness, come out of me, in Jesus' name.
15. My glory, reject evil exchanges and evil transfers, in Jesus' name.
16. Holy Ghost, arise and re-arrange my life for breakthroughs, in Jesus' name.
17. Satanic spiritual wedding garments and rings, roast, in the name of Jesus
18. Thou power of evil marriage, die, in the name of Jesus.
19. All unrepentant friends of darkness in my family, be exposed and disgraced, in the name of Jesus.
20. O God, arise and drown all my Pharaoh in the Red Sea, in the name of Jesus.
21. Every satanic pregnancy in my life, be aborted, in Jesus' name.
22. O heavens, open over my marital life, in the name of Jesus.
23. Let every mention of my marriage, become poison in the mouth of the enemy, in the name of Jesus.
24. Lord, make known to me the secrets needed for my marital breakthrough.

25. Let every imagination of the enemy against my marital life be rendered impotent, in the name of Jesus.
26. Every force magnetizing the wrong people to me, be paralysed, in Jesus' name.
27. Let every incantation, incision, hex and other spiritually harmful activities working against my marriage, be completely neutralized, in the name of Jesus.
28. I command, all forces of evil, manipulating, delaying or hindering my marriage to be completely paralysed, in the name of Jesus.
29. Let the blood of Jesus, speak against every power working against my marriage.
30. I remove the right of the enemy to afflict my plan to get married, in the name of Jesus.
31. I break, every bondage of inherited marital confusion, in the name of Jesus.
32. I bind and plunder, the goods of every strongman attached to my marriage, in the name of Jesus.
33. Let the angels of the living God, roll away the stone blocking my marital breakthroughs, in the name of Jesus.
34. O God, arise and let all the enemies of my marital breakthrough scatter, in the name of Jesus.
35. Let the cloud, blocking the sunlight of my marital breakthrough be dispersed, in Jesus' name.
36. Let all evil spirits masquerading to trouble my marital life be bound, in the name of Jesus.
37. Lord, turn away all that would jilt, disappoint or fail me, in the name of Jesus.
38. I destroy, the power of every satanic arrest in my life, in the name of Jesus.
39. All satanic-arresting agents, release me in the mighty name of our Lord Jesus Christ.

40 Spirit of the living God, quicken the whole of my being, in the name of Jesus.
41. O Lord, liberate my spirit to follow the leading of the Holy Spirit.
42. I rebuke, every spirit of spiritual deafness and blindness in my life, in the name of Jesus.
43. I choose to believe the report of the Lord and no other, in the name of Jesus.
44. You spirit of confusion, loose your hold over my life, in the name of Jesus.
45. I frustrate, every demonic arrest over my spirit-man, in the name of Jesus.
46. I cut down, all the roots of problems in my life, in Jesus' name.
47. I reject any demonic limitation on my marriage, in Jesus' name.
48. I refuse to wear the garment of tribulation and sorrow, in the name of Jesus.
49. Let every rebellion flee from my heart, in the name of Jesus.
50. Lord, let wonderful changes be my lot this year.
51. Thank God for the victory.

REVOKING EVIL MARITAL DECREES

Bible Reading Ps: 8:4-8

Make your way straight with God

Confession:

In the beginning, God created man to subdue the earth and have dominion over the fish of the sea, and over the fowl of the air and over every living thing that moveth upon the face of the earth.

The psalmist also confirms this as he writes that God has mademan to have dominion over all the works of His hands and has put all things under his feet. All sheep and oxen, yea and the beasts of the field, the fowl of the air, and the fish of the sea and whatsoever passeth through the PATHS OF THE SEAS.

The mandate every man lost to devil through Adam's disobedience has been restored unto us by Jesus Christ. I am God's workmanship, recreated in Christ as a priest, and king to reign here on earth.

Jesus Christ was made manifest that He might destroy all the works of the devil and when He was going, He said that greater works than He did I should do.

Therefore, as I go into this prayer, I hold in my hand the victory Jesus Christ purchased on the cross at calvary, when He made an open show of principality and powers. I take my position in Christ as one given power to become a son of God, even joint-heir of the kingdom of God with Christ, to execute judgment against every form of disobedience exhibited against the knowledge of God.

Greater is He that is in me, than any power on earth and in the seas. I am born of God, and I have overcome the world with my faith.

By faith, I hand over my battle to God. By faith, I come against evil strongholds of any marine kingdom. By faith, I pollute the water of the enemy with the blood of Jesus Christ. By faith, I overturn every queen enthroned against me. By faith, I trample upon her serpents and scorpions. By faith, I spoil her palace and set her captives free and bind her herself.

There shall be no reinforcement or evil reunion of any power against me. I seal my confessions with the blood of Jesus and I cover myself with the blood of Jesus. Amen.

Before you pray these prayer points, go into a period of praise and thanksgiving.

1. Any witchcraft, practised under any water against my life, receive immediate judgment of fire, in the name of Jesus.

2. Let every evil altar, under any water upon which certain evils are done against me, be roasted, in the name of Jesus.
3. Every priest, ministering at any evil altar, against me inside any water, fall down and die, in the name of Jesus.
4. Any power, under any river or sea remote-controlling my life, be destroyed by fire. And I shake myself loose from your hold, in the name of Jesus.
5. Let any evil monitoring mirror, ever used against me under any water shatter to irredeemable pieces, in Jesus' name.
6. Every marine witchcraft, that has introduced spirit husband/wife or child in my dreams be roasted by fire, in Jesus' name.
7. Every agent of marine witchcraft posing as my husband, wife or child in my dreams, be roasted by fire, in Jesus' name.
8. Every agent of marine witchcraft, physically attached to my marriage to frustrate it, fall down and perish now, in the name of Jesus.
9. Every agent of marine witchcraft, assigned to attack my finances, through dream attacks, fall down and perish, in Jesus' name.
10. I pull down, every stronghold of bewitchment, enchantment, jinx or divination fashioned against me by marine witches, in the name of Jesus.
11. Let the thunderbolts of God, locate and destroy every location of marine witchcraft covens, where deliberations and decisions have ever been fashioned against me, in the name of Jesus.
12. Any water spirit from my village, in my place of birth, practising witchcraft against me and my family, be amputated by the word of God, in Jesus' name.
13. Let every spiritual weapon of wickedness, fashioned against me under any river or sea, be roasted by the fire of God, in the name of Jesus.
14. Any power of marine witchcraft, holding any of my blessings in bondage, receive the fire of God and release them, in the name of Jesus.
15. I loose my mind and soul from the bondage of marine witches, in the name of Jesus.

16. Any marine witchcraft chain, binding my hands and feet from prospering, be broken and shattered to pieces, in Jesus' name.
17. Every arrow, shot into my life from under any water through witchcraft, come out of me and go back to your sender, in the name of Jesus.
18. Any evil material, transferred into my body, through contact with any marine witchcraft agent, be roasted by fire, in Jesus' name.
19. Every sexual pollution of marine spirit husband/wife, in my body, be flushed out by the blood of Jesus.
20. Any evil name given to me under any water, I reject and cancel with the blood of Jesus.
21. Every image, constructed under any water to manipulate me, be roasted by fire, in the name of Jesus.
22. Any evil, ever done against me through marine witchcraft oppression and manipulation, be reversed by the blood of Jesus.
23. Spirit husband/wife, release me by fire, in Jesus' name.
24. Every spirit husband/wife, I divorce you by the blood of Jesus.
25. Every spirit husband/wife, die, in the name of Jesus.
26. Everything you have deposited in my life, come out by fire, in Jesus' name.
27. Every power, working against my marriage, fall down and die, in the name of Jesus.
28. I divorce and renounce my marriage with the spirit husband or wife, in the name of Jesus.
29. I break, all covenants entered into with the spirit husband or wife, in the name of Jesus.
30. I command, the thunder fire of God to burn to ashes the wedding gown, ring, photographs and all other materials used for the marriage, in Jesus' name.

31. I send the fire of God, to burn to ashes the marriage certificate, in the name of Jesus.
32. I break, every blood and soul-tie covenant with the spirit husband or wife, in the name of Jesus.
33. I send the thunder fire of God, to burn to ashes the children born to the marriage, in Jesus' name.
34. I withdraw my blood, sperm or any other part of my body deposited on the altar of the spirit husband or wife, in the name of Jesus.
35. You spirit husband or wife tormenting my life and earthly marriage, I bind you with hot chains and fetters of God and cast you out of my life into the deep pit, and I command you not to ever come into my life again, in the name of Jesus.
36. I return to you, every property of yours in my possession, including the dowry and whatsoever was used for the marriage and covenants, in the name of Jesus.
37. I drain myself, of all evil materials deposited in my body as a result of our sexual relations, in the name of Jesus.
38. Lord, send Holy Ghost fire into my root, to burn all unclean things deposited into it by the spirit husband or wife, in Jesus' name.
39. I break, the head of the snake deposited into my body by the spirit husband or wife to do me harm, and command it to come out, in the name of Jesus.
40. I purge, with the blood of Jesus, every evil material deposited in my womb to prevent me from having children on earth.
41. Lord, repair and restore every damage done to any part of my body and my earthly marriage by the spirit husband or wife, in the name of Jesus.
42. I reject and cancel every curse, evil pronouncement, spell, jinx, enchantment and incantation placed upon me by the spirit husband or wife, in the name of Jesus.
43. I take back, all my earthly belongings in the custody of the spirit husband or wife, in the name of Jesus.

44. I command the spirit husband or wife to turn his or her back on me forever, in Jesus' name.
45. I renounce and reject, the name given to me by the spirit husband or wife, in the name of Jesus.
46. I hereby declare and confess that the Lord Jesus Christ is my Husband for eternity, in Jesus' name.
47. I soak myself in the blood of Jesus and cancel the evil marks or writings placed on me, in Jesus' name.
48. I set myself free from the stronghold, domineering power and bondage of the spirit husband or wife, in Jesus' name.
49. I paralyse, the remote control power and work used to destabilise my earthly marriage and to hinder me from bearing children for my earthly husband or wife, in the name of Jesus.
50. I announce to the heavens, that I am married forever to Jesus.
51. Every trademark of evil marriage, be shaken out of my life, in Jesus' name.
52. Every evil writing engraved with iron pen, be wiped off by the blood of Jesus.
53. I bring the blood of Jesus, upon the spirit that does not want to go, in the name of Jesus.
54. I bring the blood of Jesus, on every evidence that can be tendered by wicked spirits against me.
55. I file a counter-report, in the heavens against every evil marriage, in the name of Jesus.
56. I refuse, to supply any evidence that the enemy may use against me, in the name of Jesus.
57. Let satanic exhibitions be destroyed by the blood of Jesus.
58. I declare to you spirit husband/wife, that there is no vacancy for you in my life, in the name of Jesus.
59. O Lord, make me a vehicle of deliverance.

60. I come by faith to mount Zion. Lord, command deliverance upon my life now.
61. Lord, water me from the waters of God.
62. Let the careful siege of the enemy be dismantled, in Jesus' name.
63. O Lord, defend Your interest in my life.
64. Everything written against me in the cycle of the moon, be blotted out, in the name of Jesus.
65. Everything programmed into the sun, moon and stars against me, be dismantled, in Jesus' name.
66. Every evil thing, programmed into my genes, be blotted out by the blood of Jesus.
67. O Lord, shake out seasons of failure and frustrations from my life.
68. I overthrow, every wicked law working against my life, in Jesus' name.
69. I ordain a new time, season and profitable law, in Jesus' name.
70. I speak destruction, unto the palaces of the queen of the coast and of the rivers, in Jesus' name.
71. I speak destruction, unto the headquarters of the spirit of Egypt and blow up its altars, in the name of Jesus.
72. I speak destruction, unto the altars speaking against the purpose of God for my life, in the name of Jesus.
73. I declare myself a virgin for the Lord, in the name of Jesus.
74. Let every evil veil, upon my life be torn open, in Jesus' name.
75. Every wall between me and the visitation of God, be broken, in Jesus' name.
76. Let the counsel of God, prosper in my life, in Jesus' name.
77. I destroy, the power of any demonic seed in my life from the womb, in the name of Jesus.
78. I speak unto my umbilical gate, to overthrow all negative parental spirits, in the name of Jesus.

79. I break the yoke of the spirits, having access to my reproductive gates, in the name of Jesus.
80. O Lord, let Your time of refreshing come upon me.
81. I bring fire, from the altar of the Lord, upon every evil marriage, in the name of Jesus.
82. I redeem myself, by the blood of Jesus, from every sex trap, in Jesus' name.
83. I erase, the engraving of my name on any evil marriage record, in the name of Jesus.
84. I reject and renounce every evil spiritual marriage, in Jesus' name.
85. I confess that Jesus is my original spouse and is jealous over me.
86. I issue a bill of divorce to every spirit husband/wife, in Jesus' name.
87. I bind, every spirit husband/wife with everlasting chains, in Jesus' name.
88. Let heavenly testimony, overcome every evil testimony of hell, in Jesus' name.
89. O Lord, bring to my remembrance every spiritual trap and contract.
90. Let the blood of Jesus, purge me of every contaminating material, in the name of Jesus.
91. Let the spirit husband/wife, fall down and die, in Jesus' name
92. Let all your children attached to me, fall down and die, in the name of Jesus.
93. I burn your certificates and destroy your rings, in Jesus' name.
94. I execute judgement, against water spirits and I declare that you are reserved for everlasting chains in darkness, in Jesus' name.
95. O Lord, contend with those who are contending with me.
96. Every trademark of water spirit, be shaken out of my life, in Jesus' name.

97. Begin to thank God for your deliverance.

POWER AGAINST SPIRITUAL MARRIAGE

Before you pray these prayer points, go into a period of praise and thanksgiving.

Praise worship

1. Spirit husband/spirit wife, release me by fire, in Jesus' name.
2. Every spirit husband/wife, I divorce you by the blood of Jesus.
3. Every spirit husband/wife, die, in the name of Jesus.
4. Everything you have deposited in my life, come out by fire, in the name of Jesus.
5. Every power, that is working against my marriage, fall down and die, in the name of Jesus.
6. I divorce and renounce my marriage, with the spirit husband or wife, in the name of Jesus.
7. I break all covenants, entered into with the spirit husband or wife, in the name of Jesus.
8. I command the thunder fire of God, to burn to ashes the wedding gown, ring, photographs and all other materials used for the marriage, in Jesus' name.
9. I send the fire of God, to burn to ashes the marriage certificate, in the name of Jesus.
10. I break all blood and soul-tie covenants with the spirit husband or wife, in the name of Jesus.
11. I send thunder fire of God, to burn to ashes the children born to the marriage, in Jesus' name.
12. I withdraw my blood, sperm or any other part of my body deposited on the altar of the spirit husband or wife, in the name of Jesus.

13. You spirit husband or wife tormenting my life and earthly marriage, I bind you with hot chains and fetters of God, and cast you out of my life into the deep pit, and I command you not to ever come into my life again, in the name of Jesus.
14. I return to you, every property of yours in my possession, including the dowry and whatsoever was used for the marriage and covenants, in the name of Jesus.
15. I drain myself of all evil materials deposited in my body as a result of our sexual relations, in the name of Jesus.
16. Lord, send Holy Ghost fire into my root, and burn out all unclean things deposited in it by the spirit husband or wife, in Jesus' name.
17. I break the head of the snake deposited into my body by the spirit husband or wife to do me harm, and I command it to come out, in the name of Jesus.
18. I purge myself, with the blood of Jesus, every evil material deposited in my womb to prevent me from having children on earth.
19. Lord, repair and restore every damage done to any part of my body and my earthly marriage by the spirit husband or wife, in the name of Jesus.
20. I reject and cancel every curse, evil pronouncement, spell, jinx, enchantment and incantation placed upon me by the spirit husband or wife, in the name of Jesus.
21. I take back, all my earthly belongings in the custody of the spirit husband or wife, in the name of Jesus.
22. I command, the spirit husband or wife to turn his or her back on me forever, in Jesus' name.
23. I renounce and reject the name given to me by the spirit husband or wife, in the name of Jesus.
24. I hereby declare and confess that the Lord Jesus Christ is my Husband for eternity, in Jesus' name.

25. I soak myself in the blood of Jesus and cancel the evil marks or writings placed on me, in Jesus' name.
26. I set myself free from the stronghold, domineering power and bondage of the spirit husband or wife, in Jesus' name.
27. I paralyse, the remote control power and work used to destabilise my earthly marriage and to hinder me from bearing children for my earthly husband, in Jesus' name.
28. I announce to the heavens, that I am married forever to Jesus.
29. Every trademark of evil marriage, be shaken out of my life, in the name of Jesus.
30. Every evil writing engraved with an iron pen, be wiped off by the blood of Jesus.
31. I bring the blood of Jesus upon the spirit that does not want to go, in the name of Jesus.
32. I bring the blood of Jesus, on every evidence that can be tendered by wicked spirits against me.
33. I file a counter-report in the heavens against every evil marriage, in the name of Jesus.
34. I refuse, to supply any evidence that the enemy may use against me, in the name of Jesus.
35. Let satanic exhibitions be destroyed by the blood of Jesus.
36. I declare to you spirit husband/wife, that there is no vacancy for you in my life, in the name of Jesus.
37. O Lord, make me a vehicle of deliverance.

38. I come by faith to mount Zion. Lord, command deliverance upon my life now.
39. Lord, water me from the waters of God.
40. Let the careful siege of the enemy be dismantled, in Jesus' name.
41. O Lord, defend Your interest in my life.
42. Everything, written against me in the cycle of the moon, be blotted out, in the name of Jesus.
43. Everything, programmed into the sun, moon and stars against me, be dismantled, in Jesus' name.
44. Every evil thing, programmed into my genes, be blotted out by the blood of Jesus.
45. O Lord, shake out seasons of failure and frustrations from my life.
46. I overthrow, every wicked law, working against my life, in Jesus' name.
47. I ordain a new time, season and profitable law, in Jesus' name.
48. I speak destruction unto the palaces of the queen of the coast and of the rivers, in Jesus' name.
49. I speak destruction unto the headquarters of the spirit of Egypt and blow up its altars, in the name of Jesus.
50. I speak destruction unto the altars speaking against the purpose of God for my life, in the name of Jesus.
51. I declare myself a virgin for the Lord, in the name of Jesus.
52. Let every evil veil, on my life be torn open, in Jesus' name.
53. Every wall, between me and the visitation of God, be broken, in the name of Jesus.
54. Let the counsel of God prosper in my life, in Jesus' name.
55. I destroy, the power of any demonic seed in my life from the womb, in the name of Jesus.
56. I speak unto my umbilical gate, to overthrow all negative parental spirits, in the name of Jesus.

57. I break the yoke of the spirits, having access to my reproductive gates, in the name of Jesus.
58. O Lord, let Your time of refreshing come upon me.
59. I bring fire from the altar of the Lord upon every evil marriage, in the name of Jesus.
60. I redeem myself, by the blood of Jesus from every sex trap, in the name of Jesus.
61. I erase, the engraving of my name on any evil marriage record, in the name of Jesus.
62. I reject and renounce every evil spiritual marriage, in Jesus' name.
63. I confess that Jesus is my original spouse and is jealous over me.
64. I issue a bill of divorce to every spirit husband/wife, in the name of Jesus.
65. I bind every spirit husband/wife with everlasting chains, in the name of Jesus.
66. Let heavenly testimony overcome every evil testimony of hell, in the name of Jesus.
67. O Lord, bring to my remembrance every spiritual trap and contract.
68. Let the blood of Jesus, purge me of every contaminating material, in the name of Jesus.
69. Let the spirit husband/wife fall down and die, in Jesus' name
70. Let all your children attached to me fall down and die, in the name of Jesus.
71. I burn your certificates and destroy your rings, in Jesus' name.
72. I execute judgement against water spirits and declare that you are reserved for everlasting chains in darkness, in Jesus' name.
73. O Lord, contend with those who are contending with me.
74. Every trademark of water spirit, be shaken out of my life, in the name of Jesus.

DELIVERANCE FROM EVIL PATTERNS

NOTE: Prayer of release from evil patterns have to be done aggressively and violently. No stone should be left unturned. You must hate the evil patterns with perfect hatred. Scriptural fasting will enhance deliverance.

Scriptures reading: Exod 25:9; 25:40; Num 8:4; Josh 22:28; II Ki 16:10; 1 Chr 28:11-12; 1 Chr 28:18-19; Ezek 43:10; 1 Tim 1:16; Titus 2:7; Heb 8:5

Confession: Col. 2:14-15: Blotting out the handwriting of ordinances that was against us, which was contrary to us, and took it out of the way, nailing it to his cross; 15 And having spoiled principalities and powers, he made a shew of them openly, triumphing over them in it.

PRAISE WORSHIP

1. I apply the blood of Jesus to break all curses.
2. Sing this song: "There is power mighty in the blood (x2). There is power mighty in the blood of Jesus Christ. There is power mighty in the blood."
3. Confess your sins and those of your ancestors, especially those sins linked to evil powers.
4. I cover myself with the blood of Jesus.
5. I apply the blood of Jesus to break all consequences of parental sins.
6. O Lord, turn all the evils directed at me to good.
7. I command all powers of evil directed against me to return directly to the sender, in the name of Jesus.
8. God, make everything the enemy has said is impossible in my life possible, in the name of Jesus.
9. I release myself, from the umbrella of any collective captivity, in the name of Jesus.

10. I release myself, from any inherited bondage, in Jesus' name.
11. O Lord, send Your axe of fire to the foundation of my life to destroy every evil plantation.
12. Let the blood of Jesus, flush out from my system every inherited satanic deposit, in the name of Jesus.
13. I release myself, from the grip of any problem transferred into my life from the womb, in Jesus' name.
14. Let the blood of Jesus and the fire of the Holy Ghost cleanse every organ in my body, in Jesus' name.
15. I break and loose myself from every collective evil covenant, in the name of Jesus.
16. I break and loose myself from every collective curse, in the name of Jesus.
17. I vomit, every evil consumption that I was fed with as a child, in the name of Jesus.
18. I command, all foundational strongmen attached to my life to be paralyzed, in the name of Jesus.
19. Let any rod of the wicked, rising against my family line be rendered impotent for my sake, in the name of Jesus.
20. I cancel the consequences of any evil local name attached to my person, in the name of Jesus.
21. Pray aggressively against the following roots of collective captivity: Every effect of . . . (pick from the under listed, one by one), upon my life, come out with all your roots, in Jesus' name.

- evil physical design	- evil dedication
- parental curses	- demonic marriage
- envious rivalry	- demonic sacrifice
- demonic incisions	- inherited infirmity
- dream pollution	- evil laying on of hands
- demonic initiations	- wrong exposure to sex

- destructive effect of polygamy
- unscriptural manner of conception
- demonic blood transfusion
- demonic alteration of destiny
- fellowship with family idols
- fellowship with demonic consultants
- exposure to evil diviners
- fellowship with local idols

22. Pray against anything in your life that is following known or unknown evil patterns.
23. You evil foundational plantations, come out of my life with all your roots, in the name of Jesus.
24. I break and loose myself, from every form of demonic bewitchment, in the name of Jesus.
25. I release myself, from every evil domination and control, in the name of Jesus.
26. Let the blood of Jesus be transfused into my blood vessel.
27. Let every gate, opened to the enemy by my foundation, be closed forever with the blood of Jesus.
28. Lord Jesus, walk back into every second of my life and deliver me where I need deliverance, heal me where I need healing, transform me where I need transformation.
29. Thank God for the deliverance.

BRINGING FORTH

Praises - Sing 'How great Thou art.'

Prayer of forgiveness of sin.

Make these powerful confessions and personalise them.

Ps 31:2: Bow down thine ear to me; deliver me speedily: be thou my strong rock, for an house of defence to save me.

Ps 143:7: Hear me speedily, O LORD: my spirit faileth: hide not thy face from me, lest I be like unto them that go down into the pit.

Isa 58:8: Then shall thy light break forth as the morning, and thine health shall spring forth speedily: and thy righteousness shall go before thee; the glory of the LORD shall be thy rereward.

Luke 18:8: I tell you that he will avenge them speedily.

Ps 102:2: Hide not thy face from me in the day when I am in trouble; incline thine ear unto me: in the day when I call answer me speedily.

Jer 1:12: Then said the LORD unto me, Thou hast well seen: for I will hasten my word to perform it.

Jer 29:11: For I know the thoughts that I think toward you, saith the LORD, thoughts of peace, and not of evil, to give you an expected end.

Ps 56:9: When I cry unto thee, then shall mine enemies turn back: this I know; for God is for me.

Mal 4:2: But unto you that fear my name shall the Sun of righteousness arise with healing in his wings; and ye shall go forth, and grow up as calves of the stall.

Gal 3:13-14: Christ hath redeemed us from the curse of the law, being made a curse for us: for it is written, Cursed is every one that hangeth on a tree: That the blessing of Abraham might come on the Gentiles through Jesus Christ; that we might receive the promise of the Spirit through faith.

Col 2:14-15: Blotting out the handwriting of ordinances that was against us, which was contrary to us, and took it out of the way, nailing it to his cross; And having spoiled principalities and powers, he made a shew of them openly, triumphing over them in it.

Matt 8:17: That it might be fulfilled which was spoken by Esaias the prophet, saying, Himself took our infirmities, and bare our sicknesses.

Rom 16:20: And the God of peace shall bruise Satan under your feet shortly. The grace of our Lord Jesus Christ be with you. Amen.

Matt 3:10: And now also the axe is laid unto the root of the trees: therefore every tree which bringeth not forth good fruit is hewn down, and cast into the fire.

I Jn 3:8b: For this purpose the Son of God was manifested, that he might destroy the works of the devil.

2 Tim 4:18: And the Lord shall deliver me from every evil work, and will preserve me unto his heavenly kingdom: to whom be glory for ever and ever. Amen.

Deut 7:14-15: Thou shalt be blessed above all people: there shall not be male or female barren among you, or among your cattle. And the LORD will take away from thee all sickness, and will put none of the evil diseases of Egypt, which thou knowest, upon thee; but will lay them upon all them that hate thee.

Deut 28:4, 11: Blessed shall be the fruit of thy body, and the fruit of thy ground, and the fruit of thy cattle, the increase of thy kine, and the flocks of thy sheep. And the LORD shall make thee plenteous in goods, in the fruit of thy body, and in the fruit of thy cattle, and in the fruit of thy ground, in the land which the LORD sware unto thy fathers to give thee.

Exod 23:26: There shall nothing cast their young, nor be barren, in thy land: the number of thy days I will fulfil.

Ps 115:14: The LORD shall increase you more and more, you and your children.

Ps 128:3: Thy wife shall be as a fruitful vine by the sides of thine house: thy children like olive plants round about thy table.

1 Tim 2:15: Notwithstanding she shall be saved in childbearing, if they continue in faith and charity and holiness with sobriety.

I Jn 4:4: Ye are of God, little children, and have overcome them: because greater is he that is in you, than he that is in the world.

Phil 4:19: But my God shall supply all your need according to his riches in glory by Christ Jesus.

Ps 4:1-8: Hear me when I call, O God of my righteousness: thou hast enlarged me when I was in distress; have mercy upon me, and hear my prayer. O ye sons of men, how long will ye turn my glory into shame? how long will ye love vanity, and seek after leasing? But know that the LORD hath set apart him that is godly for himself: the LORD will hear when I call unto him. Stand in awe, and sin not: commune with your own heart upon your bed, and be still. Offer the sacrifices of righteousness, and put your trust in the LORD. There be many that say, Who will shew us any good? LORD, lift thou up the light of thy countenance upon us. Thou hast put gladness in my heart, more than in the time that their corn and their wine increased. I will both lay me down in peace, and sleep: for thou, LORD, only makest me dwell in safety.

Jesus is Lord over my spirit, soul and body for the word of God tells me that at the name of Jesus every knee shall bow. I can do all things through Christ who strengthens me. The Lord is my shepherd, I shall not want. God has delivered me from the powers of darkness and has translated me into the kingdom of His dear Son. In Jesus I have redemption through His shed blood and also forgiveness of sins. Jesus has blotted out the handwriting of ordinances that was against me which was contrary to me, and took it out of the way nailing it to His cross. I am the body of Christ. I am redeemed from the curse because Jesus bore my physical and spiritual diseases in His body. I have the mind of Christ and hold the thoughts, feelings and purposes of His heart.

While laying your hands on your womb and breasts:

1. Thank the Lord for His power to deliver from any form of bondage.
2. I confess the sins of my ancestors (list them).
3. O Lord, forgive me of all my ancestral sexual sins.
4. Ask the Lord for forgiveness.
5. Ask the Lord to forgive those sins you do not know about.
6. Let the lost glory of my family line be restored unto me, in the name of Jesus.
7. Let the power in the blood of Jesus separate me from the sins of my ancestors.
8. I cover myself with the blood of Jesus.
9. Place a wall of fire around yourself.
10. Pray that ministering angels will surround you.
11. I renounce any evil dedication placed upon my life, in the name of Jesus.
12. I break every evil edict and ordination, in the name of Jesus.
13. I take back everything the enemy has stolen from my life, in the name of Jesus.
14. I cancel all visions, dreams, words and curses contrary to conception and child bearing in my life, in Jesus' name.
15. I command every negative imagination against my child-bearing to be cast down, in the name of Jesus.
16. Lord, let Your healing power flow into every area of my body relevant to conception and child-bearing.
17. God who quickens the dead, quicken everything concerning my conception and child-bearing, in Jesus' name.
18. I bind, plunder and render to nought, every spiritual activity contrary to the peace of my home, in the name of Jesus.
19. I chase back, all stubborn pursuers and cut off every unprofitable family covenant, in the name of Jesus.
20. O Lord, let this month be our month of miracles.

21. Let my womb be purged by the fire of the Holy Spirit, in the name of Jesus.
22. Let all evil hands be removed from the affairs of my life, in the name of Jesus.
23. I break every covenant with any sexual demon, in Jesus' name.
24. I rebuke, the spirit of the dog, and cast it out of my ways, in the name of Jesus.
25. I render myself impenetrable by any occasional or regular anti-pregnancy spirit, in the name of Jesus. (Put one hand on your head, the other one on your womb.)
26. Let the fire of God, purge the whole of my body system and remove all the impurities therein, in the name of Jesus.
27. I break, every covenant of late child-bearing with the fire of God and the blood of Jesus.
28. I renounce and denounce, every bad spirit using my image against me, in the name of Jesus.
29. Breathe in the fire of God and breathe out negative things.
30. I renounce and loose myself, from every negative dedication placed upon my life, in the name of Jesus.
31. I command all demons, associated with the dedication to leave now in the name of Jesus Christ.
32. I take authority, over all the associated curses, in Jesus' name
33. Lord, cancel the evil consequences of any broken demonic promise or dedication.
34. I take authority over all the curses emanating from broken dedication, in the name of Jesus.
35. I command all demons associated with any broken evil parental vow and dedication to depart from me now, in Jesus' name.
36. O Lord, separate me completely from all the sins of my forefathers by the precious blood of Jesus.
37. Ask the Lord to remove the curse if it is from Him.

38. I command the curse of. . . to be broken, in Jesus' name.
39. Apply the oil and command all demons associated with the curse to leave at once, in the name of Jesus.
40. I command any demon afflicting the . . . or causing . . . to leave at once, in the name of Jesus.
41. Ask the Lord to heal all the damages done.
42. I dismiss from my heart, every thought, image or picture of failure in these matters in Jesus' name.
43. I reject every spirit of doubt, fear and discouragement, in the name of Jesus.
44. I cancel all ungodly delays to the manifestations of my miracles, in the name of Jesus.
45. Let the angels of the living God roll away every stone of hindrance to the manifestation of my breakthroughs in Jesus' name.
46. O Lord, hasten Your Word to perform it in every department of my life.
47. O Lord, avenge me of my adversaries speedily, in Jesus' name.
48. I refuse to agree with the enemies of my progress in the mighty name of Jesus.
49. *(Pray the next four prayer points according to the level of your faith)*
50. O Lord, I desire breakthroughs concerning . . . today, in the name of Jesus.
51. O Lord, I desire breakthroughs concerning . . . this week, in the name of Jesus.
52. O Lord, I desire breakthroughs concerning . . . this month, in the name of Jesus.
53. O Lord, I desire breakthroughs concerning . . . this year, in the name of Jesus.
54. Let there be turbulence, re-arrangement, revision, re-organisation and re-routing of circumstances to give path to my desire miracles, in the name of Jesus.

55. Let every hole present in the container of my life be sealed, in the name of Jesus.
56. I bind, plunder and render to nothing every anti-testimony, anti-miracle and anti-prosperity forces, in the name of Jesus.
57. The God who answers by fire and the God of Elijah, answer me by fire, in the name of Jesus.
58. The God who answered Moses speedily at the Red Sea, answer me by fire, in the name of Jesus.
59. The God who changed the lot of Jabez, answer me by fire, in the name of Jesus.
60. The God who quickeneth and calleth those things that be not as if they are, answer me by fire in Jesus' name.
61. I apply the blood of Jesus on my spirit, soul, body and womb.
62. Let the fire of God saturate my womb, in the name of Jesus.
63. Let every design against my life be completely nullified, in the name of Jesus.
64. Let all evil labels fashioned by the camp of the enemy against my life be rubbed off by the blood of Jesus.

Sing the song "HOLY GHOST FIRE, FIRE FALL ON ME" with full concentration and by faith.

65. I vomit every satanic deposit in my life in the mighty name of Jesus.

(Prime the expulsion of these things by coughing slightly. Refuse to swallow any saliva coming out from the mouth)

66. I break myself loose from the bondage of stagnancy in the mighty name of Jesus.
67. Lord, destroy with Your fire anything that makes Your promise to fail upon my life no matter the origin.

As you pray No 68, take 3 to 4 deep breathe determinedly flushing out spiritual contamination. Do so aggressively in the mighty name of Jesus.

68 Let the blood, the fire and the living water of the Most High God wash my system clean from:-

- unprofitable growth in my womb - evil plantation
- evil deposits from spirit husband
- impurities acquired from parental contamination
- evil spiritual consumption - hidden sicknesses
- remote control mechanisms
- physical and spiritual incisions - satanic poisons
- evil stamps, labels and links

69. Let every area of my life become too hot for any evil to inhabit, in the name of Jesus.

70. Evil growth in my life, be uprooted, in the name of Jesus.

71. Let my body, reject every evil habitation in the mighty name of our Lord Jesus Christ.

72. O Lord, reverse all evil arrangements attracted consciously or unconsciously to my life.

73. I reject all evil manipulations and manipulators in the mighty name of Jesus.

74. I break the power of the occult, witchcraft and familiar spirits over my life, in the name of Jesus.

Prime the expulsion of the following things by heaving deeply and applying little force upon the lower part of the abdomen.

75. I pass out any satanic deposit in my intestine, in Jesus' name.

76. I pass out any satanic deposit in my reproductive organs, in the name of Jesus.

77. I pass out any satanic deposit in my womb, in Jesus' name.

78. In the name of Jesus, I declare before all the forces of darkness that, Jesus Christ is Lord over every department of my life.

79. You foreign hand, laid on my womb, release me, in Jesus' name.

80. In the name of Jesus, I renounce, break and loose myself from

all: - demonic holds - psychic powers
- bonds of physical illness - bondage

81. In the name of Jesus, I break and loose myself from all curses, chains, spells, jinxes, bewitchments, witchcraft or sorcery which may have been put upon me.
82. Let a creative miracle take place in my womb and reproductive system, in the name of Jesus.
83. Father, I ask You, in the name of Jesus Christ to send out Your angels and have them unearth and break all evil storage vessels fashioned against me.
84. I loose myself, from every evil influence, dark spirit and satanic bondage in Jesus' name.
85. I confess and declare that my body is the temple of the Holy Spirit, redeemed, cleansed, and sanctified by the blood of Jesus Christ.
86. I bind, plunder and render to nought every strongman assigned to my womb, reproductive system and marital life, in the name of Jesus.
87. God who quickens the dead, quicken my womb and reproductive system, in the name of Jesus.
88. I release myself, from the hold of spirits of sterility, infertility and fear, in the name of Jesus.
89. All the spirits concerned with fornication, come out of my womb with all your roots, in the name of our Lord Jesus.
90. All the spirits concerned with sexual perversion, come out of my womb with all your roots, in the name of Jesus.
91. All the spirits concerned with spirit husband, come out of my womb with all your roots, in the name of our Lord Jesus.
92. All the spirits concerned with masturbation, come out of my womb with all your roots, in the name of our Lord Jesus.
93. All the spirits concerned with guilt, come out of my womb with all your roots, in the name of our Lord Jesus.
94. All the spirits concerned with pornography, come out of my womb with all your roots, in the name of our Lord Jesus.

95. Sing this song: ***"There is power mighty in the blood...."***
96. I reverse, every evil manipulation done against my womb using my menstrual pads or dates, in the name of Jesus.
97. I divorce, every satanic marriage to my father, in Jesus' name
98. I release myself, from every inherited womb malformation, in the name of Jesus.
99. Lord, grant unto my womb the power to retain, maintain and safely deliver my babies, in the name of Jesus.
100. Let the blood of Jesus sanitise my womb and anoint it, in the name of Jesus.
101. I command all satanic network, against my having issues to be completely broken, in the name of Jesus.
102. I break, every anti-marriage and anti-pregnancy curse, in the name of Jesus.
103. I bind every spirit of abortion and miscarriage, in Jesus' name.
104. I bind and paralyse, any strongman that is in charge of my womb, in the name of Jesus.
105. Let all the door ways of the enemy, into my life be closed firmly, in the name of Jesus.
106. All spiritual poison that entered into my body, during my wedding ceremony, depart, in the name of Jesus.
107. Spiritual poison, introduced into my womb through (pick from the under listed), I command you to depart, in Jesus' name.
    - eating in the dream - sexual activities in the dream
    - miscarriages - drinking of dirty water
    - any spiritual contamination
    - abortion - masturbation
108. I stand against (pick from the under listed) in my life, in the name of Jesus.
    - miscarriages - slippery pregnancy
    - fake pregnancy - wasteful loss of blood

109 I command any evil tree, planted in my womb contrary to the perfect growth and development of my body to be roasted and uprooted, in the name of Jesus.

110. I break and cancel, every curse, jinx and spell placed on my womb, in the name of Jesus.

111. Let all the spiritual parasites that are feeding on the seeds of my womb be roasted, in the name of Jesus.

112. Lord, correct any disorder in my ovary, fallopian tube and womb.

113. Lord, flush out of my system with the blood of Jesus any retained products or blockages.

114. Let all demonic eyes, monitoring my body functions and progress receive blindness, in the name of Jesus.

115. Terminal pains around my waist and beneath my belly, cease, in the name of Jesus.

116. Every vicious cycle of problems in my life, break, in Jesus' name.

117. Evil inner voice, speaking discouragement or unbelief to my heart, be silenced, in the name of Jesus.

118. No devourer will devour the fruit of my womb, in Jesus' name.

119. I soak my womb, fallopian tube and ovary in the blood of Jesus.

120. Lord, activate all the parts of my body with Your fire.

121. I claim the promise of God concerning child-bearing, in the name of Jesus.

122. Thank God for answered prayers.

DAILY EXERCISE:

A. Speak to your womb to retain and maintain the pregnancy till birth.

B. Barricade your spirit with the hedge of fire and blood of Jesus.

C. Bind household strongmen from both sides of the family.

D. Command the spirit of abortion and miscarriage to depart from your womb.

E. Command the spirit of death to depart from your womb.

F. Thanksgiving.

FOR BACHELORS AND SPINSTERS ON MARRIAGE

Confession: Gen. 2:18, John 15:7, Prov. 18:22, Rom. 8:34, 1 Pet. 5:7, Col. 2:14-15; Phil. 4:19

1. Lord, I thank You because You care for me and my life is in Your hand.
2. Let the power of the Holy Ghost magnetize my God-chosen partner to me, in the name of Jesus.
3. I command all evil anti-marriage marks to be removed, in the name of Jesus.
4. I break all evil covenants of false and late marriage, in the name of Jesus.
5. I cancel, every conscious and unconscious spiritual marriage, in the name of Jesus.
6. Lord, open my spiritual eyes and ears to receive divine revelation concerning my life-partner.
7. Lord, show me the secrets of any marital problem I have.
8. Let every hindrance to a happy marital life be removed, in the name of Jesus.
9. I return or cancel any spiritual bride price paid or received on my behalf, in the name of Jesus.
10. Father, send Your Angels to link me up with Your chosen partner for me, in the name of Jesus.
11. I break, any anti-marriage generational curse back to 20 generations, in the name of Jesus.
12. Let the beauty and glory of the Lord be upon me, in the name of Jesus.

13. I break, every curse brought upon me by inherited sexual sins and by my personal sexual sins, in the name of Jesus.
14. I bind, every spirit of fear, in the name of Jesus.
15. I renounce and break, all anti-marriage covenants made by me or on my behalf, in the name of Jesus.
16. I reverse, every backwardness that worry has created in my life, in the name of Jesus.
17. I cancel every anti-marriage spell, bewitchment and enchantment, in the name of Jesus.
18. Let my partner and myself be for signs and wonders amongst the nations, in the name of Jesus.
19. I bind, the spirit of error and uncertainty in my life and the life of my partner, in the name of Jesus.
20. Father Lord, reveal unto me, Your choice for my life.
21. Let all rough places concerning this matter be made plain, in the name of Jesus.
22. I stand against and break loose from:
- spirit of marriage destruction - spirit of fear
- anti-marriage covenant - spirit husbands/wives
- inherited spirits - sales of sexual birth-right
- spirit of frustration.

23. Let every blockage of the manifestation of my miracle crumble, in the name of Jesus.

BREAKING ANTI-MARRIAGE CURSES AND COVENANTS

Confessions: Col. 2:14-15; 1:13-14; Gal. 3:13-14; 2 Tim. 4:18; Isa. 53:3-5; 54:17; Rev. 12:11.

1. Thank the Lord for His redemptive power which never fails nor diminish.
2. Ask the Lord to forgive you your sins.
3. In the mighty name of Jesus, I break myself loose from every covenant of late or useless marriage.

4. I release myself in the name of Jesus from every marital, ancestral curse.
5. In the mighty name of our Lord Jesus Christ, I renounce and break all evil curses and bewitchment put upon my marriage.
6. In the name of Jesus, I take authority over and bind the strongman attached to my marital life.
7. In the name of Jesus, I break all marital curses placed on me by household enemies.
8. In the name of Jesus, I break all marital curses placed upon my life through witchcraft.
9. I command all demonic spirits, connected to the curse to release me and go now, in the name of Jesus.
10. Lord, reveal my life-partner to me during this prayer session.
11. Anything present in me that is anti-marriage in nature go now in the mighty name of Jesus.
12. I break and release myself, in Jesus' name, from every anti-marriage curse.
13. In the name of Jesus, let my would-be husband\wife be released, whom evil powers have been trying to hold back from me.
14. In Jesus' name, I cancel and revoke, any spiritual marriage or childbirth contrary to the will of God.
15. Let all family idols, from both sides of my parents, release me and my marital life, in the name of Jesus.
16. I bind, every strongman from my father's and mother's sides attached to my marital life.
17. In the name of Jesus, I refuse to follow any evil pattern laid down or programmed by any of my ancestors.
18. I reject all ancestral burdens and bondage, in Jesus' name.
19. In the name of Jesus, I stand against:

- demonic wedding rings
- demonic wedding gowns/attire
- spiritual trading of marriage for something else

- evil spiritual marriage
- instituted and remotely programmed frustration
- anti-marriage habits and imaginations
- fear of abandonment and of loneliness
- attraction to me by wrong and unserious partners
- unprofitable impatience in the mighty name of Jesus.

20. Let all the veil, hindering me from seeing what I should see be roasted by the fire of God in Jesus' name.
21. I release myself in Jesus' name from all anti-marriage curses, spells, bewitchment, hexes and covenants operating on both sides of my family.
22. Let divine marital prosperity replace all the anti-marriage curses and covenants, in the name of Jesus.

Please, note the following:

- You must repent from all your sins.
- If you have trouble with your dreams, seek for deliverance ministration or minister self-deliverance to yourself.
- Ensure that all restitutions have been made.
- Ensure that you are completely emptied of pride and anger.
- Stop all forms of crying.
- Memorize and read your Bible daily and memorize some passages.
- Seek the genuine baptism of the Holy Spirit.

PRAYER FOR ENGAGED PARTNERS PLANNING MARRIAGE

Praise worship sing: "How Great Thou Art..."

Confession: Psalm 138:8, Philippians 1:6, 2 Tim. 1:7, Col. 2:14-15, Psalm 71:21, Zech. 4:7-9, Deut. 33:26-27.

1. Thank God for His miraculous hand upon your life.
2. Confess every sin of unforgiveness, bitterness, anxiety, wrong

thinking and forgive anyone who might have hurt or disappointed you.

3. I renounce, break and loose myself from every ancestral marital curse or bondage in Jesus' name.
4. I reject and refuse to follow any evil marriage pattern in Jesus' name.
5. Father, I ask You, in the name of Jesus Christ, to send out Your angels to all the corners of the earth on my behalf, and let them bring to me the favour, provisions, blessings and materials needed for a successful marriage.
6. I bind, plunder and render to nought every spirit of marriage destruction in Jesus' name.
7. Lord, unite me with those who will bless me and keep all others away.
8. Let Your holy angels surround us. Let Your wall of fire be built around my husband/wife and I. Let the Blood of Jesus cover us throughout every stage of the marriage.
9. All evil touch and evil arrows are completely neutralised in Jesus' name.
10. Father, let the spirit of joy, liberty, grace and love fill us to the brim.
11. Lord, give me power to avoid useless quarrels that wound without achieving results.
12. Lord, give me power over angry outbursts that achieve nothing.
13. Lord, convert all the retreats that I have suffered into advances.
14. Lord, convert all my trials and tests to testimonies and triumph.

WAR AGAINST ANTI-MARRIAGE FORCES

Use these prayer points when your marriage is being threatened.

1. All evil counsels against my marital life, collapse, in the name of Jesus.

2. Any association between my husband/wife and any strange man/woman, be scattered now, in the name of Jesus.
3. Every demonic-in-law, loose your hold upon my life, in the name of Jesus.
4. Spirit husbands and spirit wives, loose your hold in the name of Jesus. (Place your hand below your stomach as you pray.)
5. Every curse that has been issued against my marriage, be cancelled, in the name of Jesus.
6. Every demonic mark, contrary to settled homes, be wiped off with the blood of Jesus.
7. Every inherited spirit, that is not of God, go, in Jesus' name.
8. Every curse, issued against my marriage or against my marital life, be broken, in the name of Jesus.
9. Let the effect of every ceremony done on the day of my wedding and which has been working against me, be cancelled and destroyed, in the name of Jesus.
10. Every spiritual bride price, collected on my behalf, I return you to the sender, in the name of Jesus.
11. The spiritual marriage of all husbands/wives to their mother, be dissolved, in the name of Jesus.
12. Any power, which says that I will not enjoy my marital life, be roasted, in the name of Jesus.
13. I command every run-away husband/wife to come back, in the name of Jesus.
14. You spirit of marriage destruction, be bound, in Jesus' name.
15. I command every curse on my marriage to be converted to blessing, in the name of Jesus.
16. I command every evil which strange friends have done against my home, to be reversed, in the name of Jesus.
17. I release my partner from every demonic cage, in Jesus' name.

PRAYERS TO UNCAGE YOUR PARTNER

Use these prayer points when.

- Your partner is losing interest in the relationship.
- A strange partner has walked into the relationship.
- Hatred has replaced love.
- The home is threatening to break.

Aggressive Confession: The word of God says I shall decree a thing and it shall be established. Therefore, I decree that my partner be released from any anti-marriage or divorce cage, in the mighty name of the Lord Jesus Christ. The word of God says, "What God has joined together, let no man put asunder." I command all the forces battling against my home to be completely uprooted, for they are trying to put asunder what God has joined together. I tread upon serpents and scorpions, in the mighty name of Jesus. Let the angels of the living God, pursue the architects of anti-marriage cages, in the mighty name of Jesus.

1. I command every spirit of division to depart from my marital life, in the name of Jesus.
2. You spirit of Egypt, release my . . . (mention the name of your partner), in the name of Jesus.
3. Let all family cages holding my . . . (mention the name of your partner) receive the fire of God.
4. Lord Jesus, wash away all anti-marriage stamps, labels and links in the mighty name of Jesus.
5. Let the spirit of love and understanding prevail between us, in the name of Jesus.
6. Let every demonic family interference,be completely severed, in the name of Jesus.
7. Holy Spirit, overshadow this relationship.
8. I command all stubborn yokes to break, in Jesus' name.
9. Let all the effects of spiritual wedding rings, clothes and shoes be completely removed, in the name of Jesus.

10. I bind all the stubborn pursuers militating against my home in the mighty name of Jesus.
11. I command the veil of hatred against me in the heart of . . . (mention the name of your partner) to be destroyed, in the name of Jesus.
12. Let the wicked spirits polluting the heart of my . . . against me receive the stones of fire , in the name of Jesus.
13. You . . . (mention the name of your partner) receive your divine senses back in the mighty name of Jesus.
14. O Lord, put the love for me back in the heart of my . . . .
15. O Lord, reveal to me,every other secret that I need to know concerning this problem.
16. Let the joy of the enemy over my home be converted to sorrow in the mighty name of Jesus.
17. You . . ., you will not follow the evil patterns of any parent or ancestor in the name of Jesus.
18. Let all the activities of the spirits from me air, water land and family idols loose their hold upon my marriage.
19. Let all the activities contrary to marriage vows in the life of ...... be paralysed, in the name of Jesus
20. Let all the spirits of fear, depression, worry and despair release me, in the name of Jesus.

SAFEGUARDING YOUR HOME

Prayers to sanitize your home and pull down past or present anti-marriage strongholds.

Confessions: Mark 10:8-9, Psl. 145:16, Col. 3:18-19, 1 Cor. 7:14-15, Isa. 43:18-19, Psl. 68:1, Job 22:28

1. You, who conspired with my husband/wife to destory our marriage and good home, I command you to remove your hand from my husband/wife in the name of Jesus. It is against God's word for you to separate us.

2. All evil counsel against our home, collapse, in Jesus' name.
3. I scatter all arrangements between you and my husband/wife, in the name of Jesus.
4. Dislike each other as from now, in the name of Jesus.
5. I get the favour and love of my husband/wife, in Jesus' name.
6. Thank the Lord for His mercies and grace.
7. Ask the Holy Spirit to help you pray to the point of breakthrough.
8. (Gird your spiritual loins and aggressively stand against the following local home-wreckers. Pray as follows:) I stand against any . . ., (fix in the items listed hereunder) and command them to release you and your marriage, in the name of Jesus.

- competition by strange women or girls\men
- financial failure and poverty, especially after the wedding
- spirit husband/wife - demonic in-laws
- demonic marks - anti-marriage destruction
- spirit of fear - spirit of Jezebel (domineering nature)
- inherited spirit from the father's and mother's side
- marriage curses - anti-marriage covenants
- spirit of misunderstanding, misinterpretation and exaggeration ungodly attachment to parents.

9. (Cancel the effects of the following things. Please pray aggressively if you are involved or feel you may be involved in them. Pray as follows:) I cancel the satanic influence of . . . upon my marriage; I bind the connected spirits and command them to loose their hold upon my marriage, in the name of Jesus.

- demonic water pouring on the feet on the wedding day
- contaminated wedding rings and shoes
- background of polygamy and multiple husbands

- familiar spirits and witchcraft spirits
- satanic deposits in the home
- collection of spiritual bride-price - incest

10. I break and loose myself in the name of Jesus from any anti-marriage curse issued upon my family.
11. Father, let the Prince of Peace reign in my marriage without any hindrance, in Jesus' name.
12. I decree reconciliation between myself and my partner, in the name of Jesus.
13. All powers conspiring with anyone to destroy our home\marriage loose your hold, in the name of Jesus.
14. All evil counsel against our home be frustrated, in Jesus' name.

PRAYERS FOR COUPLES EXPECTING PROMISED CHILDREN FROM THE LORD

To be done every morning and night.

Scriptures for confession: Psalms 148 - 150, Genesis 1:28, Exodus 23:26, Deut. 7:14, Psalm 127:1-3; 128:3; 113:9, I Timothy 2:15, Galatians 6:17; 3:13-14, Phil. 1:6, Isa. 8:18; 40:5 Exodus 1:19.

Confession - The word of God tells me that I should be fruitful and multiply. God said it and I believe it. This must come to pass in my life, in Jesus' name. My Father and my God, I bring Your word to remembrance, for You said: "No woman shall be barren in the generation of Abraham." I belong to Christ and I am, therefore, Abraham's seed and heir according to promise (Gal. 3:29). Barrenness is a curse of the law and Christ has redeemed me from the curse of the law. I must have my own child by this time next year. You devil, hear the word of the Lord: All your weapons against me will not prosper, in Jesus' name. For the Lord of hosts is with me and the God of Jacob is my refuge.

You devil, loose your hold upon my life in Jesus' name, for I bear in my body the mark of Christ. Right now, I command every hindrance to conception, disturbance, blockage in the womb and inherited spirits to depart, in Jesus' name. For it is written, "He suffered no man to do them wrong, yea, He reproved kings for their sakes, saying, 'touch not my anointed and do my prophets no harm'". So, you powers of darkness, I am untouchable, in Jesus' name. The way of fruitfulness has opened for me today. Glory be to the name of the Lord. Amen.

1. I denounce and reject, every unprofitable covenant regarding child-bearing in Jesus' name.
2. I apply the blood of Jesus Christ to my womb.
3. I bind every hindering spirit in the name of our Lord Jesus Christ.
4. Father in the name of Jesus, work the necessary miracles to enable me have the fruit of the womb.
5. I break, every curse of barrenness, in the name of Jesus.
6. O Lord, lay Your hands upon our lives, in the name of Jesus.
7. I command all contrary handwriting against me to be destroyed in Jesus' name.
8. I bind, plunder and render to nought every spirit of infertility and fear in Jesus' name.
9. I loose myself, from any curse issued against me by satanic, agent in Jesus ' name.
10. I release myself, from any inherited problem in Jesus name.
11. I cancel every bewitchment, against my reproductive organs and child-bearing in Jesus name.
12. Father Lord, send Your angels to retrieve my blessings from any hiding place in Jesus' name.
13. I renounce and denounce, all unprofitable covenants in Jesus' name.

14. Let this month, be my month of miracles in Jesus' name.
15. I release myself from every bondage of infertility and pregnancy wastage in Jesus' name.
16. I bind, plunder and render to nought every sperm-destroying and foetal-eating demon in Jesus' name.
17. I paralyse, every spirit behind impotence, ejaculation problems, ovulation failure, hormonal problems and other anti-pregnancy strategies.
18. Lord Jesus, wash away the effect of past sexual sins on my life in Jesus' name.
19. Lord, remove the effect of sexual relationships with demonized partners from my life in Jesus' name.
20. I cancel, the evil effects of contaminated menstrual pads and lost underwear in Jesus' name.
21. With the blood of Jesus, I break every bondage and all ungodly soul ties with all past sex partners.

DELIVERANCE FROM THE SPIRIT OF MARRIAGE DESTRUCTION

1. Father, let Your kingdom be established in every department of my marriage, in the name of Jesus.
2. I renounce and denounce, every evil spiritual marriage contract I have consciously or unconsciously entered into, in the name of Jesus.
3. Let all spirits of marriage destruction release me, in the name of Jesus. E.g. the spirit of:

- anger	- Ahab	- criticisms	
- strife	- jezebel	- infirmity	
- pride	- hatred	- worry	- selfishness
- impatience	- fear	- bad speaking	
- familiar spirit	- competition	- adultery	
- prayerlessness	- apathy	- fornication	

- failure - power strugglers - harsh words
- cruelty - lying - extravagance - pride
- marital unfaithfulness - lack of submission from wife
- Poor communication - poor leadership from husband
- Domineering character - spiritual backsliding

4. I release myself from the school of broken homes, in the name of Jesus.
5. I fire back, to the camp of the enemy every arrow fired at my marriage, in the name of Jesus.
6. I spoil and destabilze, every satanic plan against my home, in the name of Jesus.
7. Let every evil design, fashioned by the enemy against my life be completely destroyed, in the name of Jesus.
8. Let every curse, issued against my home be cancelled and replaced by blessings, in the name of Jesus.
9. Let every evil covenant, fashioned against my home be broken to pieces, in the name of Jesus.
10. Let the powers of household wickedness, fashioned against my home be dashed into pieces, in the name of Jesus.
11. Let every cage of the enemy, fashioned against my home, be broken to pieces, in the name of Jesus.
12. Let every negative word, spoken against my home, be nullified, in the name of Jesus.
13. Let any spiritual husband and wife sent against me be bound, in the name of Jesus.
14. Let every evil wedding ring and garments be roasted, in the name of Jesus.
15. I deliver my marriage, from the hands of home-wreckers, in the name of Jesus.
16. I command, all evil counsellors and spiritual emptiers to loose their hold upon my marriage, in the name of Jesus.
17. Let the Prince of Peace, reign in my marriage, in Jesus' name.

18. Let every satanic agent, hired against my marriage fall after the order of Balaam, in the name of Jesus.
19. Let the anointing to prosper in marital life, come upon my home, in the name of Jesus.
20. Let the Holy Spirit, transform my marriage to be heaven on earth, in the name of Jesus.

WAR AGAINST CONFLICTS AND HOSTILITY IN THE HOME

1. Make a list of all the things that are at present wrong in the home.
2. Take these things one by one and pray aggressively as follows: You . . ., (e.g. weakness, faults or problems) in my home, I root you out, I pull you down and I destroy you, in Jesus' name.
3. Let all the enemies of my good dreams and visions on my home be rendered impotent, in the name of Jesus.
4. I paralyze, every architect of conflict and hostility in my home, in the name of Jesus.
5. Let every factor, leading to maladjustment in the home be dissolved by the fire of the Holy Spirit.
6. I decree that, divine characters be planted and built in my home, in the name of Jesus.
7. I withdraw my marriage, from the hands of evil designers, in the name of Jesus.
8. Let every evil power, trying to re-draw my marriage map be put to shame, in the name of Jesus.
9. I refuse to pattern my marriage contrary to God's original design, in the name of Jesus.
10. Let all household wickedness, release my home, in Jesus' name.
11. Let every negative influence on my home by parents from both sides be nullified, in the name of Jesus.

12. Let every disease of our family altar be healed, in Jesus' name.
13. I break every curse, affecting my home negatively, in the name of Jesus.
14. Devil, I command you to take all your properties and be gone from my life, in the name of Jesus.
15. Lord, restore all that the enemies have stolen from my home.
16. Father, convert all my marital failure to success, in Jesus' name.
17. Lord, keep the wall of defense of my family constantly strong, in the mighty name of Jesus.
18. Lord, heal all broken and sore family relationships, in the mighty name of Jesus.
19. I receive deliverance from every evil plantation, designed to bring myself and my children under the bondage of the devil, in the name of Jesus.
20. I deliver myself, from bondage that my sins and those of my ancestors have provoked, in the name of Jesus.
21. Holy Spirit, break every yoke of marital failure in my life, in the name of Jesus.
22. I paralyse, every spirit of hatred and hostility militating against my home, in the name of Jesus.
23. Let peace flow, like water, into my home, in Jesus' name.
24. I stand against every spirit of---------------------

-talkativeness	- unappreciation	- stubbornness
- laziness	- manipulation	- callousness
- self-centeredness	- impotence	- passiveness
- accusation	- masturbation	- unreasonableness
- oral sex	- egotisim	- anger
-over ambitious	- possessiveness	- rigidity
- child molestation	- emotional	- inconsistency
- flirting	- insensitivity	- despondency

- intolerance - unbelief - unforgiveness
- rejection - humiliation - frustration
- impatience

Loose your hold upon my life, in the name of Jesus. I command you to be separated from me. I place the cross of Jesus between me and you. I forbid you to ever return or send any other spirit, in the mighty name of Jesus.

25. Let all demonic maternal and paternal strings, break, in the name of Jesus.

DELIVERANCE FROM THE GRIP OF HOME DESTROYERS

Praise worship.

Confession of sins and prayers of forgiveness.

Ask the Holy Spirit to direct you in this prayer session.

Take the problem areas listed under here one by one and pray these three violent prayer points on each of them.

1. Let the axe of fire from heaven, take the problem from the roots, in the name of Jesus.
2. Let the finger of God, pull down the stronghold of the problem, in the name of Jesus.
3. Let the finger of God build up the right replacements, in the name of Jesus.

- evil association - planlessness
- carelessness - weak family altar
- pride - unsaved partner or children
- foolishness - lack of knowledge of the word of God

- unprofitable imitation
- unprofitable comparison
- communication gap
- suspicion
- deterioration of relationship
- selfishness
- misplaced priority
- evil attachment to parents
- evil counsellors
- incomplete "leaving" and incomplete "cleaving" of couple.

4. Let my home be released from the hands of evil remote control forces, in the name of Jesus.
5. I command every evil wind directed at my family to be re-directed by the Holy Spirit, in the name of Jesus.
6. Let all the eaters of love and drinkers of joy release my family, in the name of Jesus.
7. Let every problem, arising from the issue of sex in the family receive divine solution, in the name of Jesus.
8. Let all extra-marital relationship with other "partners" collapse and die, in the name of Jesus.
9. Let every problem from the issue of finance receive divine solution, in the name of Jesus.
10. Let the anointing to prosper come upon my family, in the name of Jesus.
11. Let every problem arising from the issue of relatives receive divine solution, in the name of Jesus.
12. Let every problem arising from the issue of children receive solution, in the name of Jesus.
13. Lord arise and put the enemies responsible for the following conditions to flight:
    - inability to produce children
    - replacing love for wife/husband with love for children
    - showing more love to one child than the other
    - disrespectful children
    - inability to cater spiritually, physically and materially

- production of strange children (Psalm 144:11)
- Godless children
- contaminated children
- bad parental example to children
- homes that are not attractive to children
- parental disagreement on child discipline
- children possessed by demons
- in-laws conflict
- financial difficulties
- loneliness, isolation and boredom
- sexual problems
- absence of romantic love in marriage

DISSOLVING DEADLOCKS IN SETTLEMENT DISCUSSIONS

Confessions: Matt. 19:26; Mark 3:27; Jer. 32:17.

1. Thank God for all the settlement moves.
2. Thank God because with Him nothing shall be impossible.
3. Let the spirit of peace, reign within the heart of my . . ., in the name of Jesus.
4. I command every strange hand, to be taken off my marriage, in the name of Jesus.
5. I disengage, the hand of evil manipulators from my home, in the name of Jesus.
6. Let every spirit of rebellion and strife be put to shame, in the name of Jesus.
7. Let every yoke, creating deadlocks in settlement be melted away, in the name of Jesus.
8. Lord, re-write my name in the heart of . . . (mention the name

of the person).

9. I paralyse, all the enemies of peace in my home, in Jesus' name.
10. Let every yoke of disagreement be completely broken, in the name of Jesus.
11. Let all fake sympathizers be put to shame, in Jesus' name.
12. Holy Spirit, take control over all subsequent meetings and dialogues.
13. Holy Spirit, put Your own words into all contributing mouths in this matter.
14. I arrest, every creator of deadlocks and paralyse them, in the name of Jesus.
15. Let every acidic contribution to settlement discussions, be dissolved, in the name of Jesus.
16. Let every demonic storm, rising against my home be punctured, in the name of Jesus.
17. I bind, every spirit of hatred, in the name of Jesus.
18. Lord, let the hedge of thorns go into operation in every area it is needed in my marriage.
19. Let all the activities of strange man/woman fuelling the strife be rendered null and void, in the name of Jesus.
20. O God, let Your face shine upon our marital relationship, in the name of Jesus.
21. O Lord, heal all marital diseases plaguing my home.

PRAYERS TO RESUSCITATE DEAD MARRIAGES

Confessions: John 11:25; Ezek. 37:1-10; Rom. 4:17

1. Thank the Lord for His resurrection power.
2. Ask the Lord to forgive you or whoever may be directly or indirectly involved
   in the death of the marriage.
3. I command my marriage to come alive, in the name of Jesus.

4. Lord Jesus, walk back into every second of my marital life and heal all the wounds created by the enemy.
5. Let the breath of life, enter into foundations of my marriage and make it whole, in the name of Jesus.
6. Let all satanic forces contributing to killing my marriage be paralysed, in the name of Jesus.
7. Let all marriage killers be paralysed, in the name of Jesus.
8. Let every activity of household enemies on my marriage be paralysed, in the name of Jesus.
9. Let my partner begin to have dreams and visions that would lead to the resurrection of my marriage, in Jesus' name.
10. Let God arise and let the enemies of my home scatter, in the name of Jesus.
11. I remove my marriage, from the grip of powers that put asunder, in the name of Jesus.
12. Let all the enemies of settled home living around me scatter, in the name of Jesus.
13. Let the spirit of life, enter into the blood of my marriage, in the name of Jesus.
14. Let all the glory that has departed from my marriage, be restored, in the name of Jesus.
15. Let all the virtues stolen from my marriage, be restored seven-fold, in the name of Jesus.
16. Let the anointing to prosper maritally, fall upon me, in the name of Jesus.
17. Lord, let divine sense enter into our relationship, in the name of Jesus.
18. I fire back, every arrow the enemy fired at my marriage, in the name of Jesus.
19. Let all the powers sucking the peace of my home be rendered impotent, in the name of Jesus.
20. I retrieve my marriage, from the altar of satanic destruction,

in the name of Jesus.
21. Let the blood of Jesus erase all past unprofitable memories on my marital relationship.
22. I bind, every spirit of demonic independence, in Jesus' name.
23. Let the resurrection power of the Lord Jesus Christ fall upon my marriage, in the name of Jesus.
24. I remove my name from the book of broken homes, in the name of Jesus.
25. Lord, remove from the heart of . . . all excuses for not wanting to face the difficulties of marriage.
26. Lord, remove from the heart of . . . the intention of seeking "greener grass" in marriage.
27. Let the corpse of my marriage receive fire, in Jesus' name.
28. Pray in the spirit for at least 10 minutes.
29. Thank the Lord for answered prayers

RELEASE OF CHILDREN FROM BONDAGE

Confessions: Psalms 32:8; 127, Job 22:28, Col. 1:9-10; 1 Cor. 7:14, Luke 1:37, 1 John 4:4, Isa. 8:10,18, Deut. 28:7, Rom. 16:20.

1. I bind, every spirit contrary to the spirit of God preventing me from enjoying my children.
2. I bind, all spirits blinding their minds from receiving the glorious light of the gospel of our Lord Jesus Christ.
3. Let all spirits of stubbornness, pride and disrespect for parents flee from their lives, in the name of Jesus.
4. Father, destroy everything in my children, preventing them from doing Your will, in the name of Jesus.
5. Every curse, evil covenant and all inherited problems passed down to the children, be cancelled, in the name of Jesus.
6. Mention their names one by one and tell the Lord what you want them to become.

7. Let every association and agreement between my children and my enemies be scattered, in the name of Jesus.
8. My children, will not become mis-directed arrows in Jesus' name.
9. I release my children, from the bondage of any evil domination, in the name of Jesus.
10. Let all evil influences, by demonic friends clear away in Jesus' name.
11. You . . . (mention the name of the child), I dissociate you from any conscious or unconscious demonic groupings or involvement in the name of Jesus.
12. In the name of Jesus, I receive the mandate and now exercise it to release my children from the prison of any strongman.
13. Let God arise and let all the enemies of my home be scattered, in the name of Jesus.
14. Every evil influence and activity of strange women on my children be nullified, in the name of Jesus.

DELIVERANCE FOR CHILDREN

PRAYER FOR THE PRE-BORN CHILD

Confessions: Luke 1:41, Psa. 139:13, Isa. 44:2, Gal. 1:15, Jer. 1:5

1. I thank You Lord for the provision of this child.
2. I thank You Lord for this child shall be great before You and shall do exploits in Your name.
3. I decree that no sickness or plague will come over the baby, in the name of Jesus.
4. I decree soundness, health and wholeness into the spirit, soul and body of this baby, in the name of Jesus.
5. I ban this baby from inheriting any evil thing from our own family line, in the name of Jesus.
6. I speak wholeness, soundness and perfection into the heart, eyes, ears, skin, bones, teeth of this baby, in Jesus' name.

7. Let this baby be covered with the blood of Jesus and surrounded by the hedge of divine fire, in the name of Jesus.
8. I disallow this baby from having/accepting any form of infirmity, in the name of Jesus.
9. Let the respiratory, digestive and circulatory systems of this baby be normal, strong and healthy, in the name of Jesus.
10. You baby, hear the word of the Lord. Your position must be head down at birth, in the name of Jesus. The cord must be the perfect length and position, not around your neck, in the name of Jesus.
11. O Lord, let this child be saved at an early age.
12. O Lord, let this child be filled with the Holy Spirit even from the womb.

PRAYERS FOR PROTECTION AND DELIVERANCE FOR CHILDREN

(Mark 10:14-16)

1. I cut off, the flow of hereditary problems into this child, in the name of Jesus.
2. I bind every negative ancestral spirit and command them to loose their hold upon this child, in the name of Jesus.
3. Let every problem arising from the power of bad parental example receive solution, in the name of Jesus.
4. I break, every hereditary curse and bondage upon this child, in the name of Jesus.
5. Let this child be cleansed from every hereditary problems with the blood of Jesus.
6. I command, everything that will prevent my child from being a blessing to be totally shattered, in the name of Jesus.
7. I command any power that wants to convert my child to a nuisance to be completely paralysed, in the name of Jesus.
8. You spirit of . . . (pick from the underlisted), release my child,

in the name of Jesus.

-rejection	- abnormal fears	- familiar spirit
- sexual lust	- addiction	- unreasonable silence
- rebellion	- forgetfulness	- anger
- mind darkness	- confusion	- day dreaming
-stupidity	- slowness	- inactivity
- inability to read	- infirmity	- indifference
-dullness	- spiritual blindness	- ostrich behaviours
- bad sleeping	- bad dreams	

9. Let every problem, arising from . . . (pick from the underlisted) receive divine solution, in the name of Jesus.
   - a child being born after long and protracted labour
   - a child being born by caesarean operation or with surgical assistance
   - a child being born with cord around the neck
   - father dies or leaves mother
   - polygamous set up
   - parents addiction to alcohol, smoking or others
   - a child conceived outside wedlock
   - a child conceived as a result of rape or accidental pregnancy
   - a child conceived as a result of incest
   - being born to parents who do not want them
   - being spoilt and pampered
   - being born to unhappy parents who argue, fight or do not communicate
   - being born to harsh parents
   - destruction of home by fire or encountering some natural disasters

- sudden drop in the family standard of living
- a child not believed when telling the truth
- constant criticism of child by parents
- unjust discipline of child
- subjection to sexual molestation
- birth deformity
- being born with the sex opposite to what the parents desired
- sexual aggression to wife by the father in the presence of the child
- adopted child
- separation or divorce of the parents
- death of one or both parents
- boarding school
- lack of parental love and discipline
- attempted abortion during pregnancy, etc.

10. I render every bad spirit powerless in the life of . . . (put the name of the child), in the name of Jesus.
11. I bind the power and break the influence of every negative spirit militating against . . .(put the name of the child), in the name of Jesus.
12. You harmful hereditary and other wicked spirits, I loose . . . (put the name of the child) from your grip, in Jesus' name.
13. Father, let the blood of Jesus cleanse the mind, emotions, imaginations and will of . . . (put the name of the child).
14. Lord, fill this child with Your joy, glory, peace and love.

SCRIPTURES TO USE IN WEIGHT CONTROL

Psalm 34:10: The young lions do lack, and suffer hunger: but they that seek the Lord shall not want any good thing.

Psalm 42:11: Why art thou cast down, O my soul? and why art thou disquieted within me? hope thou in God: for I shall yet praise him, who is the health of my countenance, and my God.

Psalm 55:18: He hath delivered my soul in peace from the battle that was against me: for there were many with me.

Psalm 97:10: Ye that love the Lord, hate evil: he preserveth the souls of his saints; he delivereth them out of the hand of the wicked.

Psalm 103:5: Who satisfieth thy mouth with good things; so that thy youth is renewed like the eagle's.

Psalm 145:18: The Lord is nigh unto all them that call upon him, to all that call upon him in truth.

Proverbs 10:11: The mouth of a righteous man is a well of life: but violence covereth the mouth of the wicked.

Proverbs 18:20: A man's belly shall be satisfied with the fruit of his mouth; and with the increase of his lips shall he be filled.

Proverbs 23:1-3: When thou sittest to eat with a ruler, consider diligently what is before thee: 2And put a knife to thy throat, if thou be a man given to appetite. 3Be not desirous of his dainties: for they are deceitful meat.

Proverbs 25:27-28: It is not good to eat much honey: so for men to search their own glory is not glory. 28He that hath no rule over his own spirit is like a city that is broken down, and without walls.

Proverbs 30:8: Remove far from me vanity and lies: give me neither poverty nor riches; feed me with food convenient for me:

Isaiah 26:3: Thou wilt keep him in perfect peace, whose mind is stayed on thee: because he trusteth in thee.

Isaiah 40:29: He giveth power to the faint; and to them that have no might he increaseth strength.

Philip. 4:7: And the peace of God, which passeth all understanding, shall keep your hearts and minds through Christ Jesus.

Hebrews 10:35: Cast not away therefore your confidence, which hath great recompence of reward.

STEPS TO PERSONAL DELIVERANCE

When you understand self-deliverance, you will keep yourself from being demonized. You will keep yourself healthy, physically and spiritually and free from demonic pollution. Everyday, you will enjoy divine health and will not be spending your money on drugs and hospital bills.

Sometimes, there may be no minister who is anointed and knowledgeable about deliverance to help you. Sometimes, you can be heavily attacked in your dream and the next service is about four days away. What do you do? You should never allow evil spirits to reside in your life. If you lack adequate time to do self deliverance in the mornings, after your quiet time, then, when you're having your bath, you can do it.

Our environment is such that there are many evil spirits moving around and if you are not regularly cleaning your house, they may come in and lodge there, your level of education not withstanding. If a whole university professor could carry a ritual sacrifice because he needed promotion, then education is irrelevant in spiritual matters.

Let's learn a few lessons now before we go into the actual practice.

A demon is a spirit, which means it's like a wind or breath. Most evil spirits move through the breathing passage· or by any opening in the body. This is why sometimes when prayers are hot some people begin to pass out gas or emit bad odour. Now when an ambulance wants to go through a busy area and blares its siren, the purpose is to clear the traffic to ease the passage of the ambulance.

Therefore, when praying for self-deliverance, you should keep quiet after the prayer before ejecting those evil spirits. This is why at times we ask people to breath in and out. If you are praying or speaking at this time, the spirits will not go out because you have not opened the way for them.

The next lesson you must learn is this; demons can come out by simple breathing, coughing, choking, yawning, vomiting, etc. The manifestations vary according to the person and the spirit involved. All the spirits that are not deeply rooted, depart easily, but those deeply entrenched, will require more time and effort to be thrown out. The more stubborn ones will require the help of other believers. Even when they are that strong, and you continue to wound them daily, they will eventually be mortally wounded.

Also, know that if multiple spirits are responsible for one problem, all of them must be removed before total victory is assured. One thing is certain; with every inch of ground grabbed from the devil, you will notice a definite improvement in your life. This is certain. Once the spirit leaves you, there will be a change in you.

Also, remember that an evil spirit must have a legal ground for staying in a person's life.

The purpose of all these information is to enable you to do self-deliverance at home for yourself.

The process of self-deliverance is carried out in stages. Let's go through them one by one.

Step ONE - Start with praise worship. You can sing songs to praise God and to worship Him.

Step TWO - Confess out loud promising deliverance Scriptures. Let us run through a few of them:

Luke 10:19: Behold, I give unto you power to tread on serpents and scorpions, and over all the power of the enemy: and nothing shall by any means hurt you.

Ephes. 1:7: In whom we have redemption through his blood, the forgiveness of sins, according to the riches of his grace;

Romans 16:20: And the God of peace shall bruise Satan under your feet shortly. The grace of our Lord Jesus Christ be with you. Amen.

Rev. 12:11: And they overcame him by the blood of the Lamb, and by the word of their testimony; and they loved not their lives unto the death.

Col. 2:14: Blotting out the handwriting of ordinances that was against us, which was contrary to us, and took it out of the way, nailing it to his cross;

Col. 2:15: And having spoiled principalities and powers, he made a shew of them openly, triumphing over them in it.

Galatians 3:13: Christ hath redeemed us from the curse of the law, being made a curse for us: for it is written, Cursed is every one that hangeth on a tree:

Galatians 3:14: That the blessing of Abraham might come on the Gentiles through Jesus Christ; that we might receive the promise of the Spirit through faith.

Psalm 91:3: Surely he shall deliver thee from the snare of the fowler, and from the noisome pestilence.

2 Tim. 4:18 has this to say:

And the Lord shall deliver me from every evil work, and will preserve me unto his heavenly kingdom: to whom be glory for ever and ever. Amen.

You must memorize at least this one - 2 Tim. 4:18.

Step THREE - Break covenants and curses to destroy their legal hold. You pray a simple prayer like this:

"I break, any curse working against me or I break any covenant working against me, in the name of Jesus."

This is a simple prayer point with much results.

Step FOUR - Bind all the spirits associated with those covenants and curses, like this:

"I bind all the spirits attached or connected to the curses and covenants I have just broken, in the name of Jesus."

Step FIVE - Lay one hand on your head and the other on your stomach or navel and begin to pray like this:

Holy Ghost fire, burn from the top of my head to the sole of my feet, in the name of Jesus.

Begin to mention every organ of your body: kidney, liver, intestine, blood, etc. You must not rush at this level. Lay your hands on areas that the Spirit of God leads you to. Do not be afraid if you notice that you are swaying or staggering, etc.

Step SIX - Then begin to saturate yourself with the blood of Jesus. You do this by saying:

"Blood of Jesus, enter into my spirit, soul and body."

Next you say:

"I drink the blood of Jesus."

This must continue until you have a release in your spirit to stop.

Step SEVEN - It is now, that you are able to demand firmly, in the name of the Lord Jesus Christ, that any spirit that is not of God should leave you. You demand it forcefully like this:

"In the name of the Lord Jesus Christ, I come against all you hidden spirit and I bind your activities in my life. You can no longer hide below the surface because I now recognize what you have been doing; release me."

If sickness is the problem, address it like this:

"You spirit of infirmity, I speak to you directly, get out of my life now. I am redeemed by the blood of Jesus Christ, come out and go now. Go out with every breath by the power of the Holy Spirit. I prevail over you, in the name of Jesus. "

At this point, you stop talking; open your mouth and nose and begin to breath in and out. Take about three to seven deep breaths, and expel them forcefully through your mouth and nose. You may be surprised that strange things will begin to happen. Repeat this stage again and again. This will help you to flush out any deposit or impurity within your body. You may notice that you are coughing, yawning, sneezing, sweating or shedding tears, but continue and do not lose your concentration.

Step EIGHT - When you have finished the expulsion stage, you then ask for a fresh in-filling of the Holy Spirit and close the session with praises.

When you are attacked in your dream, rise up and go through the stages I have already mentioned. (Our book "Victory Over Satanic Dreams" can help you further.)

Self-deliverance keeps you from getting sick; it removes every evil seed of the enemy; it charges your body with fire. It uproots evil plantations and builds up your confidence.

Every night before you go to bed, you must remember these three important prayer points.

Pray that the walls of fire should surround you. The Bible says:

Zech. 2:5: For I, saith the Lord, will be unto her a wall of fire round about, and will be the glory in the midst of her.

Pray for cover with the blood of Jesus.

Rev. 12:11: And they overcame him by the blood of the Lamb, and by the word of their testimony; and they loved not their lives unto the death.

Also pray that the angels of God should surround you.

Psalm 34:7: The angel of the Lord encampeth round about them that fear him, and delivereth them.

No matter how sleepy you are, make sure you pray these three prayer points every night.

There is no reason why self-deliverance should not be effective. However, if the person seeking deliverance is under stubborn demonic control or hereditary strongman, and lacks sufficient faith or authority to defeat the oppressors, or is living in any known sin, the evil spirits will defend what they think is their right.

One final word of caution. For a person to be delivered, he must desire deliverance. Self-deliverance must not be done because of pride, shyness, the fear of possible public embarrassment, etc. Your motive for engaging in self-deliverance has to be pure.

Remember, deliverance is a process and the length of time it takes depends on several things viz:

- The length of time the evil spirit has stayed inside a person,
- The strength and reinforcement of the spirit,
- The experience and degree of anointing upon the person ministering the deliverance,
- The willingness of the person being delivered to be free,

- The knowledge of the word of God and your level of hatred for sin.

For self-deliverance to be very effective, a great deal of self-discipline is necessary.

Also, remember that bondage can be weak or strong. A weak hold can be broken quickly, whereas a stronghold may take a longer time. You will not realize the strength of a bondage, until you faithfully and persistently work on it. You must remember that a foothold can graduate to a stronghold if left unaddressed.

PRAYERS FOR CLEANSING THE HOUSE

How do you clean your home, your office, your car, land, farm or properties from contamination by evil spirits?

Firstly, prepare yourself by fasting and prayer and studying the word of God. Do at least, one day fast. This first stage is preparation.

Secondly, find a good prayer partner if possible. Jesus sent His disciples two by two. Try to get one partner.

Thirdly, you must have at least the following 10 Scriptures in your memory and book for the attack. You must know them;

- **Revelation 12:11:** And they overcame him by the blood of the Lamb, and by the word of their testimony; and they loved not their lives unto the death.
- **Revelation 22:3:** And there shall be no more curse: but the throne of God and of the Lamb shall be in it; and his servants shall serve Him:
- **Colossians 2:14-15:** Blotting out the handwriting of ordinances that was against us, which was contrary to us, and took it out of the way, nailing it to His cross; And having spoiled principalities and powers, He made a shew of them

openly, triumphing over them in it.

- **Galatians 3:13-14:** Christ hath redeemed us from the curse of the law, being made a curse for us: for it is written, Cursed is every one that hangeth on a tree: That the blessing of Abraham might come on the Gentiles through Jesus Christ; that we might receive the promise through faith.

- **Deuteronomy 21:23:** His body shall not remain all night upon the tree, but thou shalt in any wise bury him that day; (for he that is hanged is accursed of God;) that thy land be not defiled, which the LORD thy God giveth thee for an inheritance.

- **Deuteronomy 32:5:** They have corrupted themselves, their spot is not the spot of his children: they are a perverse and crooked generation.

- **Numbers 23:8:** How shall I curse, whom God hath not cursed? or how shall I defy whom the LORD hath not defied?

- **Numbers 23:23:** Surely there is no enchantment against Jacob, neither is there any divination against Israel: according to this time it shall be said of Jacob and of Israel, What hath God wrought!

- **II Samuel 7:29:** Therefore, now let it please thee to bless the house of thy servant, that it may continue for ever before thee: for thou, O Lord God, hast spoken it: and with thy blessing let the house of thy servant be blessed for ever.

- **Luke 10:19:** Behold, I give unto you power to tread on serpents and scorpions, and over all the power of the enemy: and nothing shall by any eans hurt you. With these Scriptures you are ready to do the work.

Fourthly, when you and your partner move into the environment, you read these Scriptures out loud, in unison or separately.

Fifthly, you pray for discernment by asking the Holy Spirit to reveal to you where you will lay your hands. Have in your possession a bottle of olive oil and if possible some anointed handkerchiefs. The Scriptures for this is found in the book of Mark, chapter 6 verse 13:

And they cast out many devils, and anointed with oil many that were sick, and healed them.

And in James, chapter 5 verse 14:

Is any sick among you? let him call for the elders of the church; and let them pray over him, anointing him with oil in the name of the Lord.

Also in Acts, chapter 19 verses 11-12:

And God wrought special miracles by the hands of Paul;

So that from his body were brought unto the sick handkerchiefs or aprons, and diseases departed from them.

THE ANOINTING AND PRAYING

(Pray this over every room in the house:) By the blood of the Lord Jesus Christ, I bind every evil spirit that is in this room and I command them to flee right now and go where the Lord Jesus Christ sends them. I claim by faith that this room is covered under the blood of Jesus Christ and no evil spirit can enter it.

After going through every room in the house, pray like this:

I dedicate and consecrate this home to the Lord Jesus Christ; and satan has no hold on it. I surrender everything in this house to the Lord Jesus Christ and claim it is under His protection.

I bind, every evil spirit that is in this house and command them to flee to where the Lord Jesus Christ sends them.

I claim by faith, that everything in this house is covered under the blood of Jesus Christ from the top of the roof, to the bottom of the footing and everything in between.

I claim by faith, that this house is surrounded by a hedge of thorns, a wall of fire, a wall of faith, and covered under the blood of Jesus Christ.

I pray that warring angels, would come to protect the four corners of this house and everyone inside.

Thank You Lord, for the complete victory we already have in Jesus Christ. Amen!

Whenever you pray on olive oil or lay your hands on handkerchiefs, asking God to anoint them, the power of God enters into the two items. Wherever they are used, evil spirits should depart.

Now you will begin to attack all the evil powers around. You verbally denounce satan and all his hosts and claim your authority over them as a believer. You walk around the place praying, commanding the spirits to depart, touching where the spirit of God directs you to touch after dipping your hand in the anointing oil.

If strange things have been happening in that house or to that machine or instrument, then call out the specific spirits. It is sufficient to call them by the name of the evil activities they sponsor, it may be the spirit of poverty, witchcraft, familiar spirits, etc. Call them out and bind them.

When you finish praying as described above then pray a wall of fire around those things and plead the blood of Jesus on them and ask for the angels of God to be stationed in the place.

If it is a home, anoint its doors, lintels and windows. You can anoint things like toys, cars, wardrobes, cupboards and equipment in the house. Then begin to praise the Lord for the victory.

Finally, if you have books and objects associated with witchcraft, astrology, good-luck charms, the occult, Christian science and strange uses of psalms or demonic prayer uniforms, prayer candles and incense, etc, ensure that they are destroyed. Set them on fire.

WITH HEALING IN HIS WINGS

CONFESSION

Malachi 4:2: But unto you that fear my name shall the Sun of righteousness arise with healing in his wings; and ye shall go forth, and grow up as calves of the stall.

1. Praise God for His mighty power that is able to heal all sicknesses.
2. Thank God for He is the Lord God that heals you.
3. O Lord, let Your healing hand be stretched out upon my life now.
4. O Lord, let Your miracle hand be stretched out upon my life now.
5. O Lord, let Your deliverance hand be stretched out upon my life now.
6. I annul, every engagement with the spirit of death, in Jesus' name.
7. I rebuke, every refuge of sickness, in the name of Jesus.
8. I destroy, the grip and operation of sickness, upon my life, in the name of Jesus.
9. Every knee of infirmity in my life, bow, in Jesus' name.
10. O Lord, let my negativity be converted to positivity.
11. I command death, upon any sickness in any area of my life, in the name of Jesus.
12. I shall see my sickness no more, in the name of Jesus.
13. Father Lord, let the whirlwind of God, scatter every vessel of infirmity fashioned against my life, in the name of Jesus.
14. Every spirit, hindering my perfect healing, fall down and die

now, in the name of Jesus.

15. Father Lord, let all death contractors begin to kill themselves, in the name of Jesus.
16. Father Lord, let every germ of infirmity in my body die, in the name of Jesus.
17. Father Lord, let every agent of sickness, working against my health, disappear, in the name of Jesus.
18. Fountain of discomfort in my life, dry up now, in Jesus' name.
19. Every dead organ in my body, receive life now, in Jesus' name.
20. Father Lord, let my blood be transfused with the blood of Jesus to effect my perfect health, in the name of Jesus.
21. Every internal disorder, receive order, in the name of Jesus.
22. Every infirmity, come out with all your roots, in Jesus' name.
23. I withdraw every conscious and unconscious cooperation with sickness, in the name of Jesus.
24. O Lord, let the whirlwind of God, blow every wind of infirmity away.
25. I release my body from every curse of infirmity, in Jesus' name.
26. O Lord, let the blood of Jesus, flush out every evil deposit out from my blood.
27. I recover, every organ of my body, from every evil altar, in Jesus' name.

PRAYERS FOR DIVINE HEALING

CONFESSION

Deut. 7:15: And the LORD will take away from thee all sickness, and will put none of the evil diseases of Egypt, which thou knowest, upon thee; but will lay them upon all them that hate thee.

Isa. 53:5-6: But he was wounded for our transgressions, he was bruised for our iniquities: the chastisement of our peace was upon him; and with his stripes we are healed.

All we like sheep have gone astray; we have turned every one to his own way; and the LORD hath laid on him the iniquity of us all.

Col. 2:15: And having spoiled principalities and powers, he made a shew of them openly, triumphing over them in it.

I am an overcomer. I overcome satan because of the blood of the Lamb and because of the words of my testimonies. I am a body of Christ and satan has no power over me.

My body is the temple of the Holy Spirit of God. I am redeemed, cleansed and sanctified by the blood of Jesus. The devil has no place in me. The devil has no power over me. No weapon fashioned against me shall prosper. The weapons of my warfare are mighty through God to pull down strongholds. I can do all things through Christ who strengthens me.

1. Praises.
2. Confession of sins.
3. Every arrow of witchcraft in my life, **come out with all your roots,** in the name of Jesus! (Lay your hands on your stomach and keep repeating the emphasized area.)
4. Every load of infirmity, planted by the enemy, come out of me and enter no more, in the name of Jesus.
5. Let all negative materials, circulating in my blood stream, be evacuated, in the name of Jesus.
6. I drink the blood of Jesus. (Physically swallow and drink it by faith. Keep doing this for some time.)
7. Lay one hand on your head and the other on your stomach or navel and pray like this: Holy Ghost fire, burn from the top of my head to the sole of my feet. (Begin to mention every organ of your body; your kidney, liver, intestines, blood, etc. You must not rush at this level, because the fire will actually come and you may start feeling the heat.)
8. Let the blood of Jesus be transfused into my blood vessels, in

the name of Jesus.

9. I command, every agent of disease in my blood and body organs to die, in the name of Jesus.
10. Let my blood, reject every evil foreign entity, in Jesus' name.
11. Blood of Jesus, speak deliverance and healing into my life, in the name of Jesus.
12. I receive creative healing in my body, in the name of Jesus.
13. I hold the blood of Jesus against you spirit of . . . (mention what is troubling you). You have to flee.
14. O Lord, let Your hand of fire be stretched out upon my life now.
15. O Lord, let Your miracle hand be stretched out upon my life now.
16. O Lord, let Your deliverance hand be stretched out upon my life now.
17. I fire back, every arrow of death and hell, in Jesus' name.
18. Let the organs of my body, be released from every altar of bewitchment, in the name of Jesus.
19. I destroy, every garment of infirmity, in the name of Jesus.
20. Every handwriting of infirmity in my life, be wiped off by the blood of Jesus.
21. O God, arise and let every enemy of wholeness scatter, in the name of Jesus.
22. I cancel, every medical or clinical prophecy, in Jesus' name.
23. Every Pharaoh of infirmity, die in the Red Sea, in Jesus' name.
24. Holy Spirit, release Your healing virtue upon my life, in the name of Jesus.
25. Every spirit, hindering my perfect healing, fall down and die now, in the name of Jesus.
26. Father Lord, let all death contractors begin to kill themselves, in the name of Jesus.
27. Father Lord, let every germ of infirmity in my body die, in the

name of Jesus.

28. Father Lord, let every agent of sickness working against my health disappear, in the name of Jesus.
29. Fountain of discomfort in my life, dry up now, in Jesus' name.
30. Every dead organ in my body, receive life now, in Jesus' name.
31. Father Lord, let my blood be transfused with the blood of Jesus to effect my perfect health, in the name of Jesus.
32. Every internal disorder, receive order, in the name of Jesus.
33. Every infirmity, come out with all your roots, in Jesus' name.
34. I withdraw, every conscious and unconscious cooperation with sickness, in the name of Jesus.
35. O Lord, let the whirlwind of God blow every wind of infirmity away.
36. I release my body, from every curse of infirmity, in Jesus' name.
37. O Lord, let the blood of Jesus, flush every evil deposit from my blood.
38. I recover, every organ of my body from every evil altar, in Jesus' name.
39. I withdraw my body, from the manipulation of every caldron of darkness, in the name of Jesus.
40. Holy Ghost fire, destroy every stubborn agent of disease in my body, in the name of Jesus.
41. I arrest, every demon of terminal disease, in Jesus' name.
42. Holy Ghost fire, boil every infirmity out of my system, in the name of Jesus.
43. I cancel, every witchcraft verdict against my life, in Jesus' name.
44. O earth, vomit anything that has been buried inside you against my health, in the name of Jesus.
45. Every tree, that infirmity has planted in my blood, be uprooted by fire, in the name of Jesus.

46 I command every witchcraft arrow, to depart from my
- spinal cord - spleen - navel - heart
- throat - between the eyes - head, in Jesus' name.

47. I bind, every evil present in my (pick from the underlisted) system
- reproductive - digestive - respiratory
- nervous - skeletal - muscular
- circulatory - endocrine - excretory, in Jesus' name.

48. Let the power in the stripes of Jesus, heal me now.

49. O Lord, heal me and I shall be healed.

50. Every organ of my body that is not functioning well, be replaced by the creative power of God, in the name of Jesus.

51. Let my body defences, resist and destroy every sickness, in the name of Jesus.

52. Let my immunity, be empowered by the blood of Jesus.

53. Thank God for your healing.

COME ALIVE

For the resurrection of dead organs or a dead baby in the womb.

CONFESSION

John 5:21: For as the Father raiseth up the dead, and quickeneth them; even so the Son quickeneth whom he will.

John 6:63: It is the spirit that quickeneth; the flesh profiteth nothing: the words that I speak unto you, they are spirit, and they are life.

Romans 4:17: (As it is written, I have made thee a father of many nations,) before him whom he believed, even God, who quickeneth the dead, and calleth those things which be not as though they were.

John 11:25: Jesus said unto her, I am the resurrection, and the life:

he that believeth in me, though he were dead, yet shall he live:

Slot in the name of the organ you are praying about into the dotted lines:

1. Let Your resurrection power come upon my . . ., in the mighty name of Jesus.
2. I bind every spirit of death operating in my . . ., in the mighty name of Jesus.
3. I command every dead bone in my . . . to come alive, in the name of Jesus.
4. You evil hand, laid on my . . ., receive the thunder fire of God and be roasted, in the name of Jesus.
5. I command, every evil monitoring gadget fashioned against my . . . to be destroyed, in the name of Jesus.
6. I breathe in the life of God and I eject every spirit of death and hell, in the name of Jesus.
7. I recover, every miracle that I have lost through unbelief, in the name of Jesus.
8. Father, let Your creative power operate afresh in every area of my life, in the name of Jesus.
9. Father, let the fire of the Holy Ghost enter into my blood stream and cleanse my system, in the name of Jesus.
10. I release my . . . from the cage of every household wickedness, in the name of Jesus.
11. Let every information about my . . . be erased from every satanic memory, in the name of Jesus.
12. Every evil plantation in my life, **come out with all your roots,** in the name of Jesus! (Lay your hands on your stomach and keep repeating the emphasized area.)
13. Evil strangers in my body, come all the way out of your hiding places, in the name of Jesus.
14. I cough out and vomit, any food eaten from the table of the devil, in the name of Jesus. (Cough it out and vomit it by faith. Prime the expulsion.)

15. Let all negative materials, circulating in my blood stream be evacuated, in the name of Jesus.
16. I drink the blood of Jesus. (Physically swallow and drink it by faith. Keep doing this for some time.)
17. Lay one hand on your head and the other on your stomach or navel and pray like this: Holy Ghost fire, burn from the top of my head to the sole of my feet. Mention every organ of your body: Your kidney, liver, intestine, blood, etc. You must not rush at this level, because the fire will actually come and you may start feeling the heat.
18. I cut myself off, from every spirit of . . . (mention the name of your place of birth), in the name of Jesus.
19. I cut myself off, from every tribal spirit and curse, in the name of Jesus.
20. I cut myself off, from every territorial spirit and curse, in the name of Jesus.
21. Holy Ghost fire, purge my life.
22. I claim complete deliverance, in the name of Jesus, from the spirit of . . . (mention those things you do not desire in your life).
23. I break the hold of any evil power over my life, in Jesus' name.
24. I move from bondage into liberty, in the name of Jesus.
25. Thank God for answers to your prayer points.

PRAYERS TO HEAL ABDOMINAL SICKNESS

CONFESSIONS

Psalm 30:2: O Lord my God, I cried unto thee, and thou hast healed me.

Proverbs 3:7-8: Be not wise in thine own eyes: fear the Lord, and depart from evil. It shall be health to thy navel, and marrow to thy bones.

Proverbs 4:20-22: My son, attend to my words; incline thine ear unto my sayings. Let them not depart from thine eyes; keep them in the midst of thine heart. For they are life unto those that find them, and health to all their flesh.

Psalm 27:1-2: The Lord is my light and my salvation; whom shall I fear? the Lord is the strength of my life; of whom shall I be afraid? When the wicked, even mine enemies and my foes, came upon me to eat up my flesh, they stumbled and fell.

1 Cor. 10:21: Ye cannot drink the cup of the Lord, and the cup of devils: ye cannot be partakers of the Lord's table, and of the table of devils.

Psalm 91:1-16: He that dwelleth in the secret place of the most High shall abide under the shadow of the Almighty. I will say of the Lord, He is my refuge and my fortress: my God; in him will I trust. Surely he shall deliver thee from the snare of the fowler, and from the noisome pestilence. He shall cover thee with his feathers, and under his wings shalt thou trust: his truth shall be thy shield and buckler. Thou shalt not be afraid for the terror by night; nor for the arrow that flieth by day; Nor for the pestilence that walketh in darkness; nor for the destruction that wasteth at noonday. A thousand shall fall at thy side, and ten thousand at thy right hand; but it shall not come nigh thee. Only with thine eyes shalt thou behold and see the reward of the wicked. Because thou hast made the Lord, which is my refuge, even the most High, thy habitation; There shall no evil befall thee, neither shall any plague come nigh thy dwelling. For he shall give his angels charge over thee, to keep thee in all thy ways. They shall bear thee up in their hands, lest thou dash thy foot against a stone. Thou shalt tread upon the lion and adder: the young lion and the dragon shalt thou trample under feet. Because he hath set his love upon me, therefore will I deliver him: I will set him on high, because he hath known my name. He shall call upon me, and I will answer him: I will be with him in trouble; I will deliver him, and honour him.

With long life will I satisfy him, and shew him my salvation.

1. Blood of Jesus, flush out every infirmity from my abdomen.
2. Every physical and spiritual poison in my abdomen, come out, in the name of Jesus.
3. I vomit, every spiritual and physical worm working against my intestine, in the name of Jesus.
4. I challenge every organ in my abdomen with the fire of God, in the name of Jesus.
5. By the stripes of the Lord Jesus Christ, I recover my abdomen from every bewitchment.
6. I break the power of any evil arrow, fired against my abdomen, in the name of Jesus.
7. Every disease agent in my abdomen, I command you to die, in the name of Jesus.
8. I command every evil plantation in my abdomen: **Come out with all your roots,** in the name of Jesus! (Lay your hands on your stomach and keep repeating the emphasized area.)
9. Evil strangers in my intestine, come all the way out of your hiding places, in the name of Jesus.
10. I disconnect, any conscious or unconscious linkage with demonic caterers, in the name of Jesus.
11. Let all avenues of eating or drinking spiritual poisons, be closed, in the name of Jesus.
12. I cough out and vomit, any food eaten from the table of the devil, in the name of Jesus. (Cough it out and vomit it by faith. Prime the expulsion).
13. Let all negative materials circulating in my abdomen be evacuated, in the name of Jesus.
14. I drink the blood of Jesus. (Physically swallow and drink it by faith. Keep doing this for some time.)
15. Holy Ghost fire, circulate all over my body.

16 I command all physical poisons inside my system to be neutralised, in the name of Jesus.

17. Let all evil assignments, fashioned against me, through the mouth gate be nullified, in the name of Jesus.

18. Bread of heaven, fill me till I want no more.

19. I command my digestive system to reject every evil command, in the name of Jesus.

20. Let all satanic designs of oppression, against me in dreams and visions, be frustrated, in the name of Jesus.

21. Holy Spirit, overshadow my life by fire.

PRAYERS TO DESTROY BED-WETTING

CONFESSIONS

Psalm 25:20: O keep my soul, and deliver me: let me not be ashamed; for I put my trust in thee.

Psalm 32:6: For this shall every one that is godly pray unto thee in a time when thou may est be found: surely in the floods of great waters they shall not come nigh unto him.

Psalm 69:15: Let not the waterflood overflow me, neither let the deep swallow me up, and let not the pit shut her mouth upon me.

Psalm 144:7: Send thine hand from above; rid me, and deliver me out of great waters, from the hand of strange children;

Matthew 8:17: That it might be fulfilled which was spoken by Esaias the prophet, saying, Himself took our infirmities, and bare our sicknesses.

1. I arrest, every power attacking my bladder and kidney, in the name of Jesus.
2. I bind and cast out, every spirit of bed-wetting, in Jesus' name.
3. Let my life be released from every oppression, in Jesus' name
4. Let the glory of the Lord uphold me by fire, in Jesus' name.

5. Holy Ghost, dry up every excessive excretory fluid, in the name of Jesus.
6. I bind and cast out, every spirit of torment, in Jesus' name.
7. I push out, any arrow fired into my urinary system, in the name of Jesus.
8. I command deliverance upon my life by fire, in Jesus' name.
9. I vomit every negative thing I have eaten or swallowed, in the name of Jesus.
10. Let the fire of the Holy Ghost, burn every satanic plantation in my life, in the name of Jesus.
11. Every evil hand, covering my urinary system, loose your hold, in the name of Jesus.
12. Blood of Jesus, shake out every power of darkness, in the name of Jesus.
13. I pass out, every problematic fluid circulating in my system, in the name of Jesus.
14. O Lord, speak healing into my bladder.
15. I dismantle, every gate of oppression giving access to my body, in the name of Jesus.
16. Holy Ghost, connect my bladder to the resurrection power of the Lord Jesus Christ.
17. Every arrow of witchcraft, fired into my life, come out now, in the name of Jesus.
18. I remove my organs, from every witchcraft bewitchment, in the name of Jesus.
19. O God arise and let every enemy of my comfort scatter, in the name of Jesus.
20. O Lord, let my life experience Your resurrection power now, in the name of Jesus.
21. I dismantle, every power of the crocodile spirit working against my life, in the name of Jesus.
22. O God, let Your power mop out the plantation of darkness in

my body, in the name of Jesus.

23. Every handwriting of darkness, move out of my spirit, in the name of Jesus.
24. O Lord, let Your anointing, break the yoke of every infirmity.
25. I pull down, the powers of darkness working against my comfort, in the name of Jesus.
26. O Lord, move Your yoke-breaking power upon me and set me free.
27. I touch the helm of Your garment, O Lord. Set me free.
28. I cast out, every deposit of the enemy in my bowels, in the name of Jesus.
29. You hereditary demon, loose your hold, in the name of Jesus.
30. Thank God for your healing.

PRAYERS TO HEAL FEVER

CONFESSIONS

Matthew 8:17: That it might be fulfilled which was spoken by Esaias the prophet, saying, Himself took our infirmities, and bare our sicknesses.

Luke 4:38-39: And he arose out of the synagogue, and entered into Simon's house. And Simon's wife's mother was taken with a great fever; and they besought him for her. And he stood over her, and rebuked the fever; and it left her: and immediately she arose and ministered unto them.

1. I rebuke every spirit of fever, in the name of Jesus.
2. Every attack on my body temperature, die, in Jesus' name.
3. I pull down, the stronghold of fever, in the name of Jesus.
4. Blood of Jesus, flush out every demon of fever, in Jesus' name.
5. Every agent of fever, dry up, in the name of Jesus.
6. Every germ, sponsoring fever, clear out of my body, in the name of Jesus.

7. Holy Ghost fire, drain out spiritual contamination from my blood, in the name of Jesus.
8. O God, arise and let the evil siren of the enemy be silenced, in the name of Jesus.
9. My body, reject every destructive strategy, in Jesus' name.
10. Let my blood receive divine power to kill every agent of fever, in the name of Jesus.
11. O Lord, after the order of Your rebuke of fever, I rebuke every fever in my life, in the name of Jesus.
12. I rebuke the fever troubling my body, in the name of Jesus.
13. O Lord, beginning from the top of my head to the soles of my feet, let me begin to experience Your healing power, in the name of Jesus.
14. As I breathe in and out now, let sicknesses flee through my breath, in the name of Jesus.
15. Every power, targeted at draining away my strength, loose your hold, in the name of Jesus.
16. I speak destruction, unto every agent of fever in my body, in the name of Jesus.
17. My blood, reject every complication of infirmity, in Jesus' name.
18. Let the power of God in my life, be ignited to suffocate and destroy every power of infirmity, in the name of Jesus.
19. Every cauldron of witchcraft, boiling my blood, be broken, in the name of Jesus.
20. Every command, working against my blood, die, in Jesus' name.
21. Thank God for your healing.

PRAYERS FOR THOSE GOING TO HOSPITAL FOR MEDICAL TREATMENT

CONFESSIONS

Psalm 91:1-16: He that dwelleth in the secret place of the most High shall abide under the shadow of the Almighty. I will say of the Lord, He is my refuge and my fortress: my God; in him will I trust. Surely he shall deliver thee from the snare of the fowler, and from the noisome pestilence. He shall cover thee with his feathers, and under his wings shalt thou trust: his truth shall be thy shield and buckler. Thou shalt not be afraid for the terror by night; nor for the arrow that flieth by day; Nor for the pestilence that walketh in darkness; nor for the destruction that wasteth at noonday. A thousand shall fall at thy side, and ten thousand at thy right hand; but it shall not come nigh thee. Only with thine eyes shalt thou behold and see the reward of the wicked. Because thou hast made the Lord, which is my refuge, even the most High, thy habitation; There shall no evil befall thee, neither shall any plague come nigh thy dwelling. For he shall give his angels charge over thee, to keep thee in all thy ways. They shall bear thee up in their hands, lest thou dash thy foot against a stone. Thou shalt tread upon the lion and adder: the young lion and the dragon shalt thou trample under feet. Because he hath set his love upon me, therefore will I deliver him: I will set him on high, because he hath known my name. He shall call upon me, and I will answer him: I will be with him in trouble; I will deliver him, and honour him. With long life will I satisfy him, and shew him my salvation.

Psalm 121:1-8:I will lift up mine eyes unto the hills, from whence cometh my help. My help cometh from the Lord, which made heaven and earth. He will not suffer thy foot to be moved: he that keepeth thee will not slumber. Behold, he that keepeth Israel shall neither slumber nor sleep. The Lord is thy keeper: the Lord is thy shade upon thy right hand. The sun shall not smite thee by day, nor the moon by night. The Lord shall preserve thee from all evil: he shall preserve thy soul. The Lord shall preserve thy going out and thy coming in from this time forth, and even for evermore.

1. Jesus, the great Physician, make Yourself known to me as I enter the hospital.
2. O Lord, come into this house with Your hands and touch the sick
3. O Lord, restore health and wholeness by fire.
4. O Lord, heal every hidden evil memory.
5. Any power, damaging my health, die, in the name of Jesus.
6. I deliver myself from evil influences of diseases, in Jesus' name.
7. Let Your Spirit, O Lord, minister healing to my life.
8. Let the healing anointing, be upon my home, in Jesus' name.
9. Every barrier to the movement of healing gifts to operate on my behalf, be broken, in the name of Jesus.
10. I sanctify, every equipment and drug that would be used for me and on me, in the name of Jesus.
11. Every eater of flesh and drinker of blood in the hospital, my body is not your candidate, in the name of Jesus
12. I cover the whole of the hospital with the blood of Jesus.
13. O Lord, build the hedge of the blood of Jesus around my life.
14. I shall not die but live to declare the works of God, in the name of Jesus.
15. Let divine wisdom enter into those who will administer my medical and nursing care, in the name of Jesus.
16. By the power that divided the Red Sea, let my weaknesses be banished and let my health be restored, in Jesus' name.
17. O Lord, I will live to glorify Your holy name, in Jesus' name.
18. I cover all the members of staff of the hospital with the blood of Jesus.
19. Wonderful Father, I put myself into Your hands before the operation, in the name of Jesus.
20. Thank God for your healing.

PRAYERS BEFORE AN OPERATION

CONFESSIONS

Psalms 34:7: The angel of the Lord encampeth round about them that fear him, and delivereth them.

Isaiah 53:5: But he was wounded for our transgressions, he was bruised for our iniquities: the chastisement of our peace was upon him; and with his stripes we are healed.

SONGS: The Great Physician or There is power in the blood or You are the Lord that healeth me

1. I cover the whole of this environment with the blood of Jesus.
2. I banish every eater of flesh and drinker of blood from this environment, in the name of Jesus.
3. I shall not die but live, to declare the works of God, in the name of Jesus.
4. Every spirit of death and hell, I bind and cast you out, in the name of Jesus.
5. I soak the personnel that will attend to me with the blood of Jesus.
6. Wonderful Father, I put myself into Your hands, in Jesus' name.
7. O Lord, deliver me from the fear of pain and from the unknown.
8. I hide behind the cross of calvary.
9. Let the water and the blood of Jesus, overshadow my life, in the name of Jesus.
10. Holy Spirit, guide the surgeon, anaesthetist and all the theatre staff, in the name of Jesus.
11. I bind any spirit, which is not of God within or outside the theatre, in the name of Jesus.
12. I shut out, every spirit of death and hell, from my vicinity, in the name of Jesus.
13. O Lord, anoint the staff of the hospital with Your healing power.

14. While I am unconscious, let my deepest feeling rest in me, in the name of Jesus.
15. O Lord, as I sleep in peace, let me awake to praise Your name, in the name of Jesus.
16. I bind every spirit of error. You shall not come close to me, in the name of Jesus.
17. O God of signs and wonders, You are the heavenly surgeon. Touch me by Your power, in the name of Jesus.
18. You evil wandering spirit, my life is not your candidate, in the name of Jesus.
19. O God, let divine wisdom be upon me and upon the hands that will carry out the operation, in the name of Jesus.
20. I bind and cast out, every spirit of complication after surgery, in the name of Jesus.
21. Affliction shall not rise again the second time in my life, in the name of Jesus.
22. Thou power of God, arrest every power that is arresting my health, in the name of Jesus.

DREAM CRIMINALS MUST DIE

Confession: Phil. 2:10-11

1. Lord, show me dreams, visions and restlessness that would advance my cause.
2. Let all satanic designs of oppression against me, in dreams and visions be frustrated, in the name of Jesus.
3. Let all the enemies of my good dreams and visions on my home, be rendered impotent, in the name of Jesus.
4. I bind, the activities of demonic manipulation in dreams and visions, in the name of Jesus.
5. I stand against, dream defeats, in the name of Jesus.
6. I claim freedom, from satanic and restless dreams, in Jesus' name.

7. Let all satanic designs of oppression against me, in dreams and visions be frustrated, in the name of Jesus.
8. I claim all the good things which God has revealed to me through dreams. I reject all satanic dreams, in Jesus' name.
9. (You are going to be specific here. Place your hand on your chest and talk to God specifically about the dreams which need to be cancelled. Cancel it with all your strength. If it needs fire, command the fire of God to burn it to ashes.)
10. O Lord, perform the necessary surgical operation in my life and change all that had gone wrong in the spirit world.
11. I recover all the good things which I have lost as a result of defeat and attacks, in my dreams, in the name of Jesus.
12. I arrest, every spiritual attacker and paralyse its activities in my life, in the name of Jesus.
13. I recover, my stolen virtues, goodness and blessings, in Jesus' name.
14. Let all satanic manipulations, through dreams be dissolved, in the name of Jesus.
15. Let all arrows, gunshots, wounds, harassment and opposition in dreams return to the senders, in Jesus' name.
16. I reject, every evil spiritual load, placed on me through dreams, in the name of Jesus.
17. All spiritual animals (cats, dogs, snakes, crocodiles) paraded against me, be chained and returned to the senders, in the name of Jesus.
18. Holy Ghost, purge my intestine and my blood from satanic foods and injections.
19. I break every evil covenant and initiation, through dreams, in the name of Jesus.
20. I disband, all the hosts of darkness set against me, in the name of Jesus.
21. Every evil imagination and plan, contrary to my life, fail

woefully, in the name of Jesus.

22. Every doorway and ladder to satanic invasion in my life, be abolished forever by the blood of Jesus.
23. I free myself from curses, hexes, spells, bewitchment and evil domination directed against me through dreams, in the name of Jesus.
24. I command you ungodly powers, to release me, in Jesus' name.
25. Let all past satanic defeats in the dream, be converted to victory, in the name of Jesus.
26. Let all tests in the dream, be converted to testimonies, in Jesus' name.
27. Let all trials in the dream, be converted to triumphs, in Jesus' name.
28. Let all failures in the dream, be converted to success, in Jesus' name.
29. Let all scars in the dream, be converted to stars, in Jesus' name.
30. Let all bondage in the dream, be converted to freedom, in Jesus' name.
31. Let all losses in the dream, be converted to gains, in Jesus' name.
32. Let all oppositions in the dream, be converted to victory, in Jesus' name.
33. Let all weaknesses in the dream, be converted to strength, in the name of Jesus.
34. Let all negative in the dream, be converted to positive, in Jesus' name.
35. I release myself, from every infirmity introduced into my life through dreams, in the name of Jesus.
36. Let all attempts by the enemy, to deceive me through dreams fail woefully, in the name of Jesus.
37. I reject, evil spiritual husband, wife, children, marriage, engagement, trading, pursuit, ornament, money, friend, relative, etc., in Jesus' name.

38. Lord Jesus, wash my spiritual eyes, ears and mouth with Your blood.
39. The God who answereth by fire, answer by fire whenever any spiritual attacker comes against me, in Jesus' name.
40. Lord Jesus, replace all satanic dreams with heavenly visions and divinely-inspired dreams.
41. Confess these Scriptures out loud: Psalm 27:1-2, 1Cor. 10:21, Psalm 91.
42. I command every evil plantation in my life, **come out with all your roots in the name of Jesus!** (Lay your hands on your stomach and keep repeating the emphasized area.)
43. Evil strangers in my body, come all the way out of your hiding places, in the name of Jesus.
44. I disconnect, any conscious or unconscious linkage with demonic caterers, in the name of Jesus.
45. Let all avenues of eating or drinking spiritual poisons in the dream be closed, in the name of Jesus.
46. I cough out and vomit, any food eaten from the table of the devil, in the name of Jesus. (Cough it out and vomit it by faith. Prime the expulsion).
47. Let all negative materials, circulating in my blood stream be evacuated, in the name of Jesus.
48. I drink the blood of Jesus. (Physically swallow and drink it by faith. Keep doing this for some time).
49. Let all evil spiritual feeders, warring against me drink their own blood and eat their own flesh, in Jesus' name.
50. I command, all demonic food utensils fashioned against me to be roasted, in the name of Jesus.
51. Holy Ghost fire, circulate all over my body.
52. I command, all physical poisons inside my system to be neutralized, in the name of Jesus.

53. Let all evil assignments, fashioned against me through the mouth gate be nullified, in the name of Jesus.
54. Let all spiritual problems, attached to any hour of the night be cancelled, in the name of Jesus. (Pick the periods from midnight to 6:00 a.m.).
55. Bread of heaven, fill me till I want no more.
56. Let all the catering equipment of evil caterers, attached to me be destroyed, in the name of Jesus.
57. I command my digestive system, to reject every evil command, in the name of Jesus.
58. Let all satanic designs of oppression, against me in dreams and visions be frustrated, in the name of Jesus.
59. I remove my name, from the register of evil feeders with the blood of Jesus.
60. Let the habitation of evil caterers, become desolate, in Jesus' name.
61. I paralyse, the spirit that brings bad dreams to me, in Jesus' name.
62. Let the fire of the Holy Ghost, destroy any evil list containing my name, in the name of Jesus.
63. Let the fire of the Holy Ghost destroy any of my pictures in the air, land or sea, in the name of Jesus.
64. I destroy, any coffin prepared for me, in the name of Jesus.
65. I cancel and wipe off, all evil dreams, in the name of Jesus.
66. I destroy, every satanic accident organised for my sake, in Jesus' name.
67. I render, all evil night creatures powerless, in Jesus' name.
68. Let the blood of Jesus wash clean all the organs in my body, in Jesus' name.
69. Let all sicknesses, planted in my life through evil spiritual food be destroyed, in the name of Jesus.
70. Let the blood of Jesus, erase all evil dreams, in Jesus' name.

71. Let the fire of God boil all river-harbouring demons, in Jesus' name.
72. Let all evil dreams be replaced with blessings, in Jesus' name
73. I command all my good dreams to come to pass, in Jesus' name.
74. I release myself, from every dream pollution, in Jesus' name.
75. Let every satanic attack, against my life in my dream be converted to victory, in the name of Jesus.
76. Let all rivers, trees, forests, evil companions, evil pursuers, visions of dead relatives, snakes, spirit husbands, spirit wives and masquerades manipulated against me in the dream be completely destroyed by the power in the blood of the Lord Jesus.
77. Every power and spirit in the likeness of snakes attacking me in my dreams, be buried, in the name of Jesus.
78. Let every demonic influence, targeted at destroying my vision, dream and ministry receive total disappointment, in the name of Jesus.
79. O Lord, enlarge my coasts beyond my wildest dream.
80. I stand against, every dream of defeat, in the name of Jesus.
81. I send the arrows or any gun shot in the dream back to the senders, in the name of Jesus.
82. I paralyse, all the night caterers and I forbid their food in my dream, in the name of Jesus.
83. Let all the contamination in my life through dreams, be cleansed by the blood of Jesus.
84. I cancel, all visions, dreams, words and curses contrary to my progress, in the name of Jesus.
85. I bind every demon, that pollutes spiritual visions and dreams, in the name of Jesus.
86. Divine revelations, spiritual visions, dreams and information will not be scarce commodities in my life, in the name of Jesus.

87. Every satanic animal in the dream, fall down and die, in Jesus' name.
88. Let all the enemies of my good dreams and visions concerning my home, be rendered impotent, in Jesus' name.
89. My imagination and dreams, will not be used against me, in Jesus' name.
90. By the blood of Jesus, I rebuke, every attacking and fearful dreams, in the name of Jesus.
91. Let the evil vision and dream, on my life, evaporate from the camp of the enemy, in the name of Jesus.
92. Every cause of demotion in the dream, in my life, be nullified by the blood of Jesus.
93. Every cause of confused and unprogressive dreams, in my life, be nullified by the blood of Jesus.
94. Every cause of harassment, in the dreams by familiar faces, be nullified by the blood of Jesus.
95. My dream will not become a nightmare, in Jesus' name.
96. Any anti-progress materials, fired into my life through dreams, be nullified, in the name of Jesus.
97. By the blood of Jesus, I nullify every dream of . . . (pick from the under listed), in Jesus' name.

- swimming in water - eating strange food
- drinking coke and fanta
- having sex with fair or dark women / men
- running without getting to a stop
- talking alone without response
- getting married with a dirty garment
- having or breast-feeding children
- having bald head or hair falling off
- sitting on a broken or cracked fence

- falling inside the mud
- eating from inside a broken plate
- getting married without a wedding suit/dress
- sleeping/playing in an uncompleted building

98. Every witchcraft hand, planting evil seeds in my life, through dreams, wither and burn to ashes, in the name of Jesus.
99. Every marine witchcraft, that has introduced spirit husband/wife or child in my dreams, be roasted by fire, in the name of Jesus.
100. Every agent of marine witchcraft, posing as my husband, wife or child in my dreams, be roasted by fire, in the name of Jesus.
101. Every agent of marine witchcraft, assigned to attack my finances through dreams, fall down and perish, in the name of Jesus.
102. Every power and spirit, attacking me in the form of snakes in my dreams, be buried, in the name of Jesus.
103. I command all my properties, captured by spiritual robbers in the dream, to become too hot to handle and revert to me, in the name of Jesus.
104. I bind, every demon that pollutes spiritual visions and dreams, in the name of Jesus.
105. Wonderful Lord, I reverse any defeat that I have ever suffered in the dream, in the name of Jesus.
106. Any dreams, that I have dreamt that are good and for God, I receive them, and those that are satanic, I reject them, in the name of Jesus.
107. Every night and dream attacks and their consequences, be nullified, in the name of Jesus.
108. I claim freedom, from satanic and restless dreams, in Jesus' name.
109. I claim freedom, from importing anxiety and shameful thoughts into my dream, in the name of Jesus.
110. I stand against, dream defeats and their effects, in Jesus' name.

111. Let all satanic designs of oppression, against me in dreams and visions be frustrated, in the name of Jesus.
112. Let the evil vision and dream on my life, evaporate and condense in the camp of the enemy, in the name of Jesus.
113. Every dream of demotion to junior school, be dismantled. I shall grow from glory to glory, in the name of Jesus.
114. By the power in the blood of Jesus, I cancel the maturity dates of any evil dream.
115. O God of promotion, promote me beyond my widest dream, in the name of Jesus.
116. Every sickness, planted into my life through dream, get out now and go back to your sender, in the name of Jesus.
117. Let life be squeezed out of my dream attackers, in Jesus' name.
118. By the power in the blood of Jesus, I command all my buried good dreams and visions to be exhumed.
119. By the power in the blood of Jesus, I command all my polluted good dreams and visions to receive divine solution.
120. By the power in the blood of Jesus, I command all dream and vision killers that are working against the manifestation of my good dreams and visions to be paralysed.
121. By the power in the blood of Jesus, I command every good dream and vision that has been stolen from me to be restored with fresh fire.
122. By the power in the blood of Jesus, I command every good dream and vision, that has been transferred to be restored with fresh fire.
123. By the power in the blood of Jesus, I command every good dream and vision that has been poisoned to be neutralised.
124. By the power in the blood of Jesus, I command every good dream and vision that has been amputated to receive divine strength.
125. Let all the contamination in my life, through dreams be cleansed by the blood of Jesus.

126. Any anti-progress material, fired into my life through dreams, be nullified, in the name of Jesus.
127. I resist, the threat of death in my dream by fire, in Jesus' name.
128. Every evil dream, that other people have had about me, I cancel them in the astral world, in the name of Jesus.
129. Every image of satan, in my dream, I curse you to wither now, in the name of Jesus.
130. I command every dream of demotion, to stop, in Jesus' name.
131. Every arrow of death, in the dream, come out and go back to your sender, in the name of Jesus.
132. Every sponsored dream of poverty, by household wickedness, against my life, vanish, in the name of Jesus.
133. I smash every poverty dream on the ground, in Jesus' name.
134. I cancel, the manipulation of every satanic dream, in Jesus' name.
135. You powers of the night, polluting my night dreams, be paralysed, in the name of Jesus.
136. Every anti-prosperity dream, die, in the name of Jesus.
137. Let all satanic designs of oppression, against me in dreams and visions be frustrated, in Jesus' name.
138. I paralyse, the spirits that bring bad dreams to me, in Jesus' name.
139. I cancel and wipe off, all evil dreams, in the name of Jesus.
140. Let the blood of Jesus, erase all evil dreams in my life, in Jesus' name.
141. My dreams, my joys and my breakthroughs that have been buried in the dark world, be exhumed now, in Jesus' name.
142. Every dream serpent, go back to your sender, in Jesus' name.
143. Every power, planting affliction into my life through the dream, be buried alive, in the name of Jesus.
144. Any evil, programmed into my life, through my dream, be dismantled now, in the name of Jesus.

145. O Lord, deliver me from witchcraft dreams.
146. Satanic dreams, go back to your senders, in Jesus' name.
147. I reject oppression, I claim liberty, in the name of Jesus.
148. I reject infirmity, I claim divine health, in the name of Jesus.
149. I reject curses, I claim God's blessing, in the name of Jesus.
150. I reject poverty, I claim wealth, in the name of Jesus.
151. I reject turbulence, I claim the peace of God, in , in Jesus' name.
152. I reject tragedy, I claim goodness, in the name of Jesus.
153. I reject satanic dreams, I claim divine revelations, in Jesus' name.
154. I reject failure, I claim good prospects, in the name of Jesus.
155. I reject frustration, I claim multiple promotions, in Jesus' name.
156. You powers of the night, polluting my night dreams, be paralysed, in the name of Jesus.
157. Every sponsored dream of poverty, by household wickedness against my life, vanish, in the name of Jesus.
158. I drink the blood of Jesus, to neutralize every satanic food or drink taken in the dream, in the name of Jesus.
159. I cancel, every evil dream by the blood of Jesus and fire of the Holy Ghost, in the name of Jesus.
160. Every instrument of satanic retaliation, die, in Jesus' name.
161. Every entrance of satanic influence into my life, die in Jesus' name.
162. O Lord, kill every internal destiny-killer.
163. Blood of Jesus, recover my stolen birthright, in Jesus' name.
164. Every power of familiar spirit, over my destiny, die, in Jesus' name.
165. I shall fulfil my divine agenda, in the name of Jesus.
166. O Lord, stir the Holy Ghost in my spirit, in Jesus' name.
167. Every anti-testimony altar, die, in the name of Jesus.

168. Every power that wants me to attend MFM in vain, die, in Jesus' name.
169. Stubborn witchcraft, I rub your pepper of affliction on your body, in the name of Jesus.
170. Amputators and emptiers, loose your hold upon my life and die, in the name of Jesus.
171. Evil birds, assigned against my mounting up, crash-land and die, in the name of Jesus.
172. Every bat/vulture/dog programmed into my dream, die, in the name of Jesus.
173. None, shall pluck my stars out of my hands, in Jesus' name.
174. None, shall pluck my stars out of my head, in Jesus' name.
175. My Glory shall not sink, in the name of Jesus.
176. Every friendly Judas, in my life, be exposed and disgraced, in the name of Jesus.
177. Evil hands, pointed against me, dry up, in the name of Jesus.
178. By the power that divided the Red Sea, let my problem die, in the name of Jesus.
179. Every river in my place of birth, release my virtue, in Jesus' name.
180. I sack, every satanic checkpoint mounted against my success, in the name of Jesus.
181. Let deliverance take place in my dream, in Jesus' name.

PRAYERS TO OVERCOME WITCHCRAFT

Psalm 59:1-17: Deliver me from mine enemies, O my God: defend me from them that rise up against me. Deliver me from the workers of iniquity, and save me from bloody men. For, lo, they lie in wait for my soul: the mighty are gathered against me; not for my transgression, nor for my sin, O Lord. They run and prepare themselves without my fault: awake to help me, and behold. Thou therefore, O Lord God of hosts, the God of Israel, awake to visit all the heathen: be not merciful to any wicked transgressors. Selah. They return at evening: they make a noise like a dog, and go round about the city. Behold, they belch out with their mouth: swords are in their lips: for who, say they, doth hear? But thou, O Lord, shalt laugh at them; thou shalt have all the heathen in derision. Because of his strength will I wait upon thee: for God is my defence. The God of my mercy shall prevent me: God shall let me see my desire upon mine enemies. Slay them not, lest my people forget: scatter them by thy power; and bring them down, O Lord our shield. For the sin of their mouth and the words of their lips let them even be taken in their pride: and for cursing and lying which they speak. Consume them in wrath, consume them, that they may not be: and let them know that God ruleth in Jacob unto the ends of the earth. Selah. And at evening let them return; and let them make a noise like a dog, and go round about the city. Let them wander up and down for meat, and grudge if they be not satisfied. But I will sing of thy power; yea, I will sing aloud of thy mercy in the morning: for thou hast been my defence and refuge in the day of my trouble. Unto thee, O my strength, will I sing: for God is my defence, and the God of my mercy.

Aggressive praise worship

1. Let every problem in my life, that originated from witchcraft, receive divine, instant solution, in Jesus' name.
2. I command, all the damages done to my life by witchcraft to be repaired, in the name of Jesus.
3. Let every blessing, confiscated by witchcraft spirits, be released in Jesus' name.
4. Every witchcraft power, assigned against my life and marriage, receive... (pick from the under listed), in the name of Jesus.
   - the thunder and lightning of God
   - hail and fire mingled with the blood of the Lamb
   - unbearable heat
   - concentrated acid

- destroying flood - destruction - raging fire
- continuous plagues - failures - confusion

5. I loose myself, from any power of witchcraft, in Jesus' name.
6. Every camp of witchcraft gathered against my prosperity, fall down and die, in Jesus' name.
7. Every witchcraft pot, working against me, I bring the judgment of God against you, in the name of Jesus.
8. I command every witchcraft pot, using remote control against my health to be broken into pieces, in Jesus' name.
9. Witchcraft opposition, receive the rain of affliction, in the name of Jesus.
10. Let the spirit of witchcraft attack the familiar spirits fashioned against me, in Jesus' name.
11. I retrieve, my integrity, from the hands of household witchcraft, in the name of Jesus.
12. I break the power of the occult, witchcraft and familiar spirits over my life in Jesus' name.
13. In the name of Jesus, I break and loose myself from all curses, chains, spells, jinxes, bewitchments, witchcraft or sorcery which may have been put upon me.
14. Let the thunder of God, locate and dismantle the throne of witchcraft in my household, in the name of Jesus.
15. Let every seat of witchcraft in my household, be roasted by the fire of God, in Jesus' name.
16. Let the altar of witchcraft, in my household be roasted, in the name of Jesus.
17. Let the thunder of God, scatter beyond redemption, the foundation of witchcraft in my household, in Jesus' name.
18. Every stronghold or refuge of my household witches, be destroyed, in the name of Jesus.
19. Every hiding or secret place of witchcraft in my family, be exposed by fire, in the name of Jesus.
20. Let every local and international witchcraft network of

household witches, be shattered into pieces, in Jesus' name.

21. Let the communication system, of household witches be frustrated, in the name of Jesus.
22. Let the terrible fire of God, consume the transportation of my household witchcraft, in the name of Jesus.
23. Every agent, ministering at the altar of witchcraft in my household, fall down and die, in the name of Jesus.
24. Let the thunder and fire of God, locate the storehouses and strongrooms of my household witchcraft, harbouring my blessings, and pull them down, in the name of Jesus.
25. Let any witchcraft curse, working against me, be revoked by the blood of Jesus.
26. Every decision, vow and covenant of household witchcraft affecting me, be nullified by the blood of Jesus.
27. I destroy, with the fire of God, every weapon of witchcraft used against me, in Jesus' name.
28. Any material, taken from my body and now placed on a witchcraft altar, be roasted by the fire of God, in Jesus' name.
29. I reverse, every witchcraft burial, fashioned against me, in the name of Jesus.
30. Every trap, set for me by witches, begin to catch your owners, in the name of Jesus.
31. Every witchcraft padlock, fashioned against any area of my life, be roasted, in Jesus' name.
32. Let the wisdom of household witches, be converted to foolishness, in the name of Jesus.
33. Let the wickedness of household enemies, overtake them, in the name of Jesus.
34. I deliver my soul, from every witchcraft bewitchment, in the name of Jesus.
35. Any witchcraft bird, flying for my sake, fall down, die and be roasted to ashes, in the name of Jesus.
36. Any of my blessings, traded with by household witches be

returned to me, in Jesus' name.

37. Any of my blessings and testimonies, swallowed by witches, be converted to hot coals of fire of God and be vomited, in the name of Jesus.

38. I break myself loose, from every bondage of witchcraft covenants, in the name of Jesus.

39. Any witchcraft coven, where any of my blessings are hidden, be roasted by the fire of God, in the name of Jesus.

40. (Lay your right hand on your head) Every witchcraft plantation, pollution, deposit or material in my body, be melted by the fire of God and be flushed out by the blood of Jesus.

41. Every evil, ever done to me, through witchcraft attack, be reversed, in the name of Jesus.

42. Every witchcraft hand, planting evil seeds in my life, through dream attacks, wither and burn to ashes, in Jesus' name.

43. Every witchcraft obstacle and hindrance put on the road to my desired miracle and success, be removed by the east wind of God, in the name of Jesus.

44. Every witchcraft chant, spell and projection fashioned against me, I bind you and turn you against your owner, in Jesus' name.

45. I frustrate every plot, device, scheme and project of witchcraft designed to affect any area of my life, in the name of Jesus.

46. Any witch, projecting himself into the body of any animal in order to do me harm, be trapped in the body of such an animal forever, in the name of Jesus.

47. Any drop of my blood, sucked by any witch, be vomited now, in the name of Jesus.

48. Any part of me, shared out amongst household / village witches, I recover you, in the name of Jesus.

49. Any organ of my body, that has been exchanged for another through witchcraft operation, be replaced now, in Jesus' name.

50. I recover, any of my virtues / blessings shared out amongst village / household witches, in the name of Jesus.
51. I reverse, the evil effect of any witchcraft summon of my spirit, in the name of Jesus.
52. I loose my hands and feet, from any witchcraft bewitchment and bondage, in Jesus' name.
53. Let the blood of Jesus, wash away every witchcraft identification mark on me or on any property of mine, in Jesus' name.
54. I forbid, any re-union or re-gathering of household and village witches against my life, in the name of Jesus.
55. Let the entire body system of my household witches, begin to run contrary until they have confessed all their wickedness, in Jesus' name.
56. Let the mercies of God, be withdrawn from them, in Jesus' name.
57. Let them grope in the daytime, as in a dark night, in Jesus' name.
58. Let everything that has ever worked for them, work against them, in Jesus' name.
59. Let them not have a cloth to cover their shame, in Jesus' name.
60. Let as many of them as are stubbornly unrepentant, be smitten by the sun in the day and by the moon in the night, in Jesus' name.
61. Let each step they take, lead them to greater destruction, in the name of Jesus.
62. But as for me, let me dwell in the hollow of God's hand, in the name of Jesus.
63. Let the goodness and mercies of God overwhelm me now, in the name of Jesus.
64. Any witchcraft practice, under any water against my life, receive immediate judgment of fire, in the name of Jesus.
65. Every witchcraft power, that has introduced spirit

husband/wife or child into my dreams, be roasted by fire, in Jesus' name.

66. Every agent of witchcraft power, posing as my husband, wife or child in my dreams, be roasted by fire, in Jesus' name.

67. Every agent of witchcraft power, physically attached to my marriage to frustrate it, fall down and perish now, in the name of Jesus.

68. Every agent of witchcraft power, assigned to attack my finances through dream, fall down and perish, in the name of Jesus.

69. Let the thunderbolts of God, locate and destroy every witchcraft power covens, where deliberations and decisions have ever been fashioned against me, in the name of Jesus.

70. Any water spirit from my village, or my place of birth, practising witchcraft against me and my family, be amputated by the word of God, in the name of Jesus.

71. Any power of witchcraft, holding any of my blessings in bondage, receive the fire of God and release them, in the name of Jesus.

72. I loose my mind and soul, from the bondage of marine witches, in the name of Jesus.

73. Any witchcraft chain, binding my hands and feet from prospering, be broken and shattered to pieces, in Jesus' name

74. Every arrow shot into my life from under any water through witchcraft power, come out of me and go back to your sender, in the name of Jesus.

75. Any evil material, transferred into my body through contact with any witchcraft agent, be roasted by fire, in the name of Jesus.

76. Any evil, ever done against me, through witchcraft oppression and manipulation, be reversed by the blood of Jesus.

77. I bind, every witchcraft control and mind-blinding spirit, in the name of Jesus.

78. I cast out, every witchcraft arrow affecting my senses (sight,

smell, taste, hearing), in the name of Jesus.

79. I command, every witchcraft arrow to depart from my:. . .

- spinal cord - spleen - navel - heart - throat
- eyes - head, in Jesus' name.

80. Let the blood of Jesus purge me of every witchcraft contaminating material, in the name of Jesus.
81. I destroy, the hand of any witch-doctor working against me, in the name of Jesus.
82. Every witchcraft spirit, attempting to build a wall against my destiny, fall down and die, in the name of Jesus.
83. I send the rain of affliction, upon every witchcraft power working against me, in the name of Jesus.
84. O sun, moon, stars, earth, water and the elements, vomit every enchantment that is against me, in the name of Jesus
85. Every power, using the heavenlies against me, fall down and be disgraced, in Jesus' name.
86. Let the stars of heaven, begin to fight for me, in Jesus' name.
87. O God, arise and scatter every conspiracy in the heavenlies that is against me, in Jesus' name.
88. I break with the blood of Jesus, all evil soul-ties affecting my life, in the name of Jesus.
89. Spirit of the living God, come upon my life and place a shield of protection around me, in the name of Jesus.
90. Every chain of inherited witchcraft, in my family, break, in the name of Jesus.
91. Every ladder, used by witchcraft against me, be roasted, in the name of Jesus.
92. Any door, that I have opened to witchcraft in any area of my life, be closed for ever by the blood of Jesus.
93. I revoke, every witchcraft verdict on my marital life, in the name of Jesus.
94. I send confusion, into the camp of household witchcraft, in the name of Jesus.

95 Stubborn witchcraft, release me, in the name of Jesus.

96. Every witchcraft power, working against my destiny, fall down and die, in Jesus' name.

97. Every incantation, ritual and witchcraft power against my destiny, fall down and die, in the name of Jesus.

98. I break the power of the occult, witchcraft and familiar spirits over my life, in Jesus' name.

99. Witchcraft opposition, receive the rain of affliction, in the name of Jesus.

100. I cancel, every witchcraft verdict against my life, in Jesus' name.

101. I command, every arrow of witchcraft in my life, come out with all your roots in the name of Jesus! (Lay your hands on your stomach and pray aggressively.)

102. I command every witchcraft pot, using remote control against my health to be broken into pieces, in Jesus' name.

103. I rebuke, the spell of any witchcraft pot, in Jesus' name.

104. I break every witchcraft pot over my life, in Jesus' name.

105. Every council of witchcraft, working against me will not prosper, in the name of Jesus.

106. I disentangle myself and my family, from every witchcraft cage and pot, in the name of Jesus.

107. I retrieve my integrity, out of the hands of household witchcraft, in the name of Jesus.

108. Every witchcraft hand, planting evil seeds into my life through dream attacks, wither and burn to ashes, in the name of Jesus.

109. Let all friendly witchcraft powers, be exposed and disgraced, in the name of Jesus.

110. O Lord, plant Your warring angels around me, to dismantle and destroy evil stronghold of internal witchcraft.

111. I exercise my authority, over stubborn witchcraft and I pull down their structures, in Jesus' name.

112. Every placental witchcraft, targeted against my destiny, what are you waiting for? Die, in the name of Jesus.
113. Placental witchcraft, manipulating my destiny, die, in the name of Jesus.
114. Every blessing, that I have lost through placental witchcraft, I repossess you, in Jesus' name.
115. Every witchcraft coven, and marine banks, release my placenta, in Jesus' name
116. Every cage of family witchcraft, release my divine partner, in Jesus' name.
117. Oh Lord, let my dreams and visions reject every witchcraft projection, in the name of Jesus.
118. Thank God for answers to prayers.

PRAYERS, CONFESSIONS FOR VICTORY DURING PREGNANCY AND AT CHILD-BIRTH

I declare according to the word of God that the Lord shall perfect everything concerning me. The Lord who has started His good work of creation in me will complete it (Phil. 1:6).

By the power in the blood of the Lord Jesus Christ, I confess that my pregnancy is perfect, in the name of Jesus. Every part of my body shall function perfectly for the formation of the baby, in Jesus' name. My blood shall circulate effectively. Everything that passes from me to the baby shall be perfect in Jesus' name for the development of the baby. I confess that I am strong. Weakness is not my lot, in the name of Jesus. I will not have morning sickness or vomiting during my pregnancy, in the name of Jesus. I reject cramps, varicose veins, piles and backaches because Jesus Christ has borne all my sicknesses. I refuse constipation, anaemia, vitamin and mineral deficiencies, swollen hands and feet, hypertension, convulsion and diabetes, in the mighty name of Jesus. My urine will remain normal, in the name of Jesus (Psalm 103: 3-5).

I confess that the activities of eaters of flesh and drinkers of blood will not prosper in my life, in the name of Jesus. I reject all negative dreams, visions, prophecies and imaginations, in the name of Jesus.

I confess God's word in Exodus 23:26, that I shall not have a miscarriage, any form of abnormal bleeding or malformation of the baby, in Jesus' name. I shall be a joyous mother of children. My womb is fruitful. I am a fruitful vine by the side of our house. My children are like olive plants round about our table. As the baby grows, every aspect of its growth, formation and development shall be perfect, in Jesus' name.

I also confess that I shall not suffer any sickness like nausea, irritation, headache, internal or external pain because by the stripes of Jesus, I am healed. I tread upon sickness and upon all the power of the devil. My body is the temple of the Holy spirit. I have the life and health of Christ in me. The Sun of Righteousness has risen, having conquered sickness, pains and satan. There is healing in His wings for me. God's will for me and my baby is to prosper and be in good health. God is at work in me now to will and to do His good pleasure. The power of the Holy Spirit is at work in me right now. It is flowing in me and perfecting all that pertains to my baby's formation, in Jesus' name.

I declare, that every disease and germ should die now, in Jesus' name. Nothing, I take into my body through the mouth shall harm me nor my baby, in Jesus' name. God's word says, if I drink any deadly thing, it shall not harm me. I confess that as I go to deliver my baby, the Lord shall direct those taking the delivery on the care suits me and the baby, in Jesus' name.

My pregnancy is established in righteousness. I am far from oppression. Therefore, I shall not fear any terror, because it shall not come near me. No evil shall befall me nor befall my baby, and no plague shall come near my dwelling place or near my family.

As the pregnancy progresses, the Lord shall fulfil the number of my days. I shall not have a premature baby, but a fully grown one. My baby shall come out alive, strong and healthy, because nothing shall harm it. I am fearfully and wonderfully made. My pelvis is wide enough to allow my baby to pass through, in the name of Jesus.

I also confess, according to Isaiah 43, that when I pass through the water, the Lord will be with me; even through the rivers, it shall not overflow me and if I walk through the fire, I shall not be burnt, nor shall the flame scorch me. Therefore, I confess that I shall pass through the child-delivering process without any pain or hurt, in Jesus' name.

The Lord shall take away from me, every sickness of pregnancy and child-bearing and any complication according to Deut. 7:14,15. I shall not fear, because I have been redeemed from the curse of the law, the curse of bringing forth the baby in agony (Galatians 4).

I boldly confess Isaiah 66:7 that before I travail, I will give birth and before any pain comes, I will be delivered of my baby. I will be saved in child-bearing because I continue in faith, love and holiness with self-control.

I confess that I shall go to the delivery room confidently, in Jesus' name. The Lord has given me perfect peace, because my mind rests on Him. My trust is in the Lord, and Jehovah God is my everlasting strength.

According to Psalm 118:17, I confess that I shall not die at child-birth, nor shall my baby suffer death. We shall both live to declare the works of the Lord, in Jesus' name. My cervix shall be fully dilated and the passage big and open enough to allow the baby pass through with ease. The delivery shall be perfect, in Jesus' name. No evil shall befall me or my baby.

No weapon of the devil that is fashioned against me nor against my baby shall prosper, in Jesus' name.

The Lord is the strength of my life, of whom shall I be afraid? He is my Deliverer, my God, my Buckler and the Horn of my salvation. The Lord is all I need to pull through on that day. He will strengthen the bars of my gate. He has blessed my children within me. Therefore, through Him I shall do valiantly. I will live to be the happy mother of my baby. None of us shall see death, in Jesus' name. I refuse prolonged labour and reject all pains from the devil during labour and afterwards.

I look forward to the rearing of the children after birth. I confess that my husband and I shall bring them up in the way of the Lord. The children shall grow up to know and love the Lord from their youth. I also confess that the Lord shall supply all our needs during pregnancy and for the babies after their delivery in Jesus' name.

Glory be to the name of the Lord, because I shall have what I say, in Jesus' name.

PRAYER POINTS

Stand against the following things aggressively every morning and night, in the mighty name of Jesus.

1. Early morning sickness
2. Miscarriage
3. Swollen hands and feet
4. Abnormal vaginal bleeding and anaemia
5. Backache, cramps, varicose veins
6. Convulsion in pregnancy
7. Hypertension and diabetes mellitus
8. Complicated and aided child delivery, e.g any form of surgical intervention.

9. Unnatural tiredness or weakness during pregnancy
10. Demonic midwives and doctors
11. Blood transfusion
12. Premature or late delivery
13. Anti-pregnancy satanic dreams
14. Spirit of fear and still-birth
15. Satanic dreams of blood and the activities of pregnancy-sucking spirits
16. Demonic exchange of the baby in the womb
17. Evil observers, satanic diary and wicked date calculators.

Be violent spiritually. Pray occasionally in the spirit and be aggressive. Try and do occasional short vigils. Form the habit of laying your hands on the pregnancy and prophesy good things on your baby.

PRAYERS FOR THE BREAKING OF COVENANTS, YOKES AND CURSES

Confessions: Col. 2:14, Gal. 3: 13 & 14, 2 Cor. 6 14 - 18, Gal. 6:17, 2 Cor. 5:17

RENOUNCING MEMBERSHIP OF EVIL ASSOCIATIONS

1. I reject, revoke and renounce my membership of the following evil associations (mention them), in Jesus' name.
2. I release myself, from the hold of Jezebel spirit, marine spirits, water spirit, queen of the coast, mermaid spirits, familiar spirits, witches and wizards and spirits of the dead, in the name of Jesus.
3. I withdraw and cancel my name, from their registers with the blood of Jesus.
4. I reject and renounce all such names, given to me in any of the evil associations, in the name of Jesus.
5. I resign my position, in any of these associations and

withdraw my services and responsibilities permanently, in Jesus' name.

6. I reject, all the evil works I have done to innocent people through my membership of these evil association and beg the Almighty God to forgive me and wash me clean with the blood of Jesus.
7. I purge myself, with the blood of Jesus, of all evil food I ate in the evil associations.
8. I bind you water spirits, marine spirits, queen of the coast, Jezebel spirits and familiar spirits operating in my life with hot chains and fetters of God. I cast you into the deep and seal you with unquenchable fire of God, in Jesus' name.
9. I withdraw, any part of my body and blood deposited on evil altars, in the name of Jesus.
10. I withdraw my pictures, image and inner-man from the altars and covens of the evil associations, in Jesus' name.
11. I return the things, the instruments and other property of evil associations I was connected with, at my disposal for the execution of duties, in the name of Jesus.
12. I hereby confess total separation, from the evil associations, in the name of Jesus.
13. Holy Spirit, build a wall of fire round me, that will completely make it impossible for these evil spirits to come to me again.
14. I break, any covenant binding me with any of these evil associations, in the name of Jesus.
15. I break, all inherited covenants and all covenants I consciously and unconsciously entered into, in Jesus' name.
16. I bind, the demons attached to these covenants and cast them into the deep, in the name of Jesus.
17. I resist with the blood of Jesus, fire, brimstone and thunder of God, every attempt to return me to the evil associations.
18. I renounce and revoke, all the oaths I took while entering the evil associations, in the name of Jesus.
19. I break and cancel with the blood of Jesus, every evil mark,

incision and writing placed in my spirit and body as a result of my membership of the evil associations. I purify my body, soul and spirit with Holy Ghost fire, in Jesus' name.

20. I break, all covenants inherited from my ancestors on my father's side and my mother's side, in the name of Jesus.
21. Lord, break down, every evil foundation of my life and build a new one on Christ the Rock.
22. I command the fire of God to roast and burn to ashes, every evil bird, snake or any other animal attached to my life by the evil association, in the name of Jesus.
23. I dismantle, every hindrance, or blockage put on my way of progress by my involvement in these evil associations, in the name of Jesus.
24. All the doors of blessings and break-through shut against me due to my involvement in these evil associations, I command you to open, in the name of Jesus.

CURSES

1. I break and cancel, every inherited curse, in Jesus' name.
2. Lord, remove from me, all the curses placed upon my ancestral families as a result of their evil associations involvement, in the name of Jesus.
3. I break and cancel, every curse placed upon me by my parents, in the name of Jesus.
4. I break and cancel, every curse, spell, hex, enchantment, bewitchment and incantation placed upon me by my involvement with evil association, in the name of Jesus.
5. I break and revoke, every blood and soul-tie covenant and yokes attached to them, in the name of Jesus.
6. With the blood of Jesus, I purge myself of all the evil food I ate in the evil world. I purify myself with the fire of the Holy Ghost, in the name of Jesus.
7. All demonic spirits, attached to all these covenants and curses, be roasted with the fire of God, in the name of Jesus.
8. I declare my body, soul and spirit a no-go-area for all evil spirits, in the name of Jesus.

DELIVERANCE PRAYER AGAINST SPIRIT HUSBAND OR WIFE

1. I divorce and renounce my marriage with the spirit husband or wife, in the name of Jesus.
2. I break, all covenants entered into with the spirit husband or wife, in the name of Jesus.
3. I command the thunder fire of God, to burn to ashes the wedding gown, ring, photographs and all other materials used for the marriage, in the name of Jesus.
4. I send the fire of God, to burn to ashes the marriage certificate, in the name of Jesus.
5. I break every blood and soul-tie covenants with the spirit husband or wife, in the name of Jesus.
6. I send the thunder fire of God, to burn to ashes the children born to the marriage, in the name of Jesus.
7. I withdraw my blood, sperm or any other part of my body deposited in the altar of the spirit husband or wife, in the name of Jesus.
8. You spirit husband or wife, tormenting my life and earthly marriage, I bind you with hot chains and fetters of God and cast you out of my life and into the deep pit; and, I command you not to come into my life again, in Jesus' name.
9. I return to you, every property of yours in my possession, including the dowry and whatsoever was used for the marriage and covenants, in the name of Jesus.
10. I drain myself with the blood of Jesus, of all evil materials deposited in my body as a result of our sexual relationship.
11. Lord, send Holy Ghost fire into my root and burn all unclean things deposited in it by the spirit husband or wife, in the name of Jesus.
12. I break the head of the snake, deposited in my body by the spirit husband or wife to do me harm; and I command it to come out, in the name of Jesus.

13. I purge myself with the blood of Jesus, every evil material deposited in my womb to prevent me from having children on earth.
14. Lord, repair and restore every damage done to any part of my body and earthly marriage by the spirit husband or wife, in the name of Jesus.
15. I reject and cancel every curse, evil pronouncement, spell, jinx, enchantment and incantation placed upon me by the spirit husband or wife, in the name of Jesus.
16. I recover all my earthly belongings in the custody of the spirit husband or wife, in the name of Jesus.
17. I command the spirit husband or wife to permanently turn his or l back on me, in the name of Jesus.
18. I renounce and reject, the name given to me by the spirit husband or wife, in the name of Jesus.
19. I hereby declare and confess that the Lord Jesus Christ is my Husband for eternity, in the name of Jesus.
20. I soak myself in the blood of Jesus and cancel the evil marks or writings placed on me, in the name of Jesus.
21. I set myself free, from the stronghold, domineering power and bondage of the spirit husband or wife, in Jesus' name.
22. I paralyse, the remote control power and work used to destabilise my earthly marriage and or hinder me from bearing child for my earthly husband or wife, in Jesus' name

BREAKING OF COVENANTS AND YOKES

1. I break every evil covenant with water spirits and the yokes attached to it, in the name of Jesus.
2. I break and cancel, every covenant with any idol and the yokes attached to it, in the name of Jesus.
3. I break and cancel, any evil covenant entered into by my parents on my behalf and all the yokes attached to it, in Jesus' name.
4. I command the fire of God, to roast the forces of hindrance and paralyse the power, in Jesus' name.

5. Lord, let the Holy Ghost effect an immediate breakthrough, in every area of my life, in the name of Jesus.
6. I confess that my deliverance shall never to be reversed, in the name of Jesus.

PRAYERS FOR PARENTS DESIRING GODLY SPOUSES FOR THEIR CHILDREN

Scriptures: Matt. 7:7, Josh. 24:15, Isa. 54:13,17; 49:25.

1. Thank God because He alone is the perfect matchmaker.
2. Lord, release the man/woman You have preordained as my daughter's/son's husband/wife.
3. Lord, cause the 'divine match' to come forth soon.
4. Lord, let it be a person who loves You wholeheartedly
5. Lord, establish their home in accordance with Ephesians 5:20-28.
6. Father, let all satanic banners keeping them from meeting be dissolved, in the name of Jesus.
7. Lord, send forth Your warring angels to do battle on their behalf.
8. Lord, I believe that You have created my daughter/son for a special man/woman of God. Bring it to pass in Jesus' name.
9. I stand in the gap and call him/her out of obscurity into his/her life, in the name of Jesus.
10. I reject the provision of a counterfeit by the enemy, in the name of Jesus.
11. I cut off, the flow of any inherited marital problems into the life of my children, in the name of Jesus.
12. Let patience reign in the life of . . . *(mention the name of the person)* until the right person comes in Jesus' name.
13. Father, in the name of Jesus, just as Abraham sent his servant to find his son, Isaac, a wife, send the Holy Spirit to bring my son's/daughter's a wife/husband.

POWER OVER ANGER

Anger is a great spiritual sin and robber. It has incapacitated many useful lives. Read these Scriptures and pray aggressively. Job 5:2, Psl. 18:48, Prov. 16:32; 25:28; 29:22, Eccl. 7:9, Eph. 4:27; 4:31.

1. Thank God for Calvary.
2. Ask the Lord to forgive you for every fit of anger you have ever allowed.
3. Holy Spirit, help me to crucify my flesh, in Jesus' name.
4. Let all the works of the flesh in my life be dismantled, in Jesus' name.
5. Lord, give me grace to overcome every iota of fear, pride and selfishness in my life, in the name of Jesus.
6. I bind, plunder and render to nought every spirit of anger, in the name of Jesus.
7. O Lord, help me to repair all the good altars that anger has broken down in my life.
8. Lord, emancipate me from the works of the flesh.
9. All evil desires and lust should be crucified in Jesus' name.
10. Lord, help me to develop and manifest the fruit of the Spirit.
11. Lord, help me to put off anger or loss of temper and put on tenderheartedness.
12. Lord, help me to be quick to listen, slow to speak and dead to anger, in the name of Jesus.
13. Father, give me the power to violently resist the devil so that he will flee from me.
14. Lord, help me to hear the voice of the Holy Spirit whenever I am being provoked, and make me unprovokeable.
15. Lord, create in me, a new heart by Your power.
16. Lord, renew the right spirit within me.
17. I renounce my rights to anger.
18. Lord, remove from me, the root of irritation that keeps anger alive in me.

19. I reject the thought that I will never change, in Jesus' name.
20. Spirit of God, cleanse me and control anger in my life.
21. Lord, increase in me the power of self-control and gentleness.
22. I reject, all that robs me of the joy of my inheritance in Your kingdom.
23. I speak to evil mountains, and break their power over my life, in the name of Jesus.
24. Lord, enable me to hear Your voice.
25. Lord, by the power in the blood of Jesus, remove from my life any hindrance to my breakthroughs.
26. Lord, drive away all darkness in my life.
27. Lord, shield me from deception.
28. Lord, illuminate Your truth to my understanding.
29. Lord, let me see You more clearly with the eyes of my heart.

PRAYERS FOR THOSE DESIRING SOUND SLEEP

Sleeplessness or insomnia is not from the Lord. The prayers points should be prayed aggressively. If you had a bad night, you're likely to have a bad day.

Confession: Psalms 3:5; 4:8; 127:2, Prov. 3:24, Eccl. 5:12, Isa. 29:10, Luke 9:32, Psalm 121

Lord Jesus, I thank You for Your day time and for Your night time. I know You never sleep but constantly watch over me. I know You have placed Your guardian angels all around me.

Lord, I give You all my cares and my worries of the day. I give You all my fears.

Satan, I bind you, in the name of Jesus. All spirits of fear, especially fear of the dark, you are bound, in the name of Jesus. I rebuke the fear of fire and fear of intruders, in the name of Jesus. Spirits of insomnia, nervousness, tension, worry, I cast you out, in the name of Jesus.

Lord, please go into the darkest recesses of my mind, into my subconscious, into the dream area, and heal all painful memories and trauma.
Lord, I ask You to fill me with Your divine love, Your peace, Your calmness. I pray You will allow me to sleep soundly all night and wake up feeling refreshed in the morning. I commit myself to You. It's in the name of Jesus that I pray. Amen.

1. Thank you Father, for the protection offered under Your unsleeping eye, in the name of Jesus.
2. I commit my body, soul and spirit to Your care, O Father, as I sleep, in Jesus' name.
3. Father, in the name of Jesus, let me not go through any part of this night unaccompanied by Thee.
4. I claim sound and refreshing sleep, in the name of Jesus.
5. I claim safety, from all perils of the night in Jesus' name.
6. I claim protection, from the arrows of destruction and pestilence of the night in Jesus' name.
7. I claim freedom, from satanic and restless dreams in Jesus' name.
8. I claim freedom from importing anxiety and shameful thoughts into my dream in Jesus' name.
9. Father, let me experience the brightness of Thy presence.
10. Intercede in the spirit, for all those who cannot sleep due to pain or anxiety.
11. Thank the Lord for His redemptive power and the power of the Cross to deliver from the chains of the enemy.
12. I release myself from the bondage of sleeplessness, in the name of Jesus.
13. I break the yoke of the oppressors, in the name of Jesus.
14. I bind every spirit of fear or infirmity preventing me from enjoying a sound sleep, in the name of Jesus.
15. I release myself, from the bondage of early unprofitable

waking up, in the name of Jesus.

16. Let every emotional strain, nightmare, anxiety or depression initiating sleeplessness be melted away by the fire of the Holy Spirit, in the name of Jesus.
17. I receive deliverance, from the bondage of sleeping tablets, in the name of Jesus.
18. I claim sound and sweet sleep in the mighty name of Jesus.
19. Let every sleep disturbance originator, be eliminated from my life, in the name of Jesus.
20. I bind every spirit of faintness, dizziness, headache, tremour, unusual sweating, poor concentration, palpitation diarrhoea and any other spirit causing difficulty in sleeping in Jesus' name.
21. Every sleeplessness, attached to previous horrifying experiences, be dismantled, in Jesus' name.
22. The fear of going to sleep, be eliminated from every area of my life, in the name of Jesus.
23. Let the name of the Lord be glorified in every area of my life.

POWER AGAINST POLYGAMY

1. Bring quality repentance unto the Lord for all sexual sins.
2. Every foundation of polygamy in my family line, be broken, in the name of Jesus.
3. I refuse to follow, the evil marital pattern of my father's house, in the name of Jesus.
4. Every ancestral marital power caging my marriage, release me, in the name of Jesus.
5. Thou power of God, dismantle every polygamy witchcraft, in the name of Jesus.
6. Every immoral flow of my father's house, dry up, in Jesus' name.
7. Every spirit sponsoring polygamy in my life, I bind you and cast you out, in the name of Jesus.

8. Every familiar spirit, targeting me for polygamy, I destroy your power, in the name of Jesus.
9. Every magnet of polygamy, be destroyed by the power in the blood of Jesus.
10. Every curse and covenant of polygamy, break, in Jesus' name
11. Evil power of envious wives over my life, die, in Jesus' name
12. Evil plans of marriage failure, be cancelled with the blood of Jesus.
13. Thou power of family idols, die, in the name of Jesus.
14. You stronghold of polygamy in my life, die, in Jesus' name.
15. Every problem connected to polygamy in my life, be solved by the blood of Jesus.
16. Let my destiny, be released from the grip of polygamous power, in the name of Jesus.
17. Polygamous witchcraft embargo, die, in the name of Jesus.
18. Every evil plantation, acquired through polygamy, be uprooted, in the name of Jesus.
19. I bind and cast out, every demon of lust in my life, in the name of Jesus.
20. Every stealing of virtue, be cancelled, in the name of Jesus.
21. Marriage destroyers, will not prosper in my life, in Jesus' name.
22. Every placental bondage, be broken, in the name of Jesus.
23. My foundation, shall not disgrace my marriage, in Jesus' name.
24. Oppressive arrows, of my father's wives, die, in Jesus' name.
25. Every war waged on my mother that is now affecting me, die, in the name of Jesus.
26. My star, reject polygamous cages, in the name of Jesus.

POWER AGAINST WIFE ABUSE

2 Sam. 22:3; Mal. 2:6

1. I cover myself with the blood of Jesus.
2. I restrain and bind, every violent behaviour targeted against me, in the name of Jesus.
3. Every physical and psychological abuse targeted against me, be neutralized by the blood of Jesus.
4. I recover my life, from every inherited evil family pattern, in the name of Jesus.
5. Every desire to punish, manipulate and control me, be neutralized, in the name of Jesus.
6. Let the Prince of Peace reign in my marriage, in Jesus' name.
7. Every arrow fired against my marriage, backfire, in Jesus' name.
8. Thou power of verbal abuse, in my marriage, die, in Jesus' name.
9. I stand against, intimidation, accusations, name calling, deception, insult and profanity in my marriage, in Jesus' name.
10. Every power, assigned to convert my marriage to a misfired arrow, be dismantled, in the name of Jesus.
11. I cut off, every satanic programme arranged to hurt, maltreat or injure me, in the name of Jesus.
12. Let the power of emotional abuse be dismantled, in the name of Jesus.
13. Every satanic silent power in this home, be dislodged, in the name of Jesus.
14. I stand against (pick from the under listed) in my marriage, in the name of Jesus.
    - lack of support
    - attack by any object
    - lack of compliments
    - neglect
    - abandonment
    - lack of funding
    - isolation from family and friends
    - returning home at unreasonable time
    - forcing sexual compliance
    - slapping and beating

- sleep deprivation
- kicking and hair pulling
- throwing objects
- use of weapons

15. Every strongman of family destruction, I bind you, in the name of Jesus.
16. Every evil carryover, of my father's house, into my marriage, be destroyed, in the name of Jesus.
17. Every evil carryover, of my mother's house, into my marriage, be destroyed, in the name of Jesus.
18. Every consequence of childhood abuse, on my marriage, die, in the name of Jesus.
19. O Lord, make Your way plain before my face and give me wisdom to handle my situation, in the name of Jesus.
20. Let Your power of salvation, fall upon my family, in Jesus' name.
21. I cry out for divine intervention, in this matter, in Jesus' name.
22. I receive the power to receive respect from my mates, in the name of Jesus.
23. O Lord, I shall not fear, for Your power is with me, in the name of Jesus.

PRAYER FOR WIDOWS

Psalm 68:5

1. I cover myself and all that is mine with the blood of Jesus.
2. I release myself from the grip of the power of abandonment and desertion, in the name of Jesus.
3. O God, be my ever-present companion at these difficult times, in the name of Jesus.
4. Let every form of anger, depart from my soul, in Jesus' name.
5. I barricade my life, against any form of depression, in the name of Jesus.
6. O Lord, compensate me in Your way my loss of companionship, in the name of Jesus.

7. I refuse to be locked up in the past, in the name of Jesus.
8. Help me, O Lord, to raise the children.
9. Help me, O Lord, to receive financial breakthroughs, in the name of Jesus.
10. Make Your way plain before me in all my future activities concerning my situation, in the name of Jesus.
11. I refuse, to be consumed by self-pity, in the name of Jesus.
12. O Lord, empower me to get my priorities right at this point in my life, in the name of Jesus.
13. I refuse to drown myself in sorrow, by comparing myself with others, in the name of Jesus.
14. O God, pour the soothing oil of the Holy Spirit into my aching heart, in the name of Jesus.
15. O God, be my sufficiency in these hard times, in Jesus' name
16. Let me feel Your presence closers, O Lord.
17. O God, I know You will not forsake me. Arise and fight my battles for me, in the name of Jesus.
18. I bind and cast out, every plantation of dream criminals, in the name of Jesus.
19. I barricade my dream life, from any negative influence, in the name of Jesus.
20. Help me Lord, to rebuild my life in You, in Jesus' name.
21. Every attack of the oppressor, be neutralised, in Jesus' name.
22. Glory of God, overshadow my life, in the name of Jesus.
23. O God, be my rock and my stay at these times, in Jesus' name.
24. Any power, contesting for my benefit, loose your hold, in the name of Jesus.
25. I shall arise and possess my possession, by the power in the blood of Jesus.

1. Be Prepared
2. Breakthrough Prayers For Business Professionals
3. Brokenness
4. Criminals In The House of God
5. Dealing With Local Satanic Technology
6. Dealing With Witchcraft Barbers
7. Dealing With Hidden Curses
8. Dealing With The Evil Powers of Your Father's House
9. Dealing With Unprofitable Roots
10. Deliverance: God's Medicine Bottle
11. Deliverance By Fire
12. Deliverance From Spirit Husband And Spirit Wife
13. Deliverance of The Conscience
14. Deliverance of The Head
15. Drawers of Power From The Heavenlies
16. Dominion Prosperity
17. Evil Appetite
18. Fasting And Prayer
19. Failure In The School Of Prayer
20. For We Wrestle . . .
21. Holy Cry
22. Holy Fever
23. How To Obtain Personal Deliverance (Second Edition)
24. Limiting God
25. Meat For Champions
26. Overpowering Witchcraft
27. Personal Spiritual Check-up
28. Power Against Coffin Spirits
29. Power Against Destiny Quenchers
30. Power Against Dream Criminals
31. Power Against Local Wickedness
32. Power Against Marine Spirits
33. Power Against Spiritual Terrorists
34. Power Must Change Hands
35. Pray Your Way To Breakthroughs (Third Edition)
36. Prayer Rain

37. Prayer Strategies For Spinsters And Bachelors
38. Prayer Warfare Against 70 Mad Spirits
39. Prayers To Destroy Diseases And Infirmities
40. Praying To Dismantle Witchcraft
41. Release From Destructive Covenants
42. Revoking Evil Decrees
43. Satanic Diversion Of The Black Race
44. Smite The Enemy And He Will Flee
45. Spiritual Warfare And The Home
46. Strategic Praying
47. Strategy Of Warfare Praying
48. Students In The School Of Fear
49. The Enemy Has Done This
50. The Evil Cry of Your Family Idol
51. The Fire Of Revival
52. The Great Deliverance
53. The Internal Stumbling Block
54. The Lord Is A Man Of War
55. The Prayer Eagle
56. The Serpentine Enemies
57. The Slow Learners
58. The Snake in The Power House
59. The Spirit Of The Crab
60. The Tongue Trap
61. The Vagabond Spirit
62. Unprofitable Foundations
63. Victory Over Satanic Dreams (Second Edition)
64. Violent Prayers Against Stubborn Situations
65. When God Is Silent
66. Wealth Must Change Hands
67. When You Are Knocked Down
68. Woman! Thou Art Loosed.
69. Your Foundation and Destiny
70. Your Mouth and Your Deliverance
71. Adura Agbayori (Yoruba Version of the Second Edition of Pray Your Way to Breakthroughs)

72. Awon Adura Ti Nsi Oke Nidi (Yoruba Prayer Book)
73. Ojo Adura (Prayer Rain in Yoruba)
74. Pluie de Pri res
75. Esprit Vagabondage
76. En Finir avec les Forces Maléfiques de la maison de Ton P re
77. Que l'envo tement perisse
78. Frappez l'adversaire et il fuira
79. Comment recevoir la délivrance du Mari et de la Femme de Nuit
80. Comment se delvrer soi-m me
81. Pouvoir Contre les Terroristes Spirituels
82. Pri res de Percées pour les hommes d'affaires
83. Prier Jusqu' Remporter la Victoire
84. Pri res Violentes pour humilier les probl mes opiniâtres
85. Le Combat Spirituel et le Foyer
86. Bilan Spirituel Personnel
87. Victoire sur les R ves Sataniques
88. Prayers That Bring Miracles
89. Let God Answer By Fire
90. Prayers To Mount With Wings As Eagles
91. Prayers That Bring Explosive Increase
92. Prayers For Open Heavens
93. Prayers To Make You Fulfill Your Divine Destiny
94. Prayers That Make God To Answer and Fight By Fire
95. Prayers That Bring Unchallengeable Victory and Breakthrough Rainfall Bombardments

BOOKS BY PASTOR (MRS) SHADE OLUKOYA

1. Power To Fulfil Your Destiny
2. Principles Of A Successful Marriage
3. The Call of God
4. The Daughters of Phillip
5. When Your Destiny is Under Attack
6. Violence Against Negative Voices
7. Woman of Wonder
8. I Decree An Uncommon Change

The Books, Tapes and CDs (Audio and Video)
All Obtainable At:

- Battle Cry Christian Ministries
  322, Herbert Macaulay Way, Sabo, Yaba, Lagos
  Phone: 0816-122-9775, 0803-304-4239
- MFM International Bookshop
  13, Olasimbo Street, Onike, Yaba, Lagos
- MFM Prayer City
  Km 12, Lagos/Ibadan Expressway
- 54, Akeju Street, off Shipeolu Street
  Palmgrove, Lagos
- All MFM Churches Nationwide
- All Leading Christian Bookstores
- Battle Cry Christian Ministries
  Abuja Zonal Office & Bookshop
  No 4, Nasarawa Street, Block A, Shop 4, Garki Old Market.
  Phone: 0813-499-3860